# SUPERSTRUCTURE AND STRUCTURE

*An Essay on the Genesis of Economic Development*

אֵ A L E F
Series of works on universal logic and philosophy directed by
Michele Malatesta and Rocco Pezzimenti
A   Allgemeine Logik Und Philosophie
L   Universel Logik Og Filosofi
E   Logica Universale E Filosofia
F   Logica Universal Y Filosofia

Volume 5: Rocco Pezzimenti, *Superstructure and Structure.*
*An Essay on the Genesis of Economic Development*

# SUPERSTRUCTURE AND STRUCTURE

*An Essay on the Genesis of Economic Development*

Rocco Pezzimenti

GRACEWING

First published by GRACEWING in 2004
as *Politics and Economics.*
*An Essay on the Genesis of Economic Development.*
This edition revised with new title published
by GRACEWING in 2015.

GRACEWING
2 Southern Avenue
Leominster
Herefordshire HR6 0QF
United Kingdom
www.gracewing.co.uk

No part of this publication may be reproduced, stored in a retrieval system, or transmitted in any form or by any means, electronic, mechanical, photocopying, recording or otherwise, without the written permission of the publisher.

The right of Rocco Pezzimenti to be identified as the author of this work has been asserted in accordance with the Copyright, Designs and Patents Act 1988.

© 2015 Rocco Pezzimenti

ISBN 978 0 85244 889 2

*To Juan Avella Pinzon*

# FOREWORD

This book was published in 2004 with the title *Politics and Economics. An Essay on the Genesis of Economic Development*. The present edition differs not only in its title but also has a completely revised first chapter, a new section in chapter two starting from II.37, and an added chapter eleven. It also has a preface by Professor Paolo Savona, a new bibliography and a new index of names.

The aim of this new edition is to emphasise the basic theme of this study. Contrary to the view held by a number of contemporary economists, the conviction is fast gaining ground that before the socio-political situation can be changed it is first necessary to change the economic processes, these last being seen as the structure on which the superstructure is built (an interpretation shared by Karl Marx and Adam Smith, in different, though symmetrical, fashion).

This book attempts to show that history in fact demonstrates, frequently, the opposite. However, an attempt has also been made to further emphasise that what in the past was defined as superstructure was not only – in a derogatory sense – ideology but also rights, values and moral traditions, and many other things as well, without which no development, naturally including economic development itself, can be stable and lasting.

# Contents

|      | PREFACE by Paolo Savona ....................................................... 9 |
|------|---|
| I.   | INTRODUCTION .................................................................. 11 |
| II.  | ECONOMIC ACTIVITY IN THE ANCIENT WORLD<br>From "the market" to "state socialism" ...................... 45<br>A commonplace about the economy<br>of the High Middle Ages ............................................. 74 |
| III. | THE MIDDLE AGES AND LATE SCHOLASTICISM ........... 87 |
| IV.  | INSTITUTIONAL PRECONDITIONS<br>FOR THE ENGLISH ECONOMIC TAKE-OFF ..................... 123<br>A note on economic thought in Italy<br>in the eighteenth century ............................................. 143 |
| V.   | A SPOTLIGHT ON ECONOMIC DEVELOPMENT<br>An analysis of *Das Kapital* ........................................ 151 |
| VI.  | NEEDS AND LIMITATIONS<br>Connections between politics, economics,<br>morality and other matters ........................................... 177 |
| VII. | THE DANGERS OF INVOLUTION IN A FREE MARKET<br>SOCIETY ........................................................................... 199 |
| VIII.| BUREAUCRACY: THE PURSUIT OF EFFICIENCY<br>A gnoseological problem ............................................. 211 |
| IX.  | RISK LIMITATION AND<br>THE CRISIS IN INTELLIGENCE ..................................... 223 |
| X.   | CONCLUSION OF THE WORK? ........................................ 239 |
| XI.  | THE STRENGTH OR WEAKNESS<br>OF THE CHINESE ECONOMIC SYSTEM? ......................... 243<br>1. A giant with feet of clay ........................................... 244 |

    2. Analogies with the case of China ...... 246
    3. State Capitalism ...... 247
    4. A precedent of not so long ago ...... 256

XII. APPENDICES ...... 259

WORKS CITED ...... 263

INDEX OF NAMES ...... 273

# PREFACE
## by Paolo Savona

I read this work in its first English version* and was interested in the direction taken by the research. It was outside the usual schemata of an economist or a political expert but it also brought back to my attention problems that have never been absent from the agenda of economic policy research because so far they have not been solved. I invite the reader to examine further the broader problems brought out in the work and here limit myself to recalling the origins of the debate on the historical roots of development as well as the continuing search for the best possible combination of the rights of economic freedom with the duties of social solidarity.

The author agrees with the idea that the roots of development are to be found in an increasingly keen awareness of a lack of resources – due, among other things, to population growth and the needs of "civilised" human beings – and the need for their use to be rational: the labour expended to obtain needed goods and services has to be increasingly productive. The complications arising from this conception of the economic problem appear when people work for other people and not for themselves. This has brought out the problem of the value of their work performance, especially when social groups have carried this dissociation to an extreme. This dissociation has thereby

---

* R. Pezzimenti, *Politics and Economics. An Essay on the Genesis of Economic Development*, Gracewing Fowler Wright Books, Leominster, 2004.

taken on capitalistic connotations that are often confused with those inherent in the market. Capitalism is a form of organisation of people in society in which the accumulation of capital has been placed at the top of the scale of social values. This has given rise to the exploitation of labour. Given these tendencies, politicians have found themselves facing a choice: that of not opposing them, allowing the market to operate or attenuating their effect by having parliaments put a brake on them, or redistributing the excessively concentrated income and wealth.

Rocco Pezzimenti does not have the least hesitation in indicating the first solution, that of a competitive market, while, however, assigning to political forces an important duty: that of encouraging the meeting of demands for solidarity in order that people in a country and on the entire planet may live together in an acceptable way. This means that there should be fewer legal constraints and greater acceptance of the principle of solidarity. The market option has led to a forward leap in the logic of the evolution of economic thought. After being raised to the level of a science, such thought disengaged from the moral sciences through study and not a negation of their importance but then brought them back together after they had followed a long "independent" path. The government of the distribution of wealth, in fact, returned to the centre of the political arena with the proposal for an advanced welfare state in the mid-twentieth century. Subsequently, however, this discipline once again broke away using the extension of logical and mathematical formalisation in studies of the economy and their division into specific analyses, something which led to the loss of an overall view of social development. Some historians have focused their attention on this point and have even expressed doubts about the possibility of outlining an all-encompassing history of people in society and not just certain aspects of their collective action. This is perhaps why the tormented path of economic science attempting to free itself of the moral sciences has been forgotten, and to the point that scientific and social considerations have progressed together and not in parallel.

More recently, political and social events have brought new shocks. The privatisations and liberalisations of the Thatcher and Reagan duo significantly modified the trends toward redistribution by parliaments and governments and left the task of deciding upon the distribution of income and wealth to the market in its new forms of more intense globalisation and greater size. The direction taken has placed the examination by economists of moral matters in the forefront.

Rocco Pezzimenti's seismograph records the tremors of these upheavals at a logical and practical level, upheavals that arose from the deep-seated conflict involved in resolving the forces of the market, the law and volunteer service. This is the reason why his work is "modern", even before being a pleasure to read and instructive, as long as readers do not ignore the events that have followed one another over the centuries and there is a wish to avoid returning to an itinerary whose extreme sides – *laissez-faire* and Communism – history has already condemned.

# I. INTRODUCTION*

**I.1** In the editorial "What is Europe" on 12 February 2000, *The Economist* asked the serious question, though veiled in a certain irony, what the Old Continent could possibly have in common which would be capable of guaranteeing the future of the Union. I believe that the pages which follow are a partial response. The relationship between politics and economics, certainly not always well-balanced, can be found throughout our whole history, even in those periods which are wrongly reckoned to be least susceptible to economic issues. This relationship, thanks also to a number of reflections such as those of Smith and Marx which in many ways are specular, was broken in the second half of the eighteenth century, in favour of the supremacy of economics. We are witnessing today "Weak states, strong markets, very strong economies (…) The tendency towards political decline is one of the most problematical sides" (Possenti, 105 and 109), in short, a political sphere which is weak and subject to the economic sphere. A problem emerges, even though few seem to realise it, because a political sphere incapable of carrying out its role compromises every serious possibility of development, as I shall attempt to show.

**I.2** *Why this title?* Originally, the title of these introductory pages was intended to be *An essay on the genesis of capitalism*. Then the thought occurred to me that such a title echoed the many writers who have always analysed this

---

* This Chapter has already appeared in the review "Metalogicon", n°. 1/2001.

subject by concentrating on certain prerequisites and also on specific historical contexts. These were also modified on the basis of the intentions of the study – often conditioned by quite a few ideological prejudices. So I preferred to adopt the phrase "economic development" rather than the much-abused and not infrequently misunderstood term "capitalism", as it seems to me less compromised and also more directly suited to what I am seeking to understand and analyse. The word capitalism will certainly recur frequently in these pages, but it must not be understood in the reductive sense in which it has been presented, in particular by certain sociologists. In this essay, by capitalism, I seek to show that we are dealing with a complex phenomenon which has far more ancient roots than those usually considered up to now. It is an expression which has to be stripped of a number of uncertainties and injustices, but which nevertheless can still constitute a useful source of study for the analysis of economic progress. All this will be possible only if it is agreed that certain commonplaces should be abandoned: for example, that of structure and superstructure, which for far too long has poisoned a debate both on the part of the political right and left, which ought to be first and foremost a scientific one. We should remember that the term in question here embraces an ensemble of disciplines, since the phenomenon is not confined to the science of economics.

**I.3** Commenting on the famous work of Max Weber, the editor of an Italian edition rightly observed that for too long much has been made of economic *policy* and not enough of economic *life*, since the state has been studied more than the individual private producer and the reasons which urge him to produce (cf. Sestan, 11). While this interpretation is quite true, it is also true that from then onwards, especially since the growing success of neo-liberalism, there has been a move in exactly the opposite direction. From this comes the fact that from Adam Smith onwards, in specular fashion, economic analysis has been based on one basic notion: the relation between natural society and artificial society, or if preferred, the relation between structure and superstructure. Liberalism has always tended to give greater weight to the former, valuing its merits and its capacity to "maintain" the latter which, when it "trespasses" beyond its boundaries, only creates imbalances and anti-economic consequences. In short, the liberal order of the state is nothing more or less than the benevolent neutrality of the state in economic life. The opponents of liberalism see the phenomenon in what I would term specular fashion, and see the superstructure as the protective wrapper of economic activity. From here come the two different political and economic conceptions with which we are all too familiar. Both consider the economic system in certain senses in abstract fashion, having "reduced it to a unity, though it is not in fact reduced to unity even today" (Sestan, 42), even within the same country, however developed or otherwise it may be.

**I.4** What I intend to illustrate in this essay is that the juridical and moral "superstructure" is not merely a consequence and a projection of the economic structure, but also a preliminary condition which permits the birth and development of the structure itself which, as it gradually develops, is able to improve and enrich both law and morality. The relation between the so-called structure and superstructure is so close and binding that to ask which is the cause of the other is rather like asking the famous chicken-and-egg question. Certain social and juridical conditions make the birth of economic activity easier, especially when they make no claim to enter the decision-making and managerial phase of this activity. In short, they function as preconditions: the English Industrial Revolution was possible because the English had first brought about the revolution in legal rights which guaranteed certain possibilities of action and enterprise. This, however, does not mean that the institutional moment must be placed above the economic moment, because otherwise it is the economy itself which undergoes an involution. The greatness of the *Pax*

*Romana*, and later that of the *Pax Britannica*, was such because certain governments guaranteed rights but did not rule the economy – so much so that it is true, as used to be said even in the ancient world, that such political systems govern little.

**I.5** As any number of thinkers have reminded us, Tocqueville, for one, observed that in a social situation founded on commerce, the citizens love order, appreciate recognised morality, and show preference for practical activities rather than theory. This is one of the most salient characteristics of western civilisation, which for this reason has invented the market, and has held that the future of society should be founded on stability and competition, and everything which derives from it (cf. Novak, SDC, 119 and 205). These elements have become almost the spirit of the democracies, and have been added to other requirements which have become equally indispensable, so that they could be described as the bread of life of a living democracy. It is equally true that there is, ultimately, the tracing out of the outline of the anthropological vision of a given era. Who can deny that the "economic spirit" is closely connected to the idea that humans have of wealth, its use, and its aims at a certain moment of history? Who can deny that the lawfulness of the use of some means varies in accordance with the understanding of relationships with others.

**I.6** Such "aspects of the life of the spirit" do in fact enter economic life. To have pointed to them is perhaps one of the greatest merits of Max Weber, who also analysed other essential components of social and economic life. But even he did not perceive why those elements which could be the inspirational motives of a certain kind of capitalism subsequently ended up by being annihilated by capitalism itself. For example, if we take for granted that capitalism was generated by a certain kind of religious spirit, we cannot forget that for some it later became "at least foreign to any religious spirit and ethic" (Sestan, 48). It seems as if such a spirit must have been merely a matter of convenience, or at least, superficial. A work which has been too hastily forgotten, *Capitalism and Slavery*, by Eric Williams, shows how numbers of men who were "devout and exemplary" in their private and public lives were the main artificers of that slavery of black people which assisted the take-off of the economy in the North American lands. Williams also reminds us that the phenomenon not only affected black people, who in fact only began to be used as slaves when the sources of white labour from Europe dried up. This had been, for example, the fate of the majority of the Irish taken prisoner by Cromwell. This demonstrates a fact which many tend to set aside: religious intolerance gave a boost to slavery, and upheld it for nearly a century. How could all this have happened? Weber, too, seems to put this question to himself when he maintains that in the land where the capitalist spirit and its consequences seem to find their greatest affirmation, "the United States, the pursuit of wealth, stripped of its religious and ethical meaning, tends to become associated with purely mundane passions, which often actually give it the character of a sport" (Weber, PE, 182).

I.7 The spirit of "capitalism" was certainly present long before the age of the Reformation. How can we ignore the entrepreneurial and commercial activity of the republics and Venice and Genoa, and the other maritime republics or cities, such as those of the Hanseatic League? But above all, when we consider the country which has become identified with early capitalism, Great Britain, how can we ignore the fact that "Scotland, the country with the strongest element of Calvinism, has less importance in the economic life of Britain at this time"? (Sestan, 52). I am led to the conviction that the religious spirit, whose importance is certainly not secondary, cannot constitute the sole foundation for the phenomenon under discussion. I shall in fact try to show that mediaeval economic phenomena, although inspired by religion, find their true guarantee elsewhere. In this context I would like to point out that the mediaeval period shows an aspect which Weber seems reluctant to stress. To say that the "greater otherworldliness of Catholicism, the ascetic character of its highest ideals, must have brought up its adherents to a greater indifference towards the good things of this world" (Weber, PE, 40), means ignoring the difference between indifference and detachment. Weber himself points to the economic progress achieved by the Poles, who are Catholics, as against Russia and East Prussia, comparing them to those of Galicia and suggesting that the motives for the difference are more of a social and political than a religious kind (cf. Weber, PE, 39). The same is true of the ancient economic phenomena which developed in the absence of specific religious motives, but always in the presence of precise guarantees.

**I.8** Even Weber himself seems to admit implicitly that the latter are important, when he says that only the West has produced "parliaments of periodically elected representatives" (Weber, PE, 16). But this achievement was certainly not due to chance, nor is it a benevolent gift of nature. As I sought to show in my book *The Open Society and its Friends*, this has been a toilsome and slow achievement, based on those guarantees and rights which later, as I shall try to show, also permitted the birth and slow growth of the mercantile, and then the entrepreneurial, spirit. I do not believe that it is merely by chance that the rebirth of those mediaeval republics to which I made reference earlier, took place and developed in the same era as the rediscovery of Roman Law, and of private law in particular. And certainly it is not a mere chance that a large number of the first documents of our modern languages show the need to convey in the vulgar tongue, comprehensible to all, the content of the contracts which affect the lives of uneducated people, or of entire communities which did not have a sufficient understanding of legal Latin. Again, Weber seems once more implicitly to admit this when he maintains that "the rational capitalistic organisation of (formally) free labour" is typical only of the West, in that the rest of the world lacks "a rational organisation of apprenticeship in the handicrafts like that of our Middle Ages" (Weber, PE, 21). This shows that the economic phenomenon with which we are dealing was slowly built up in the West, and can be found in the DNA of the old continent because these same achievements of the Middle Ages cannot be said to have emerged from nothing. Again Weber seems to admit all of this when, with regard to a number of statements, including economic ones, by the Reformers, he says: "The relationship of all the Reformation Churches to the Catholic past in all was very complex and, according to the point of view which is emphasized, one or another most closely related to Catholicism or certain sides of it" (Weber, PE, 242 note 108). The same observations on the dangerousness and temptation of riches made in the context of the Reformation, for example by Baxter (cf. Weber, PE, 163) were apparently already made by Aquinas, who extended them to profit as well as to riches.

**I.9** Before real capitalism, it cannot be said that "a really accurate calculation or estimate" existed "these are points affecting only the *degree* of rationality of capitalistic acquisition" (Weber, PE, 19). This statement leads me to make two observations: The *first* is that an achievement of the kind rests on a number of other presuppositions, which show that the whole process comes from far back, and the more distant prerequisites are no less important than the others: in short, without guarantees of personal rights and property, every calculation would be useless and precarious. The *second* is that, as has been adequately shown, the rationality of the calculus with its implications, among them the double-entry book-keeping, was not in fact invented in the context of Calvinism but long before the Reformation in the shadow of the convent (one could cite Luca Pacioli), even though, as I have already said, the religious motives may here concern the interpretation of the fact and not the fact itself. We only need to examine the point where, to use Weber's own words, "our rational business book-keeping" begins (Weber, PE, 22). This "book-keeping, the registration in double entries of the facts of management in journals, or 'zornali', the master book (...) the practice of double-entry writing must already have been in wide use in Venice – as Alfieri shows – in the fourteenth century". Basically Pacioli, at the end of the fifteenth century, "is expounding what the Venetian mercantile firms had already been using for some time" (Fazio, viii). Perhaps it is worth mentioning too that Venice, somewhat like Rome in antiquity, was for some centuries sovereign in the trade of the world. And her institutions were republican; it would be interesting (though this is not the place) to assess the origins of those institutions. In any case, it was in Venice that "the mechanisms of mercantile control enjoyed the greatest development and the finest applications (...) The trade was the effective cause of her riches". But the important thing was that the Venetians dedicated themselves particularly to *overseas and maritime trade*. "The Republic, generally, forbade mainland trade to its subjects, so as not to expose them to dangers". Here the motif of security returns, crucial to any economic activity; but it is particularly important that "transit trade" became important here, meaning the launching of a "transformation" economy. All the goods had, in fact, to pass through the port of Venice; it was forbidden for them to be unloaded elsewhere. This means that not only the goods which could be directly sold on the spot arrived at the port, but also those that first had to be transformed – hence the numerous textile industries which grew up in the Venetian hinterland (cf. Alfieri, 1-2).

**I.10** In the preface to his book *The Crisis of Global Capitalism: Open Society Endangered*, George Soros, in a summary statement on the problem of economic risks (cf. Soros, CGC, xiii-xiv), raises a most interesting speculation. Is economic risk truly as hazardous as usually supposed? Is not real economic activity that which tends to reduce risks as much as possible? If this is so, does all this not demonstrate the close link existing between politics and the economy to the point that the latter only develops when it is guaranteed by the former? If this notion is true, as I believe it is, does this not overturn the classic interpretation of the liberal school? Thus it is politics, not the centralist kind with its socialist or statist overtones, but the politics of guarantees and regulations, which can ensure economic development, guarantee the markets and the possibility of enrichment for all. Otherwise, as happened in the early Middle Ages, is there anything but barbarism, with uncertainty of sea and land communications, of markets and trade, and with an absolute absence of legality? It is surely the sea routes reconquered by the maritime republics, the safe circulation in certain territories guaranteed by their revival, and above all the security of possession ensured by the rediscovery of Roman private law (I should mention again that it is no coincidence that the first documents in modern languages are almost all contracts) which guaranteed the new economic take-off. In other words, a discipline was not created by the imposition of foreign bodies, but produced by the agreement of a number of parties.

**I.11** The examples from the past to which I intend to refer, the Latin world, the mediaeval world which was shattered by absolutism, and the contemporary world, especially that of England, seem all to have the common denominator of a search for stability which is the crucial element of economic life. I believe that this is what is meant when it is stated that "financial capital is even more mobile than direct investments. Financial capital moves wherever it is best rewarded; as it is the harbinger of prosperity, individual countries compete to attract it" (Soros, CGC, xix). But in order to attract it, there must be guarantees, because these are what allow it to bear more fruit. Those who do not believe in this can be defined, as Soros says, as the market fundamentalists, because they continue to delude themselves, despite the evidence of history, that the markets correct themselves of their own accord. They oppose any kind of metaphysical notion, even where, as in religious subjects, the effort proves useless and meaningless, and then they ascribe a kind of absolutism to the market itself, against which it is pointless to intervene. They are sceptical about any moral principle, and thus they judge the market operators to be free of any defects and of any stain of guilt, ascribing divinatory capacities and qualities of justice to the market itself, capable of placing it above everything, even temptation. From here comes the belief that "the markets are self-correcting" (Soros, CGC, xix). This conviction, like the whole fundamentalist market faith, is a potential menace not only to the economy, but obviously to the very society which we refer to as "open". Perhaps we should all reflect a little more on the following statement: "I am not saying that market fundamentalism is diametrically opposed to the idea of open society the way fascism or communism were. Quite the contrary. The concepts of open society and market economy are closely linked and market fundamentalism can be regarded as merely a distortion of the idea of the open society. That does not make it any less dangerous. Market fundamentalism endangers the open society inadvertently" (Soros, CGC, xxii). The threat is serious because political failures, in this case the failures of democratic rule, are more dramatic and lasting than those of the economy. If this is true, it is the confirmation that not only are capitalism and democracy interdependent, but while the former may meet with moments of crisis, which are perhaps also contingent upon it, the latter can never abdicate without generating dangerous and often irreversible crises.

**I.12** These considerations should not encourage pointless pessimism. Healthy realism is more optimistic than might be thought. In this context, we may add two important reflections raised by studies which start out from very distinctly different viewpoints. The *first* is that human actions are by their very nature fallible because there exists no complete correspondence between the thought of individual subjects and the real state of things. All this produces unforeseen consequences of human actions, and this is not necessarily a bad thing, because what is imperfect can be improved; it is only necessary to have the honesty to admit one's own errors (cf. Soros, CGC, 18-19). The *second* is that when we speak about trade and the capacity to create riches, we must not forget that such objectives cannot be attained at all costs, ignoring moral and juridical rules which safeguard the weak, and the pacific coexistence of all. The fact that unscrupulous individuals may make vast fortunes in the most total disregard for legality should not make us forget that the world has seen certain standards of morality undergo a progressive improvement, and moreover time shows human beings clearly that immoral activities only produce the ephemeral and generate selfish wealth. Even Schumpeter maintained that the growth of industry and the change of generations removed the creative urge from management and left economic activity in the hands of the bureaucrats. Modern aristocracies, like ancient ones, ended by coming to ruin with the passing of the generations. Perhaps to avoid this danger, even from feudal times onward, certain families subjected their eldest sons to a demanding education, full of difficulties and sacrifices, in order to prevent them from being incapable of facing periods of crisis which might arise.

**I.13** I do not want it to be thought that when I mention crises, especially in the economy, I am referring in some way to the irrationalist temptations present in some interpretations of Simmel's analysis. Here crisis has to be understood as a possibility of overcoming closed schemes which refuse all possibility of change: closed schemes which refuse, in their turn, to be considered as provisional solutions and not completely final ones. The economy, and even more the institutions, constitute and gradually give shape to points of orientation in an unending process. If we wish to speak about crises at all, we must understand the incompleteness of human phenomena which are always susceptible to transformation: in a word, openness – plurality of the motives which keep a genuinely free society on its feet (cf. Cavalli-Perucchi, 10 and 14). Perhaps because of this and in contrast to those who wish to see a particular element in a particular era which generates phenomena such as capitalism, I believe that facts like economic development or capitalism are the product of a complex interweaving of factors, within which it is complicated to establish which has been more determinative than others. This does not mean, though, that even in these introductory pages, certain factors may not be held to be definitely influential.

**I.14** Among these, the modern world has witnessed (in a special way in comparison with other ages, though it was present then also), the phenomenon of economic calculus and the primary relationship with money. We could say that the economy has brought to completion what Galileo had realised by analysis of nature: the "growing tendency to quantification and to the transformation of quality into quantity" (Cavalli-Perucchi, 17). All this has resulted, in part, in the impoverishment of the economic "moment" since there is no one factor which can alone be capable of exhausting the total nature of any reality – thus the fact that two men mutually exchange their products is not, in itself, an economic-political datum (cf. Simmel, 55). However, there are present a series of conditions, connections and consequences which cannot be called by nature exclusively economic. Without wishing to do as Simmel does, and downplay aesthetic motives, there is no doubt that there are also factors present which, in the broad sense, we may describe as belonging to custom and in the strict sense to the moral and juridical spheres.

**I.15** The exclusive quantification of the economy certainly leads to many problems for those who are concerned not only with economic progress but with the full satisfaction of humankind – or one might even say the attempt at the pursuit of happiness. The first concern is that in a society of such a kind, as Rosmini supposed, there is the dominance of means over ends with all the repercussions that this causes in the context of the human spirit and its will. The dramatic problem which the Frankfurt School sums up in the famous term *the destruction of reason* originates here: an irrationalism which in social and economic terms also means losing oneself behind the immediate, with a consequent incapacity for planning ahead and hence for developing the intelligence understood as creativity and possibility of defining and reaching precise objectives. All this ends up by changing mankind in its essence, making it lose its sense of the concrete and developing its faculty for abstraction. It is curious that a person such as Simmel should unconsciously almost underwrite certain statements by Rosmini: the *yearning* for all the other things is limited by the rules of the subject's capacity for assimilation; possession does not any longer assume the form of specific objects, but rather of money (cf. Simmel, 330-1). Equally clear is that instrumentality and "technicality" acquire an objectivity which causes a subordination of the subject, so that one may even go as far as saying, of certain services, that they are "work for hire". We witness a growing liberation of needs, but in a *completely monetarised society*, all this does not always correspond with an effective increase in liberty, often sacrificed to "undeniable" objective claims.

**I.16** It could thus be said that even capitalism can give in to the *temptation to perfectionism*. Behind this term there is in fact a very complex way of defining economic action. At times the latter not only "generates consumerism (...) but also a deformation of the conscience" (Baggio, 104). In other words, today's reflection on capitalism "still has too many echoes of a polemical attitude linked to the era of contraposition between capitalism and socialism, and to the desire to settle accounts with the left" (Baggio, 109). I think that this may mean that if capitalism has triumphed over socialism, this does not signify that capitalism should believe itself capable of realising the socialist utopia: i.e. the perfect society. *The disillusionment with the socialist "paradises" must not lead us to maintain that now capitalism is in a position to realise the perfect society with which socialism failed.* Capitalism must take account of a series of errors inherent in its own tradition, and in its present manifestation. Not to admit its own errors would create a fatal presumption which could worsen, perhaps irremediably, its worst points rather than correcting them. There are certain thinkers, even Catholic ones, who do not see how social injustice can strike even at the mechanisms of production in all its dynamisms, and even go so far as to forget that the poverty of some can be the product of non-participation in the economic dynamism of the system, even if not only of that. Such thinkers do not fully understand the impact of subsidiarity, just as other thinkers of the opposite camp perhaps exalt it beyond what is due (cf. Baggio, 106-7).

**I.17** It is curious that a certain way of seeing things has even ignored the term subsidiarity which may perhaps be correctly understood apart from its etymological meaning. The term derives from the Latin *subsidium*, a word from military jargon which meant help kept in reserve for those who were unable to achieve what they were supposed to do. It is thus not an assistance to be given in an unconsidered way by taking the place of the one who was supposed to perform the action, as the statists would have it, but nor is it a disenchanted aid which never arrives, as the extreme liberalists assert. It is strange that the first to use the term in the twentieth century was Pius XI, holding it to be a due act of assistance to those members of the social body who by themselves alone were not in a position to attain certain targets. It is more a matter at times of setting in motion those intermediary bodies towards the objectives which the state, to paraphrase Tocqueville, could not always reach in a fuller and less costly way, rather than merely reaching them. In short, it is not legitimate to take away from individuals what the individuals are capable of undertaking by their own initiative and by their own means.

**I.18** That capitalism *per se* is not in a position to ensure social justice and limit unbridled competition, even Novak seems to maintain when he states that it is a matter for Catholic ethics to correct and amend the spirit of capitalism. Basic moral choices may characterise certain of the decisions of capitalism in order to direct society towards a full realisation of the common good (cf. Baggio, 95-6). This means that in and of itself, although capitalism may be better than many other systems, it may present anomalies and warrant correctives. The problem is to decide from whence and from whom such correctives should come.

**I.19** But behind these questions there lies a problem which requires greater attention. Despite the fact that the whole civilisation of the Middle Ages, and later of the communes and the Maritime Republics may have shown the contrary, and despite the fact that the efforts of certain thinkers have sought to reinvigorate this tradition, recent Christian thinking "has been mainly critical towards capitalism" (Baggio, 96); a clear sign that the era of ideological conflict is reluctant to pass away, and the real detachment of analysis is yet to come. This is witnessed by the fact that either too many collectivist prejudices end by coming up headlong against unbridled individualism, and the best of the moral analysis which concerns the person, as the Christian tradition would call it: or the subject, as other cultural interpretations would put it, becomes sacrificed in an absurd battle of opposites.

**I.20** It used to be said that healthy realism is optimistic, above all if it does not become bogged down in the scepticism which may be generated by the objective incapacity to control all events in human existence. "Recognizing the limitations of social sciences does not mean that we must give up the pursuit of truth in exploring social phenomena. It means only that the pursuit of truth requires us to recognize that some aspects of human behavior are not governed by timelessly valid laws. This should encourage us to explore other avenues to understanding" (Soros, CGC, 35). Truth, as I wrote in one of my own previous works (cf. *Homo Metaphysicus*, ch. 6), on the existential plain, is not only a target to be aimed at, but more often a path to be undertaken.

**I.21** We have mentioned the need to improve certain *standards* of morality. On this rests the true legitimisation of the development of capitalism, and from this derive those rules which legitimise it and permit it to develop. Otherwise the market, like the individual activities of human beings, risks taking a path which may also mean the loss of the requirements which have guaranteed the birth and development of capitalism itself. Because of this we can say that "free competition does not express the criterion of justice; it is in fact justice which legitimises and governs it"(D'Addio, LA, 140) because it keeps in mind not only the formal rules of a society, but all the moral presuppositions from which such rules derive. If we stop at mere juridical formalism, and do not rise beyond to examine the moral problems, we forget one of the crucial problems of human life, imbued as it is with good and evil, that have a determining influence in the realisation of a certain social life. Some fundamental observations arise out of this: "The first consideration to be made is that external goods do not promote happiness; in fact if they procure a sort of pleasure or contentedness, it is usually a matter, as experience teaches, of short-term satisfactions, which are then the source of 'infinite disquiet and incredible troubles'" (D'Addio, LA, 18). Should we reject external goods, then? Certainly not. But to enjoy their effective value and obtain real satisfaction, it is essential to understand that it is not only the needs of nature that exist, and that our capacity for desire, on which economic activity rests, will never be completely satisfied, because our moral needs, even when not completely perceived, are very much broader. Our disquiet, in order not to become anguish, has need of the totally moral awareness that economic goods, however basic for the development of peoples and of individuals, will never satisfy our expectations completely. If it were not so, economic development would sooner or later have to be exhausted. What has been said above has been more amply demonstrated by Tocqueville and by Rosmini, when they criticised the "primacy of the economic sphere and the related science of well-being" which would lead to the prevalence of technology over theoretical problems of scientific research and to the "primacy of the faculty of abstraction over that of thought" (cf. D'Addio, LA, 88, note). All this causes an obsessive search for means or instruments to satisfy immediate expectations and needs, and leads to the forgetting of the real aims of life. The result is that as time passes, a situation of growing uncertainty develops, which causes a crisis in economic life, and then in the institutions which have generated it. And indeed all this has been shown by quite a few sociological research activities concerning phenomena such as anomie.

**I.22** This is why I do not believe that freedom of enterprise, markets and competition can on their own guarantee development and progress without an adequate moral and juridical backing, which in my view integrate one another. In the past, these (and as we shall see, other) elements have assisted economic development only after an exit from a climate of uncertainty. I must refer briefly to the role of law and to its rediscovery after the unstable centuries of the invasions of the Dark Ages. We only have to think of what it meant for contracts, without which there is no economic certainty; for the statutes of free cities, for the recovery of the sense of private property, and so on. Perhaps it would be necessary to look at many other aspects of the Roman world which, already in ancient times, favoured the development and the diffusion of wealth, such as the security of maritime commerce, for instance (it is in this light that the term *mare nostrum* should be seen, which came to be used after the destruction of the pirates who had returned and spread during the Dark Ages), and the security of the roads which were the pride of Roman trade, the culture of which was based on the *negotium*. This was the exact opposite of *otium*. Its real significance was working activity, and derived from the verb *negotiari*, which in fact meant conduct affairs, trade. The revival of this conception is demonstrated by the rebirth of the maritime republics, cities administered on the model of the classical republic, and dedicated to trade in those seas which, thanks to a great effort, were beginning to regain security and peace.

**I.23** *Commercium et pax* is not only the proud motto of the port of Amsterdam, but it is the condition which, from the Roman world right down to the threshold of our own times, and throughout the rebirth after the first millennium, accompanies every serious stage of development. This is witnessed by what the Latins used to say concerning *negotium*. No less significant is the evidence from the Fathers of the Church, for example St John Chrysostom, who believed that trade was capable of developing the material bond between peoples. But it is also shown by the mediaeval thinkers who saw in peace the basic condition for the development – and not only the spiritual development – of humanity. The supreme political authority should in their view be a guarantee of peace, as the title of Marsilio's work sums up quite well: *Defensor Pacis*. A far more modern idea than one might imagine, if one examines the texts carefully – I have dealt with this theme elsewhere (cf. my work on *The Open Society and its Friends*, ch. VII). Moreover, when Montesquieu writes that "peace is the natural effect of trade", he does so with an eye to the results of the ancient *Pax Romana*, and of what would later be called the *Pax Britannica*.

**I.24** I said that no definition of capitalism can be exhaustive, any more than that of any other human phenomenon. However, some preconditions can be distinguished which remain indispensable for the shaping of any phenomenon. Apart from the relationships existing between *economics* (with calculation, estimate, degree of rationality of profit, etc.), *law* and *morality*, from which numerous corollaries arise, there is also a series of psychological motives which urge individuals – whether they be the merchants of the ancient world or entrepreneurs in the modern one – to act in an economic way. A similar observation can be derived from a series of very valuable studies on the matter: suffice to mention the names of Sombart, Weber, Pellicani or Novak. The latter maintains that with Christianity the enhancement of human activity contributed to the development and enrichment of the human race, by revealing the vocational aspect of economic activity. Such an attempt was already made by earlier major scholars, though in too sectorial a way, because it was too limited – for example in Weber's limitation to the world of Protestantism. Here, in contrast, the discussion is broadened. In short, all begins from a personal factor, to be discovered and realised, through the assistance of a community, to arrive at the realisation of a product which is also useful to others, to whom we transfer part of ourselves and give part of our personality.

**I.25** The interior motivation of the economy, which from a Christian point of view had already been analysed by Rosmini, has aroused interest with many scholars. Among these, Werner Sombart deserves to be mentioned; he aids us in broadening the vision of the "prerequisites" of economic activity. The need for luxury is one of the motives which has made it possible to increase economic activity. It first appeared in the courts, for example the Papal Court of Avignon, and then went on to become first an aristocratic and then a bourgeois phenomenon. The fact that it began with the papal court, then followed by a large number of the "princes" of the church, confirms what Pellicani has stated: the Church had, on an economic and worldly plane, anticipated that modernity, or secularisation, which in the following centuries was to be judged as too permissive by the reformers who demanded a turning back in history, causing the Church itself in the period of the Reformation, to become more rigid towards its own recent past (cf. Pellicani, MS, 12). To return to Sombart, the need for imitation led the rich to imitate the worldly splendour of the courts. From here came the transformation of life-style, with the consequent spread of consumer goods. In embryo, this was the first step towards "well-being". Out of this there also came an important phenomenon which involved the first symptoms of a social process: "the impoverishment of the ancient houses, and their substitution". Luxury manifested itself in every sector. The luxury of the table was accompanied by that of the wardrobe, and in time by that of the dwelling and the city. And this in turn involved the development of theatres, concert-halls and ballrooms, luxury hotels and restaurants (cf. Sombart, vol. I, ch. 48). I do not see what Sombart says as being valid only for a certain era; it represents a constant of economic progress. The luxury which begins at the table and reaches to the theatre is a constant of development, just as valid for ancient cities and civilisations, as for contemporary ones. The manners and modes for realising certain aspirations, and even the social presuppositions from which certain necessities arise, may change, but the *quest for luxury*, which we could discuss at length, *does constitute another constant of economic history.*

**I.26** The search for, and hence the production of, certain goods occupies the minds of certain people to the extent that we may be led to say that the "formation of capitalism is a history of personality": according to some, entrepreneurs, according to others, merchants or mere businessmen. The fact remains, however, that these were able to operate because, apart from the social necessities of the moment, they also found moral, juridical and political conditions which permitted their actions and also favoured the development of certain economic conditions, such as credit, for example, with the consequent creation of banks. This involves another necessity: trade with distant lands and the development or transformation of means of transport for the exchange of goods. This shows, as we have already pointed out, *another constant* of the economic history of any time: *the security of trade*: that *commercium et pax* which we mentioned earlier and to which we will return. Safe transport was a basic precondition of mercantile activity, both of the states and of private individuals. To the security of trade we might also add *security of business*, which seeks more and more to obtain safeguards by legal guarantees. Everything derives from that notion of contract which as Sombart himself admits, begins to make its presence felt in all the sectors of public and private life from the late Middle Ages onward (cf. Sombart, vol. II, ch. 5. § 1) – though I believe that it was also present in the ancient world, and after the rediscovery of Roman Law, can be found in the high mediaeval period with the birth of academic studies.

**I.27** Reflection on the figure of the merchant is, anyway, of great importance whether they found the legal and political conditions to guarantee their activities already existing, or whether they themselves determined them. The fact remains that specifically thanks to them, to this diligent élite of savers, the original accumulation which forms the departure point of the capitalist economy became possible. This position, on the other hand, was rejected by Marx, who was convinced that riches emerge from conquest, subjugation, assassination and violence (cf. Pellicani, SGC, 27). There is no need to stress that such a viewpoint does not consider economic activity linked to any moral presupposition or any need for improvement felt by those who are economically active. How this morality could then suddenly and unexpectedly make its appearance once the socialist society is achieved, is still to be made clear. That petty theft and riches gained by violence are not enough to start up economic development is clearly shown by historical analysis. The wealth accumulated by Spain and Portugal was not enough to guarantee the original accumulation. "Which means that in the Marxist scheme of explanation, *the essential is lacking*: i.e. there is no discernment of the *specific differences* which have made the historical parabola of the western economic situation unique" (Pellicani, SGC, 34).

**I.28** This certainly developed as a result of the action of certain remarkable men, but also because, as scholars such as Peter Kriedte, Hans Medick and Jurgen Schlumbohm have shown, since the high Middle Ages others laid the foundations of a lasting increase in population; a transformation of the agrarian economy took place, and there was an attempt to remove everyday activity from uncertainty (cf. Pellicani, SGC, 255-6). Social mobility also benefited from this – a basic phenomenon in any age of economic development. But all this goes to show one basic fact: in and of itself, the economic situation not only does not ensure a real development, but neither does it guarantee that genuine modernisation of which it should be the guarantee. There are still many states in the twentieth century, especially in Asia, which show how modernity (understood as guarantees, morality, law, participation, etc.) and scientific, economic, and industrial progress are not the same things.

**I.29** The relationship between morality and economics, however it may be judged, is an ancient element in the western notion. It can be found throughout the whole Greek and Roman tradition, and according to certain classical historians it actually predates it. Cicero is illuminating in this respect when summing up a mode of thinking that was widespread and ancient he maintains that "we need to eliminate every lie in contracting obligations", and he refers to what had already been stated by Tuberon he says "it is the property of the wise man to take account of his own patrimony without doing anything contrary to morality, the laws and traditions. We do not wish to be rich merely for ourselves, but for our children, relations, friends and above all for the state. The wealth and possessions of individuals are the riches of the city" (Cicero, DO, III, 15, 61 and 63). Many people have quoted this passage from Cicero, but no one seems to mention a subsequent passage in which Cicero reminds us that here the reference to morality and the laws is not a general admonition but refers to the *mores maiorum* of tradition, and the specific laws of contract proper to civil law. In fact, we find the following: "as regards contracts dealing with fixed assets, with us, civil law allows that at the act of sale the defects known to the seller must be declared. In fact while the Twelve Tables held that what was 'explicitly declared' was sufficient for responsibility, and if someone did not fulfil this he must pay a fine of double the sum, the jurists established a penalty for concealment" (Cicero, DO, III, 16, 65). It is here noteworthy that *the jurists, or jurisconsults*, showed a way of common understanding, thanks to tradition, *broadened* what was established in the Twelve Tables to reinforce a law which, though anchored in fundamental principles, showed itself flexible in assessing the daily requirements of the citizens.

**I.30** The legal guarantees and the need for certainty of law caused a genuine social upheaval which Sombart himself seems to admit when he says that the idea of contract is also rooted in those ranks of the population which had remained excluded from power. It is here that the mercantile and bourgeois spirit was born in the Christian mediaeval world – a spirit which would give rise to the economic revival. Long before modern economists, it was held that it was necessary to keep faith with promises, the real strongpoint of private law. As Alberti stated, nobody in a family such as his failed to keep his given word, or renegued on a contract, and all activity was carried on under the banner of honesty and truth. Parsimony, moderation and diligence were at the basis of the great families which made the economic take-off possible, just as Franklin was to say: industry and frugality (cf. Sombart, vol. II, ch. 5, § 1-2) Novelties emerged typical of modern economic activity, such as competition, but the frame of moral reference of economic activity would still be that of mediaeval Christianity. We need only mention the social and religious bonds summed up in the *timor Dei*, which led to the idea of honest gain and the justness and nobility of profit. In the light of this and other considerations already discussed, one can discern *capitalism as a result of a long and* (in various eras) *contested economic life*, which in its process of development maintained, strengthened and updated certain constants which have become characteristic elements of capitalism itself. It could be said that there were particular attitudes towards economic activity which made certain presuppositions necessary, and that these afterwards became indispensable – even though from time to time they were strongly disputed: the recognition of private property can be taken as an outstanding example. But another example may be offered by the *conception of work*, understood as a social factor, which was subjected to a certain kind of order as time matured. The actual conception of division of labour, as Sombart recalls, only asserted itself gradually and does not appear casually in the modern era, but is already present in certain ancient and mediaeval reflections such as Aquinas (cf. Sombart, vol. I, ch. 1, § 3).

**I.31** All this – without counting that which seem to us today to be characteristic elements of modern capitalism (such as the flight from the countryside, the disorderly concentration in industrial areas, etc) – may prove to be characteristic of a precise era, rather than the foundation aspect of the whole capitalist society. The *new economy* reasserts the relationship between man and work in terms which we could call more "classical". As in the era of handicrafts, the new workers will probably work in the comfort of their own homes, recreating that duality of home and work which was typical of the mediaeval world.

**I.32** The moral presuppositions of capitalism were even recognised by those who like Marx held that it would be useful and necessary to overcome capitalism itself. As has been rightly noted, Marx rejected the idea according to which capitalists could have obtained their profits by underhand or dishonest methods (cf. Giddens, CMST, ch. 4, § 1). With reference to the now well-known reflection of Marx on capitalism, to which I shall dedicate a brief chapter, I believe that the German philosopher was the victim of a contradiction which was not of an economic nature, but in fact of a mainly philosophical or (I would say) even metaphysical one. In fact his aim, expressed even in *Das Kapital*, was that of analysing the dynamic of bourgeois society thanks to the economic laws of the movement of that society, a dynamic determined by the productive forces operating in society itself. The crisis of capitalism, it can be seen, was to come about with the failure of that dynamic, and with the cancellation of economic conflict – a static state which is outside the realm of history, because it would mean the end of the mobility of labour, of transformation and the adaptability of the same – characteristics which (together with others), rather than being typical of a particular moment in the crisis of capitalism are constants of any phase of transformation and major economic development. For Marx, on the other hand they were apocalyptic symptoms of the end of times and a constructivist and perfectivist expression of a regenerated world and society.

**I.33** As well as the chapter dedicated to Marx, and an earlier one dedicated to a paradox in Smith's writings, I shall examine some more remote facts of which some readers may be unaware. In fact I believe that at least on this matter, Parsons may be right. There is no doubt that a theoretical system, in order to be considered correct, must demonstrate a series of facts to which reference is to be made and on which it is to be based. This is a rule of honesty, based on the fact that such facts must not only be known, but also accessible to all other scholars who may wish to dispute them, remembering, however that the above mentioned facts should be considered bearing in mind the expectations, and I would add the objectives, of whoever has formulated the theory (cf. Parsons, 8). These facts, in my case, serve to show how economic development is not only a broader phenomenon than capitalism, but indeed finds its roots in far distant times, since the desire for satisfaction and well-being is one of the most ancient aspirations of the human race. In the light of this, I fully agree with the other interpretation by Parsons, according to which the facts acquire a scientific value when they are expressed in such a way that they assume a precise meaning by being placed in a particular conceptual scheme (cf. Parsons, 41 ff).

**I.34** I have said from the outset that the opposing economic conceptions, which in other terms we may define as "liberalist" and "centralist", have a specular mode of analysing the economic phenomenon in relation to structure and superstructure. It has recently been said very succinctly that "Individualism and instrumentality are thus two sides of the same coin". Not only that: both of them, by leaving out the relational dimension of economics, are in fact limited in their understanding of many economic situations. Thanks to the introduction of the *Game Theory*, which, however, cannot be considered an exhaustive one, economists have begun to look at economic behaviour not only in rational terms, but also in strategic ones (cf. Bruni, 43-6), going well beyond the traditional ways of understanding the science of economics. Another attempt has been that of the *we-rationality*. This idea, which also finds some of its origins in certain classical economists, maintains that "in deciding what action to undertake, a person may think not only 'this action has good consequences *for me*', but rather, 'this action is *my part* of an *our action*, which has good consequences *for us*'" (Bruni, 48). To sum up, as emerges from the explicit title of a book by Hollis (*Trust within Reason*) there is a trust in this way of understanding rationality, in that this seems to be a correlative of the notion of sociality, which means maintaining that trust is a relationship of reciprocity.

**I.35** Trust does not derive from the simple fact of giving to our actions aims which are not merely individualistic. Apart from individual selfishness, there is also that of the group. This is amply shown by various ways of understanding the behaviour of a team in a sporting competition, which (and I do not want to dwell on this at the moment) although not being individualistic may even so be instrumental. Here, on the other hand, we are talking, on a level with the 'Three Musketeers', about persons moved by "a logic which makes way for the sense of belonging, for the desire to follow social rules, for duty, and love, etc.". All this is possible when a strong sense of belonging exists in a community; when the relationship with others takes on a central value, and among other things, when there are guiding ideals which play a key role (cf. Bruni, 50-5). But does all this not bring us back to our basic problem: in order for an economic activity to take place, and for its consequent development, are there a series of prerequisites – whether they be moral or legal or more broadly cultural – which stimulate and encourage that economic activity? Of course, we must not be fatalistic. Where such requirements do not exist, they must be created. Certainly all this is easier if these requirements exist, and if certain basic notions are accepted: this seems to me to be the meaning of certain experiences such as those of the "economy of communion". In fact, I ask myself: where the *value* of the person, and a series of guarantees which safeguard it, do not exist, is such an experience possible?

## II. ECONOMIC ACTIVITY IN THE ANCIENT WORLD
### From "the market" to "state socialism"

**II.1** In tracing the origins of capitalism, Lujo Brentano maintained that it developed in the West when the monetary economy revived in the Middle Ages. But in fact it was to the West that this economy returned, for, after the crisis of Byzantium, the West continued to use Byzantine "capitalism", while the latter in its turn had taken up the different heritages of the Phoenicians, the Greeks, the Egyptians and the Romans, as they were beginning to merge into one after the second Punic War. Brentano then replied to Sombart, who maintained that the concept of a business company was absent in the ancient world, that within the context of the way of thinking of the time, this notion was already present in embryo in Babylonian civilization, which had passed beyond the stage of the domestic community. Even though the term "business company" cannot be applied to the ancient world in the sense in which we use it today, in a broader sense it already existed in Latin civilization when a Roman bestowed or a slave or a freedman an inheritance that was to be assessed by means of contracts, services or financial evaluations (cf. Brentano, 13-14, note 2). However debatable it may be, this statement seems to me in line with what was asserted in my first chapter: the psychological, institutional and cultural reasons which permit a real economic development are far more ancient than one might suppose.

**II.2** Economic activity has always been present in history. If I have chosen to examine it here in the context of the Roman world, it is because in that world, (as was to be the case with British civilisation in the modern world), thanks to law, and in particular private law, to certain institutional developments, and to peace and a generally widespread social consensus, it found the possibility of spreading in a way that had never been possible until the threshold of modern times. The right of property had a sacred sense for the Romans. It derived from the juridical *persona*, who exercised his own personal free will over everything that was his own. Ancient landed property already identified a boundary as something sacred. The boundary, the *terminus*, was very quickly recognised as a sacred object. "O *Terminus*, you who assign frontiers to the peoples" exclaimed Ovid, in the context of a society which had even dedicated a feast, the *Terminalia*, to *Terminus*. The boundary indicated the respect for the right of everyone; in fact it symbolised a juridical and religious sovereignty which went back to the times of the monarchy of Numa (cf. Meslin, 38-9). This contributed to guaranteeing riches, and what we today term the process of accumulation. Marx himself maintained that "Ancient Rome, in its later republican days, developed merchant's capital to a higher degree than ever before in the ancient world" (Marx, K, vol. III, 332). However, it is curious that little consideration is given to the fact that all this had been rendered possible thanks to a tranquillity of trade, by sea and land, achieved as a result of the defeat of the pirates, which had taken place at the hands of Pompey. This rendered maritime trade less problematic than it had been at certain times of the year. The uncertainty of the future results of an expedition led certain masters of law to coin the term "the condition of legal trade: *si navis ex Asia venerit*" (Pisani Sartorio, 7). This *venerit* not only showed the uncertainty about the result of a commercial venture, but already revealed the need to render the traffic of goods secure, and a possible insuring of commercial activity. These were then already extremely developing notions, so much so that Marx could also affirm "not commerce alone, but also merchant's capital, is older than the capitalist mode of production, is, in fact, historically the oldest free state of the existence of capital" (Marx, K, vol. III, 325).

**II.3** Trade is generally condemned by the ancient theorists. It should not be forgotten that for Aristotle, cities should be built far from the sea in order to be spared the recurring novelties which trade might bring with it (cf. my *The Open Society*, vol. I, ch. IX, 10). The revulsion shown by the theorists, however, finds no reflection in practice. Above all in the Roman world it is backed by specific rules which regulate the *negotium*, as indeed also contracts and exchanges in general (cf. vol. I, 21 and 22). Cicero seems to represent this conflict between intellectuals and men of action quite well. He holds, in fact, that knowledge cannot exempt itself from the "obligation to protect mankind; that is, human sociability". Furthermore, theoretical knowledge "seems to be going astray in sterility and solitude" without the practice of virtue (cf. Cicero, DO, I, 44, 157). This explains why Cicero, even though he holds, in the tradition of Cato the Elder, that agriculture is the greatest occupation, and considers trade "exercised on a small scale" indecorous, he praises it on the other hand "if it is on a grand scale, involving all sorts of goods from all over the place and distributing them to many without recourse to fraud" (Cicero, DO, I, 42, 151). Two observations may be made on this: the *first* arising out of my surprise when I consider how many have condemned statements of this kind as the mere fruit of sterile moralism, as if trade must take for granted fraud and lies rather than its rules. The *second point* is that many critics have not wanted to consider the novelty of this statement, which underlies a genuine social situation active and busy in large-scale trade, in contrast to the timorous position of Aristotle in accepting not only trade but also riches in themselves as an element of social upheaval.

**II.4** Cicero, like many other western writers, always ascribed great importance to the search for well-being, as long as it was pursued with legitimate means. He also translated a book of Xenophon, a disciple of Socrates, entitled *Oeconomicus*, although he did not consider it innovative. He was in fact convinced that "this whole argument relating to gain and investment of money (...) is more practically discussed by certain men of substance (...) than by all the philosophers in all their schools". Cicero marvels that so many intellectuals consider certain "curiosities" useless, when in fact they are "elements of knowledge which should be had" (Cicero, DO, II, 24, 87). The search for utility is not to be condemned.

**II.5** These conclusions did not escape von Hayek, who, however, gives me the impression of carrying them to extremes. It is true, as he himself states, that the modern ideal of liberty is based on the Stoics and on Cicero in particular (I have in fact dedicated my work on *The Open Society and its Friends* to this conviction). It is true, because for Cicero public utility and justice eventually coincide, as many jurists and mediaeval and modern thinkers have reminded us. James Harrington quite rightly stresses that "the public interest (...) was only the common law and justice, to the exclusion of any kind of partiality or private interest", in other words, identical to the *"imperium* of the laws, not of men". Cicero shows, in fact, that *"iustitia est habitus animi, communi utilitate conservata, summa cuique tribunes dignitatem"*. This statement is taken by von Hayek as the search for a justice not to be understood in the sense of constructivist utilitarianism (cf. Hayek, 2 and 155, note 13). The conclusion is certainly true, but to discard constructivism does not allow us to talk of spontaneity as an end in itself, of which Cicero was certainly not in favour. Taking up a well-known passage from the *De Re Publica* (3.13), which says *"iustitiae non natura nec voluntas se imbecillitas mater est"*, von Hayek believes that he can say that neither nature nor will, but only intellectual weakness – i.e our ignorance – is the mother of justice. "Our ignorance as to the effects of the application of the rules to particular subjects makes justice possible in a spontaneous society of free individuals" (cf. Hayek, 127 and 187, note 19). But this ignorance of ours is nevertheless regulated and not left to its own devices. We are free only in the context of the laws: this is the great teaching of Cicero. If this is so, this is the proof that the politico-normative moment is not superstructure, does not come forth from the economic moment, but flanks it and provides it with the rules for functioning: rules which can certainly be changed, but which cannot be absent, otherwise anarchy generates injustice, and as time goes on, crisis.

**II.6** What we have said also finds confirmation in relation to the problem of property. As I have already written elsewhere, the position of Cicero, and in general of all the Roman jurists, is different from that of the Greeks in this matter, and from all those who take their reference from them. For the Roman, the natural man, who for the Greeks was already a political animal, is different from the social man, and it is in point of fact the spirit of property which shows this. In the natural dimension where all belongs to all, property does not exist. This (and in the negative sense, Marx showed it very clearly), arises with the juridical dimension when the multitude becomes a society – i.e. gives itself laws: *ubi societas, ibi ius*. Without the juridical guarantees and the political strength to make them respected, no property is safe (cf. my *The Open Society*, I.26). In the first paragraph of his *Grundisse*, Marx arrives at the same conclusions, despite the fact that he then goes on to accept the position of Smith and other classical thinkers relating to structure and superstructure. He says, in fact: "History shows rather that common property (for example among the Indians, the Slavs, the ancient Celts, etc.) is the most original form, a form which like community property also plays an important role for a long time. Here we will not go again into the question of whether riches develop better under one or another form of property". However, this question is in fact crucial for a society, and I shall try to respond to it in this present essay.

**II.7** Before going any further, however, it will be as well to remember that agriculture, such a basic activity for the ancients as to be described as "primary", does not reflect an elusive and romantic dream but is a genuine economic activity, which is carried on to produce profit and increase wealth. Every anti-economic action has to be eliminated. "No one, in fact, who is in his right mind, would be ready to encounter heavy expenses in cultivation if he sees that they cannot be recovered", as "the smallholder does not bring his goats to pasture in land where young shoots are growing" (Varro, DRR, I, 2, 8 and 17). That land could simply mean riches for agrarian activity is a ridiculous conclusion of our own times. Varro, like his contemporaries, knows perfectly well that one can carry out other activities on land which we would today call those of productive service. His words leave us in no doubt: "if a holding is situated beside a road, and is in a good position for travellers, places for rest and refreshment should be built there which, while they are fruitful, have no connection with agriculture" (Varro, DRR, I, 2, 23) Shortly, when I discuss transport systems, we shall see how widespread this opinion was: one need only mention the halting areas for carts, parking spaces, as we would say today. And then if one wants to cultivate a land holding, one must take good count of its location and the possibilities of transportation which it possesses for its produce. "The possibilities of transport for its produce render the holding itself more profitable, if there are roads where carts can pass easily or navigable rivers in the vicinity. It is well known that with both these means it is possible to establish an export-import exchange *(evehi atque invehi)* with many estates" (Varro, DRR, I, 16, 6).

**II.8** Agriculture, in order to be genuinely productive, must follow two paths: experimentation and imitation. Imitate where convenient "and try with some experiments to find new ways" (cf. Varro, DRR, I, 18, 7-8). This is not only true for labours of the field in the narrow sense "since I hold that in the rural economy there are three activities carried out for the purpose of gain, i.e. agriculture, the breeding of cattle and the rearing of farmyard animals" (Varro, DRR, III, 1, 9). Speaking of the first activity it should be remembered that whoever wants to make a profit must first consider the territory where he is to operate. "For this reason, where conditions are not salubrious, cultivation is nothing less than a risk to life and the patrimony of the proprietor" (Varro, DRR, I, 4, 3). As can be seen, even in rudimentary form, *risk has always been an economic category*. There are also notable suggestions for the breeding of livestock, beginning with the fact that peacocks offer greater possibilities of gain than hens (cf. Varro, DRR, III, 4, 1). Still on the subject of peacocks, if one wants to look with a more careful eye to gain than to beauty, the females should always be more numerous than the males (cf. Varro, DRR, III, 6, 1). Similar advice is given for other beasts. It is, however, really odd that Varro writes a different account if, along with gain, it is sought to take account of quality also. He reminds us in fact that the habit of keeping certain beasts in closed cages in order to make them fatten more rapidly was beginning to appear (cf. Varro, DRR, III, 12, 15).

**II.9** It should also be remembered that the products to be cultivated on a farm do not depend only on the quality of the land, but also on its location; if it is situated near to more or less large urban areas, or actually near a city, some of the nearby inhabitants may have a sufficient income to possess wealthy villas. Varro also suggests that in order to make agriculture more profitable, it is desirable to involve the workers actively; they are only rarely to be termed *serfs*, while more often they are called *famuli* – which indicates a quite different kind of relationship and involvement. These people need places where they can rest from the fatigues of their work, and from the heat and cold. Cicero too had spoken of weekly rest (see my *The Open Society*, I.21), and Varro was to say the same (cf. I, 16, 4). The personnel employed in work in particular conditions might also not be made up of serfs. In certain areas, it might be easier and more profitable to employ bleachers, workers and general personnel for service on the basis of annual contracts, not to mention useful artisans, to avoid taking the agricultural workers away from their more specific tasks (cf. Varro, DRR, I, 16, 3-4). At times provision was made, in certain work, even for assuming specialised day labourers (cf. Varro, DRR, I, 17, 2).

**II.10** The same wealth of reflection is presented by Varro concerning the activity of cattle trading, for which he warns us that every action of purchase and sale must proceed according to the civil laws. A legal act is needed to ensure that what belonged to someone else becomes mine. But this is not enough in itself; apart from the stipulation of the contract, the payment of money is needed, and the fixing of certain conditions concerning the quality and health of the cattle (cf. Varro, DRR, II, 1, 15). Thanks to this "the purchaser, by virtue of the act of sale, may condemn the vendor if he does not deliver the goods to him, even if he has not yet paid the money, just as the latter (the vendor) may have the purchaser condemned if he does not pay him the agreed price" (Varro, DRR, II, 2, 6).

**II.11** The legal guarantees and favourable political conditions permitted the Romans to provide economic activity not merely with development, but even with a specialisation which favoured the establishment of certain activities and certain professions, such as that of the financier *(argentarius)* who provided for capital needs, or at other times arranged the exchanging and testing of money as well as the servicing of deposits and cash-supply and loans. This type of operator is not just an occasional figure; they were active in the Roman world between the fourth century BC and the third century AD. Thus there is a period of about six centuries during which this category was becoming more and more common. Proof of this can be found in the legal texts which deal with them up to the age of Severus (see also for this era Callistratus, Papinianus, Paulus and Ulpian). The term *argentarius* like many others (see, for example, the case of the word *imperium*, discussed in my *The Open Society*, ch. VIII) changed in meaning from the fourth to fifth century onward. The profession which "kept the bench" (or banker, as we should say today) spread all through the Roman world, but with a substantial difference between the eastern and western parts, to the extent that it characterised the distinct future development of these two areas. *It was only in the West, in fact, that the activities carried on by the bank and its operators were in the hands of private individuals.* From the republican period onward, state interventions were by way of being exceptional (cf. Balbi De Caro, 37-8 and 40-1). We shall see that one of the basic motives for the crisis of the Roman Empire, neglected up to the present, can be traced to the growing interference of the political authorities in economic and financial questions. Over a period of time, *the emperors become only guarantors, and set out to support an economy and an industry which was approved by the régime*, and thus began to head towards monopoly. I would stress once again the main thesis of this work: *the political structure is the reason for economic development, but it can also be the cause of its suffocation.* Politics may have the pre-eminence over the economic sphere, but only on condition of its *radical separation.*

**II.12** We have mentioned that the *argentarius* provided for the testing of coinage, because "ancient coinage, in contrast to that of the present, was a metallic coinage with a real and intrinsic value". It was thus necessary to check that it effectively contained the corresponding quantity of noble metal, or if, on the other hand, it was to be regarded as counterfeit. Once ancient coinage was put into circulation, it freely moved everywhere, even beyond the limits of the state which had issued it, specifically because of the proven quality of the corresponding metal. This explains why noble metals such as silver, generally the most commonly used in Rome during the ages of its ancient history, were boycotted when popular policies were undertaken, in favour of bronze, for example, which had much greater difficulty in reaching distant markets (cf. Balbi De Caro, 7-9). It could be said that the prestige and role of the financiers grew at a rate corresponding to the growth of the importance of cities. The movement of huge quantities of liquid capital on the Rome marketplace improved the credit system of those who wanted to conduct business; for the first time in the West, everything was done on private initiative and under an organisation removed from the political authority, even though obviously not in conflict with the latter. The term "on the Rome marketplace" *(piazza)* should not be taken merely in a figurative way, but in a concrete sense. It originates in fact from the "piazza" of the Forum itself, where from the times of the Kings onward, it seems that the *tabernae* existed. These, which initially sold basic necessities from meat to clothes, gradually yielded the prime position to the moneychangers. In a short time these occupied three sides of the forum, in order to operate in a place where meetings, business deals and the stipulation of contracts were easy. From then on, wherever there was a market the "tables of the moneychangers" multiplied, first in other areas of the city, then in other cities which entered into the Roman commercial orbit (cf. Balbi De Caro, 12-15).

**II.13** The state exercised a controlling role, to ensure that the rules would be respected. Cicero mentions that, near the Temple of the Dioscuri the *tables of the moneychangers were* *laid out.* The same could be said for the use of interest, frequently regulated by law, which if not respected involved substantial fines for those contravening; at times they could even be suspended from their activities. That this was a profession also recognised by Roman law we are led to suppose by Ulpian, who in a fragment preserved in the *Digest* also speaks of the sale of the right to carry on the profession independently of the sale of the premises where such a profession is exercised. This leads us to believe that many *argentari* carried on their profession in public places, but on a private basis, until the time when – perhaps in other areas of the city – they might purchase premises of their own (cf. Balbi De Caro, 20 and 23). These financial operators played an important role in the markets specialising in wholesale distribution; they acted as auctioneers in auction sales and hence permitted the passage of goods to various sales points. A modern scholar "presents us with an example of the sale of olives in which the seller is a wholesaler established in the city *(foraneus)* while the buyer is a wandering salesman *(circumforaneus)* who is to sell the produce acquired at the auction in the surrounding countryside" (Andreau, 602): a fact of remarkable importance which once again shows the constant social intercourse which took place in Roman commercial society. Those who carried out such activities were for the most part freedmen, and not infrequently slaves.

**II.14** The development of economic activity was also favoured by an absolute lack of customs protectionism, which drove many operators to carry on their activities in the West rather than in the East, where (under the Ptolemies, for example), there were heavy customs duties. The opportunism and far-sightedness of Augustus, who certainly had every interest in avoiding further radicalism which would have created greater lack of confidence, fixed things so that the imperial policy provided for structures which would be capable of ensuring spontaneous economic development. Not only was the principle of *laissez faire, laissez aller* accepted, but there was a notable faith in private initiative, guaranteed by the law of the same name (cf. Oertel, EU, 382-6). The stability produced and defended by Augustus produced both direct and indirect benefits. A new and efficient middle class rediscovered the conditions for a new flowering of trade and of its own gains; for its part, the government found in this new middle class a tacit and widespread consensus which rapidly extended to all the provinces. By means of this, it could consolidate the institutional transformations which had been rendered necessary during the long period of civil strife.

**II.15** In the first century, the political establishment favoured commercial activity in every possible way, building ports equipped with quays, piers, lighthouses, etc., digging canals, improving the roads and easing the rules for obtaining passports. This is the explanation for the growing interest in foreign policy, which in the age of Claudius even involved the establishment of international relations with the King of Ceylon, Maraboduo. The middle class, which gave its backing to Augustus with a growing consensus of support, demanded new luxury products, and this explains why there were trade relations with India, where great quantities of Roman coins have been found. It also explains the refining of a number of oriental crafts, such as blowing and colouring glass, and creating jewellery from amber or mirrors from silver. According to Pliny the Elder, these objects were even used by humble peasants and slaves. The lowering of taxation produced advantages for all purchasers, and for every commercial operator. All were beneficiaries of this, even the workers, if one remembers that, especially in the West, in many craft activities there was a preference for employing free or semi-free labour, rather than slaves. There were several motives for this. First of all, it was because the capital destined for the purchase of slaves could be used in other activities; then there was the fact that a slave had to be maintained for ever, and finally the slaves, because of their lack of expertise, could produce only less sophisticated goods, or at least those destined for what we would now call the mass market. Free labourers, on the other hand, were sufficiently skilled to enable certain firms to specialise in particular objects. We need only mention the fact that the metal supports for furniture made in Pompeii were manufactured in Capua (cf. Oertel, EU, 388-92). The phenomenon of slavery would become more and more widely established as the Empire became progressively orientalised. With regard to specialisation, and the refinement of some western crafts, it is perhaps worth rethinking certain preconceptions, which assumed that these workers were always seeking to imitate the elegance and precision of the East. There are works in glass or precious metals of the highest artistic value, with new polychrome features, varying from each other. I am thinking particularly of a Murano vase of the first century, or the Portland Vase from the same period, preserved in the British Museum (both reproduced in the volume with the essay by Oertel quoted here).

**II.16** There is a whole series of activities in this period, revealed by the discovery of numerous archaeological finds, which not only show how great the dimensions of trade were, but also how it could not ignore the most elementary laws of the economy and of prices. We may recall the production of Modena lanterns, which have been found all over the Empire. Oertel suggests that they should be chemically analysed, since, if they really did all come from the same origin, we are faced here with an industry of world dimensions. It should not be forgotten, either, that *goods used for the transformation or manufacture of others* were also traded, from herbs used for medicine and ointments from the Far East, to sand, taken from Koptos, used for sawing marble. Strabo also tells us that in order to maintain price-levels, there was no hesitation in destroying surplus – just as happens today, for example, with products such as coffee; the producers of papyrus from the Nile Delta had no compunction about destroying part of their produce in order to maintain stable prices (cf. Oertel, EU, 398-9). Food and medicinal industries also developed major trade between the East and West, with a great variety of products ranging from dried fruit to figs, pure honey to dried mushrooms, vegetables such as carrots, to game, and cheeses, and sea food such as tuna and oysters.

**II.17** It is interesting to note that where, as in Spain, production and prosperity grew alongside each other, there was also a notable demographic increase, and wherever there was an excess of production, export business expanded so as to create a world market. The means of transport underwent a real development, reaching the point where they transported hundreds of businessmen, or rather their agents, and tons of merchandise. Indications of a tendency towards quite complex economic and currency operations can be deduced from the special commercial centres built in the port of Ostia, in Trajan's Forum, and in other places (cf. Oertel, EU, 412-3 and 415). To this should be added a road system which crossed the entire empire, constantly growing in size and efficiency, and which, in the periods of greatest fortune for trade, was strong and secure.

**II.18** Along these communication routes heavy and valuable goods also travelled. One of the industries which flourished most in the moments of prosperity was that related to building. Evidence of a great variety of refined materials has been found in every part of the Empire, but especially where other economic activities flourished with greater facility. Apart from materials strictly linked to building, such as marbles, columns or various kinds of brick, we must also remember that there were fountains, nymphaea, or elements for both external and internal adornment, such as mosaics, stuccos and different types of decoration. All this means the marketing of various materials, and not rarely the movement of skilled craftsmen (cf. Guidobaldi, 209-19). It is remarkable to think that they were able to market materials of the kind derived from the Red Sea in the Iberian peninsula, and vice versa. Heavy goods were also transported, and at the same time fragile objects like capitals, or sarcophagi with their covers and sides finely decorated (cf. Pensabene, 304 ff).

**II.19** Speaking of communications routes, it should be mentioned that the actual roads and the vehicles that travelled along them constituted a source of economic activity of the first importance. We need only mention that the main road network, (leaving out the roads of minor importance), spread out over 150,000 kilometres, which had not only to be surveyed and maintained, but had to be supplied with indispensable services along their whole length – for travellers, for animals and for the means of transport themselves. There were posting-stations *(mansiones)* equipped with hotels *(hospitia)* in addition to storehouses and stables *(stabula)*. In addition, every five miles there were what we call today service areas, where once could find a change of horses and whatever was needed for refreshment (cf. Pisani Sartorio, 9). All this helps us to understand the great range of economic activity which we could define as a support system for trade, and which once the security of traffic had faltered, not only weakened to the point where it no longer existed, but caused the whole of economic activity to retreat into the more modest but certainly less risky manorial economy.

**II.20** The assertion that the Latin world ascribed great importance to the road system is supported by the fact that as early as in the laws of the Twelve Tables minimal measures for the roads were laid down, beginning with the criterion which ruled that when they curved they had to observe a certain measure in relation to the straight stretches, so as to allow two transport vehicles to pass comfortably without having to stop.

For the construction of the roads, a study of the route was necessary, then it had to be prepared and stratified, then consolidated and finally paved. From then onwards, the work of maintenance began immediately. On top of all this, there had to be planning for the building of drainage outlets, gutters and sewers, which were usually sited under the sidewalks so as to avoid damaging the solid road surfaces during repairs. Special operations, too were often necessary, such as bridge-building, viaducts and tunnels, which needed other support structures such as embankments, etc. Very many of these civic constructions are still in use; without moving far from Rome, we can find the tunnel leading from the Via Flaminia to the Furlo. But the most interesting point about these works is that the whole complex favoured the development of other professions, such as the *mensores* and the *architecti*, who not only planned the operations but also employed the workforce to carry them out. At this point, the profession of *curator* also entered the scene; to him was entrusted the task of managing the roads (cf. Quilici, 18-19 and 31). It was only then that the traffic of carts and carriages, mainly but not exclusively commercial, began. It is worth remembering that it is from the word *carrus* that we derive the words for the means of transport in many of the most commonly spoken modern languages – for example *carro* in Spanish or *car* in English.

**II.21** It is obvious that the traffic was not exclusively commercial. A number of public activities were linked to the roads – not only military ones, but many others such as postal services or movements simply due to personal reasons. But all this increased even more the economic activities linked to the construction of carts, for example. We can deduce the variety of the systems of transport from the laws relating to transport, archaeological material and coinage. We can also ascertain the number of people and the weight of the merchandise which they could carry; their speed, their dimensions and the number of animals used for transportation. The animals varied according to the geographical location and the fauna. Horses were not always preferred when camels or dromedaries or other animals could be used. It may be surprising to find that certain means of transport were forbidden access to the cities, sometimes completely, sometimes at limited hours. This caused other professions to arise and flourish in the suburban areas near the great gates of the cities. There was provision for the possibility of hiring lighter carts, and of leaving the bigger vehicles which could only enter the city by night parked in designated official areas *(area carruces)*. And one could hire a driver in some of the outlying areas, just like a modern taxi (cf. Pisani Sartorio, 14-5). The carts and carriages also served as representational vehicles, or for casual outings and competitions. All this was to increase the variety of means produced and marketed, as it would also increase the number of occupations involved in their maintenance and repair.

**II.22** The building of means of transport, even before their completion and marketing, involves other activities and hence forms of employment. Pliny and Vitruvius show the importance of this period in wood-cutting and the choice of wood from among the various types available. We have various illustrations of the different stages of manufacture, which show that the technical side was linked to the quest for good taste and the different demands of those who purchased the goods. Purposes ranged from agriculture to parades, from luxury vehicles decorated with rich inlay work to triumphal chariots. However, all show two requisites of the ancient Mediterranean civilisation: solidity and functional efficiency. The market for these types of means of transport was enormous: the corporation of carpenters *(fabri tignarii)*, was one of the most important in the first two centuries of the Empire (cf. Pisani Sartorio, 17-21). Apart from the constructors, the drivers also formed a leading corporation, with prestigious offices near the most important meeting-points for business and trade. The significance of this category, divided into carters, cabmen, coachmen, sedan-chair bearers and others can be seen if we bear in mind that as for many other activities, there was competition between the private and public sectors. For urban and suburban transport, there was a sort of taximeter, which fixed the tariff according to the best route.

**II.23** The transport of goods and foodstuffs of long-term preservation was carried out with special carts, not only very large but also equipped with wide-mesh netting or canvas flaps bound to the sides of the cart with cords, just as we see today on big lorries on the motorways. Special vehicles also existed for the carriage of the sick or of elderly people. These consisted of a cart known as the *arcera*, on which it was possible to lie the person down on blankets or carpets (cf. Pisani Sartorio, 61 and 65). It is worth noting that for certain types of transfer, there was a sort of *roulotte*, the so-called *carruca dormitoria,* almost always privately owned, intended for medium to long-distance moves, which could also be used for a certain number of family members. These were large carts, sufficiently so for Juvenal to remark sarcastically that they looked like entire houses (cf. Pisani Sartorio, 56-9).

**II.24** While the robust qualities of the vehicles may not have varied from one social class to another, their elegance certainly did. It is clear that according to the social standing of those who carried on economic activities, the movement of capital and the rates of interest granted to those who asked for loans also varied. People of knightly rank or senators had ways of demanding less excessive rates of interest from the money-lenders. But every activity also varied in relation to the various economic situations, apart from the social status of the people involved in the world of business – to such an extent that (once again from Cicero) we learn that Senator Considius allowed, at a moment of economic crisis, some postponements in the payment of interest and capital lent, even though this reached the substantial sum of fifteen million sesterces. Cicero also points in many of his descriptions to the fact that the society of his time was dynamic in requesting and granting loans, as in undertaking all sorts of financial activities. Writing to his friend Atticus, who was particularly skilled in business matters, he shows how even high-ranking persons (Julius Caesar, for instance) had considerable recourse to loans – as did people in leading positions far away from the city. We can deduce, among other things, that in that period there was a substantial movement of capital from Rome to the distant provinces and vice versa (cf. Balbi De Caro, 30-2). This also explains why, in time, the central mint alone proved insufficient, and beginning with Gaul, others sprung up, not merely for local use.

**II.25** In a passage in the *Digest* (42, 5; 24, 2) with the precision of a jurist, Ulpian points out the difference existing between the non-productive deposit and the profit-bearing loan. The first is characterised by the "gratuity of the relation between depositor and depositary". The nature of the second is different, and allowed the operator to use the deposited cash. In this case "the right to receive the interest on the part of the depositor initiates not from the moment of the deposit, but from the point at which the sum has been put to use". It is only from that date, in fact, that the contract changes nature and from a "contract of deposit" is transformed into a "contract of usury". Between the two parties, whichever does not respect the terms of the contract, even if only temporary, will be obliged to pay a fine in terms of interest. The banking operator was in any case obliged to effect a series of operations for the customer who had deposited the sum; provide exact statements of account for the operations, and the interest matured, and make payments on behalf of his own client. To all this (again as shown in the *Digest*), must be added that the client could withdraw the sums deposited by him at the time and place desired: *quae quando voles et ubi voles confestim tibi* *numerabo*. The law also regulated the way of cancelling a bank account with particular precision; according to whether it was active or not; it dealt with calculation of interest and other procedures (cf. Balbi De Caro, 39-40). I think that the definition of a usury contract – a term which in time assumed an almost outrageous significance – would have signified at the beginning simply a contract for the use of wealth. Moreover *usura*, in many parts of Cicero's correspondence, means use of capital loaned. All this is confirmed by the word *usurarius*, which as we gather from some of the comedies of Plautus, is one who has the use or the enjoyment of money, a provisional and temporary use, for which someone may acquire a legal interest. With reference to interest, it should be said that as is the case today and always has been, this varied, even in the legal context, according to the risk of the operation, but also the social and political prestige of the person who sought to obtain it. In the age of Justinian, the maximum limit of interest that could be charged was 12%, but it fell to 8% for merchants of rank, and could even go down to 4% for particularly illustrious people.

**II.26** To say that banking activity had to be carried on in the context of legality means that there had to be, for every operation, a series of documents which could be presented at need to the legal authorities. For this reason, those working in banking had under normal circumstances to keep an account book *(codex rationum)* with all the operations and the signatures of the operators, which had full validity as written proof. These books were to be handed on to the heirs, and in the case of necessity, to the slaves when the banker died, or simply if he had retired from business. If the bank was made up of several shareholders, it was the responsibility of the person who had actual possession. With the spread of parchment manuscripts, it seems that they no longer took the form of rolls, but of genuine registers contained in ordinary files, with chronological indices. After the date came all the useful information: names, including those of witnesses, amount of the sum, place where the deed was compiled, expiry date of the contract (and since the Romans were accustomed to fixing them at the calends of each month), the timetable came to be known as the *calendarium* (cf. Balbi De Caro, 58 ff).

**II.27** The credit activities of these bankers were varied, as were the classes which made use of such financial operators. A well-known scholar of these phenomena of the ancient world maintains that the components of the "municipal aristocracies, on whose affairs we are less well informed, were probably the most habitual clients of the professional bankers who thus carried on a form of short term commercial credit with the merchants, similar in its economic function (but not in mode or juridical characteristics) to the modern discount institute" (Andreau, 602). It is to this same scholar that we owe the certainty that the term *argentarius* was applied to those who undertook banking activities. Until the fourth century of the Christian Era, the Latins never confused the *argentarius* with the landed proprietor or the merchant who lent out money. Passages from the commentary of Donatus on the comedies of Terence show that already by the fourth century, no payment was any longer made in the bank. All this finds confirmation in the interesting seventh letter of St Augustine, in which he calls himself a *collectarius*, to whom was entrusted a deposit of money, but there is no longer any mention of an *argentarius*; the term was in process of taking on a new meaning (cf. Andreau, 605-6). The *collectarius* did not previously have these functions, but was limited to testing the money and being an agent of exchange. The new functions taken on, which denote a radical change in Roman economic life, are mentioned several times by Augustine. In those times, what was going on was what we might call a *juridical popularisation* consisting in the use of terms of Roman law which every classical jurist would have avoided, and no legislator would have dared to introduce into the *Corpus iuris*.

That the Bishop of Hippo had perceived the difficulty of wriggling out of a law which was already in decay, is shown by the subsequent letter, in which, given "the complexity of the rights of property in post-classical judicial practice" he advises Victor to avoid bringing a controversy before the bishop's court, in part because since it concerns a problem relating to the Jews, the question must be resolved by a Jewish judge, because of the privileges accorded to the Jews by Roman Law (cf. Carrozzi, XLV-LI).

**II.28** The fact that a change was going on, even in terminology, moves us on to understand that within the empire, a monetary, financial and commercial transformation had taken place, of a kind which led in the West at least to the disappearance of certain specific professions. All this – even though it should not be understood in terms of a sign of a "global catastrophe", since the banking profession was not the only cog in the wheel of monetary circulation – must not be taken as a mere incidental fact. The *argentari* could, in fact, provide short-term credit, thus allowing the merchants to restock more rapidly, without waiting for purchasers to pay the price of the products sold. They could thus buy more even though they did not immediately have the sums required. The transactions might indeed be modest, but they were nevertheless numerous and they came specifically from that middle class which had made its fortunes and the greatness of Rome indivisible (cf. Andreau, 612-14). While it is true that "however abstract it may be, the notion of the market is not one and indivisible (...) In Italy, the transformations which were produced between the third and first centuries BC seem to me to reveal an extension of the market as a conglomerate of independent markets". Then the disappearance of the banking operators, and hence of credit, "marked a recession in the market". Even though they may have been small in dimensions the numerous transactions which formerly existed marked a strong reduction in trade when they finally came to an end, and a notable fragmentation between markets and the poverty of exchange. All this, again, confirms the end of so many small entrepreneurs who, scared by political uncertainty, withdrew their savings and were reluctant to allow them to circulate (cf. Andreau, 615). Scarcity of available goods and monetary inflation, also caused (as I shall shortly show) by a reduced real value in coinage, forced the central governments to intervene more and more in economic affairs. We only need recall the example of Commodus, who managed even to fix prices (cf. Balbi De Caro, 26). We are coming close here to something that some scholars have described as the age of *State Socialism*, a phenomenon which was progressively realized when the encroachments of the central government, and also of local governments, forced private entrepreneurs progressively to withdraw from economic activity, or to move it to contexts far removed from political control. Thus there arose a mutual distrust between the political and economic spheres – a possibly underestimated cause of the crisis of the ancient world.

**II.29** I said in my *The Open Society and its Friends* that the Roman political authority succeeded in building a long and durable consensus because it "governed little". This guaranteed an undoubted prosperity, which was evidenced above all in the economic prosperity of the first century AD. The central governments guaranteed an unquestionable freedom of action of what we today call the bourgeoisie, even going so far as to encourage their economic enterprises. In every part of the empire, commercial centres and markets developed, which became more and more specialised. All this was facilitated by the fact that the authorities protected the communication routes on land and sea, by rivers and canals; that new ports were created even in lands previously far from the commercial routes, and that new roads were built even at the confines of the Empire, while the more ancient ones were improved or extended. The customs dues imposed were minimal at this time, and such as to ensure commercial guarantees but not to discourage trade itself (cf. Oertel, ELE, 232-5). New cities were also founded, favouring the formation of an indigenous bourgeoisie which willingly accepted the Roman laws and institutions which guaranteed them stability and prosperity. *The real reason which impeded the formation of a proper capitalist system, as we understand it today, lay in the fact that apart from the problems of the labour force, with which I shall deal in the next chapter, the bourgeoisie never succeeded in becoming a majority class in a situation where the primary activity always remained that of agriculture.* The new cities and the new local middle classes acquired greater and greater autonomy. From lands which at the outset were destined only to provide raw materials, they were now transformed into places where work was carried on *in loco*, and manufactured goods of various kinds were created and exported. Many of the provinces became self-sufficient and competition improved the products (cf. Oertel, ELE, 236). The point was almost reached of the creation of real industries such as the manufacture of bricks, lanterns and glass, which also moved to those territories where logistical and marketing conditions made them most profitable. Raw materials too, like lead, tin and gold were extracted where it proved to be most convenient, and this was also the case with agricultural goods: grain, oil, and wine were produced where facility of transport and consumer markets gave rise to the promise of highest profit. The same could be said of fish.

**II.30** The zones of greatest development were those where manufactures were established for the growing demand for prime necessity goods, such as food, but also for materials and the dyeing of these, which served not only for the soldiers, but also for their families, once certain production centres became established in particular zones along the Rhine. Stability and peace facilitated commercial exchanges with people who had hardly been taken into account in other epochs. There is evidence of trade with the people of central Russia and Scandinavia, not to mention India. The exchanges were long-lasting, profitable and constant. India was in fact a point of passage between the Roman world and China, and beyond, towards Sumatra and Indo-China. It is now well-established that the Roman geographical notions, very advanced for the time, were, in contrast to the Greek ones, indebted to research by undoubtedly brilliant scholars, based on practical and concrete presuppositions. These triggered off economic and commercial interests which obliged those in power and even the Emperors themselves, from the time of Augustus, to cultivate geographical studies. It was thus that geographers such as Strabo, who certainly did not add any new conceptions to the study of physical geography already formulated by Eratosthenes, nevertheless notably increased the social, economic and political awareness of their day (cf. Cimino, 4)

**II.31** The practical importance of geographical studies is demonstrated by certain works, such as the anonymous *Periplus Maris Erythraei,* which show the great interest that the commercial traffic had in knowledge of the naval routes which facilitated the relations between the Roman world and India The flat, inelegant style, the constant information on the best routes, and best periods to undertake journeys, make it clear that the readers aimed at by this work were precisely those engaged in the trade – the merchants, in other words. Moreover, the text, written in far from stylish Greek and nowadays dated to the first century AD shows that it was directed not only in general terms to merchants, but perhaps specifically to those who, in the eastern territories of the Empire, both Greek and Arab, were the agents of the major companies importing goods to the western Roman world. The existence of the *Tabula Peutingeriana*, with its interesting notations, also shows that the existence of commercial traffic with India was by no means just occasional. The existence of a *Templum Augusti* indicated in those far distant parts points to the existence of free points of exchange there, and also of small colonies (cf. Cimino, 8-10). Among other things, the desire of Augustus to achieve a sort of *pax romana* seems certain to have obtained the consensus of India, which sent a diplomatic mission to Rome in the conviction that both these extensive territories would derive benefit from a policy which tended to surround the "inconvenient" peoples of the Parties. It is worth recalling that well before the time of Augustus, expansion towards the East had been the dream of Caesar who, in this matter sought to emulate Alexander the Great. We have various witnesses to this intention, from Propertius, Virgil, Tibullus and others, pointing to the fact that the murder of Caesar was due not, as a romantic vision of the past would have us believe, to the heroic action of certain lovers of liberty. It arose, in contrast, from the action of an upper middle class which saw in the policy of Caesar a useless waste of resources, both human and economic, in order to acquire territories "full of sand", from which valuable merchandise could be acquired simply from the increase of maritime trade, or, in certain periods, of caravans. And this explains the eastern policy of Augustus.

**II.32** It was in fact trade which made clear the liberal principles on which the Roman economy was based. The economic power of some of the provinces grew notably, reaching the point where it enjoyed almost a position of monopoly in the exchange of certain products, and consequently obtained a different political weight. Then a new debate began on what might be the best roads for traffic with the East, even to the point of speculating on the best possible silk road to China. This is the period in which, says Strabo, communications with the East became almost regular, so that each year about 120 ships left the Red Sea directed towards India. Until the time of Constantine, and even later, the commercial traffic continued, though with considerable difficulty, until the upper middle class was reduced to impotence by a more and more precarious and centralised economic policy (cf. Cimino, 25, and 28-30). It should be remembered that one of the reasons for the crisis in the Empire can be found precisely in these exchanges, as the monetary system was such as to involve a progressive loss of real riches on the part of those who purchased. In order to confront this crisis, the alloy with which the coinage was made became progressively less valuable, and this involved a mounting increase in prices and a dizzy increase in the public debt. In order to appreciate the huge amounts of money used for the commercial exchanges, it is sufficient to mention that, as was clearly shown, every year India took from the Roman Empire not less than 50 million sesterces (cf. Pliny, VI, 23, 26).

**II.33** All this shows that the market was no longer aiming merely for self-sufficiency and certainly could not be said to be a closed economic system. Trade and the related economic activities were not merely occasional, but became systematic; we need only point out today the size and importance of certain commercial ports such as ancient Ostia. This was also the moment at which a substantial circulation of coinage began, and this in turn raised problems by no means easy to solve. It should be added that warehouses, deposits, bazaars, markets and fairs developed almost everywhere. Commercial associations and corporations developed and the merchants – we have evidence of repeated and lengthy movements – voyaged constantly from the East, even the Far East, by way of the caravans of Palmyra, to the West, and vice versa. Perhaps, if Sombart had considered the phenomenon of the movements of these merchants, he would have added a few extra pages to the beginning of the fifty-first chapter (entitled *Foreigners*) of the first volume of his famous work on capitalism, already mentioned in the introductory pages of this book. The importance of the superstructure for development is shown by the fact that the maximum prosperity was reached when, under the Antonines, security became a real benefit from which all could draw their own advantages. Roads were built, such as the new Trajan Way *(Via Traiana)* which linked important cities, making possible exchanges not only of goods, but also of culture and religion.

**II.34** In the midst of such prosperity and political stability, more than one person has speculated as to why there was no radical economic transformation of the ancient world capable of remodelling the social texture of that historical moment. However, I think the question is wrongly framed. It would, in fact, be better to keep in mind that since the necessity of economising labour did not exist, *one of the fundamental laws of economics did not come into play:* that of attaining the maximum result with the minimal possible effort. This also explains why, when free labour was gradually becoming established, especially in the western world, the latter entered a crisis due to the additional costs, while in the Orient, where slavery was culturally more deeply rooted, it survived longer and also enjoyed a longer period of prosperity (cf. Oertel, ELE, 242-8 and 253-4). This is the origin of the decay of that western finesse, which, as tends to happen in all civilisations with markets and institutions in crisis, brought with it the *triumph of a certain kind of mediocrity.*

**II.35** A progressive levelling in production and in consumption, a fiscal system at the limits of survival, due to the politico-military transformations of the Empire, involved the crisis of that economic liberty which had favoured the establishment of prosperity. It also allowed the progressive realisation of state socialism, characterised by the omnipotence of the state, by its control by a paternalistic administration, which meant the disappearance of the economic fortunes of private individuals. The immediate needs required more and more extraordinary taxation. The insecurity of transport caused certain shortages, generating a climate of growing lack of confidence (cf. Oertel, ELE, 255-6). In order to remedy these problems, certain governments began debasing the coinage. Its real value was obviously affected, and inflation began. Among the most immediate consequences was the poor financial profitability of certain professions. The public offices which, in the past, had been undertaken voluntarily and quite often *pro tempore*, now became obligatory with increasingly fictitious privileges and pay. A widespread lack of commitment was found everywhere, increasing the inadequate fulfilment of public offices, and immorality in their performance. The sole remedy proposed was always that of further taxation and devaluation. A climate of growing lack of trust caused a decrease in births, also due to other motives, and protests of various kinds which led to what amounted to strikes (cf. Oertel, ELE, 257-9 and 261-2). The East, Africa, the Rhineland territories and Britannia all managed to withdraw themselves from the general crisis, but in the rest of the Roman world there was the ruin of the bourgeoisie which, when it was able, fled to the territories where prosperity still prevailed. This intensified certain forms of banditry, to repress which extraordinary measures were demanded. It was thus that special police forces were accepted, and without particular resistance the advent of the absolute State was also accepted. On the economic level, this achieved a situation of *total state socialism.*

**II.36** In the third century, the state, after having become the greatest landowner, appropriated directly to itself the quarries and mines, and after a time it also came to control certain special types of industry. These included mints, brick-works, textile manufactures, but above all foundries and arms production centres. Moreover wholesale and on-the-spot trade in other goods was placed more and more under government control. Then there was the phenomenon of the *anabolicae species,* i.e. genuine forms of nationalisation which even affected means of transport. In short, there was "an evolution towards oriental forms of economic organisation". With regard to the local situation, the West was heading towards a type of economic feudalism, which showed the future to be tending to a more and more closed economic system (cf. Oertel, ELE, 272-5). The most important thing, however, was the progressive appropriation by the state of the mercantile marine. The effect was that of carrying the economy back towards primitive forms of barter, and while the recession was not equal everywhere in the Empire, the monetary catastrophe made itself felt sooner or later all over the place. With the price policy adopted by Diocletian, the economy was already heading towards a system of planned production. A certain type of individualism, which saved a great part of ancient culture, was that of the aristocratic classes, and of the first forms of property introduced by Christianity, so that at least the cultural unity of the Mediterranean was saved (cf. Oertel, ELE, 277-81).

## A commonplace about the economy of the High Middle Ages

**II.37** Even a historian such as Henri Pirenne, in his famous *Histoire économique de l'Occident Médiéval*, claimed that movements of a commercial and economic nature can be identified as existing only after the beginning of the second millennium. In his view, the return of the merchant – supported by an increasingly urban life – who rediscovered ancient juridical institutions and updated them; the emerging maritime republics and the renewed safety of travelling by water; and the rediscovery of the ancient itineraries between Northern and Southern Europe which were developing hand in hand with those between East and West: all favoured an increase and shifting of wealth which had seemed for centuries only something to yearned for. On closer inspection, however, such is not the case. An attentive scholar such as Morghen speaks of continuity rather than rebirth. Indeed, there was "a state of affairs which, *de iure*, had never completely disappeared, but had only in actual fact been interrupted for contingent causes. Once these were removed, it was more than natural to return to the ancient'. In that period of transition, however, even ecclesiastical law, the rules produced by General Chapters, and "the *canones* took on a positive juridical value" (Morghen, 53 and 68). Even the concept of sovereignty, so important to the modern state, can be traced back to that "tradition of ancient Rome which attributed concrete and exemplary value to that conception of sovereignty, law and political relations" (Morghen, 99). This concept of sovereignty, which was characteristic of the Church, was handed down to the emerging state, as Le Goff himself appropriately points out. It is no accident that this French historian refers to the Church as the most advanced of the modern states and the holder of the largest amount of money, even though, naturally, the uses to which it was put had to be seen in a particular and single perspective (cf. Le Goff, 2010, ch. VI). Even the revenue system had its special development. What I must point out in particular, however, is that behind the revenue collection system there was a monetary system which throughout the High Middle Ages revealed a need for continuity, perhaps understood as a guarantee of stability. Indeed, money for all those lands that had been part of the ancient Empire represented "one of the rare tools for unification", tranquillity and prosperity. This is why the Anglo-Saxon sovereigns of Kent, in the High Middle Ages, still sought to issue a currency which imitated the Roman (cf. Le Goff, 2010, ch. I).

**II.38** As regards stability, it should be observed that monetary stability was one of the major issues addressed throughout the Middle Ages. This had been the case ever since national currencies had needed – it was felt – safe and strong international currencies to which to refer. This was the case for the long period of time when the ducat of Venice and the Florentine florin carried out this function and became standards of reference. As the Middle Ages drew to a close, currency questions become more and more complicated. The need was thus felt to specify the relationship between currencies with greater clarity. A meeting of experts and diplomats was thus held at Bruges in 1469. Louis XI, Edward IV, Frederic III, Charles of Burgundy and the Venetian ambassadors took part (cf. Le Goff, 2010, Ch. XII). It should be no surprise that the Papacy, which, according to Le Goff was "perhaps the most prodigious institution of the West", was not present. The economy tended to free itself from religion, which, throughout the Middle Ages, placed the economy and every other activity in a precise perspective. Every pattern of life and system of thinking could not, indeed, be measured in monetary terms since Christianity had, as its point of departure, the act of divine love of giving freely offered gifts, to which believers somehow had to relate. The humanistic view of the idea of wealth certainly did not appear suddenly. For centuries, various examples and matters for reflection had emerged but there is no doubt that the concept of *caritas* was fundamental and permeated every human activity. As Polanyi has quite clearly pointed out, it is not that trade and wealth did not have value, indeed they were central to the action of the Church, but that this system of values in its entirety was always subordinated to *caritas*.

**II.39** What has been said is also confirmed in the trade carried out in the early Middle Ages. Recent excavations in the *Portus Romae* bear witness to this. A drop in trade was attributed to the political crisis underway in the city, in part due to a population crisis which had reduced the number of inhabitants. Yet a grain supply was never lacking. From the beginning of the seventh century to the first thirty years of the eighth, when Emperor Leo the Isaurian confiscated the Italian papal holdings in southern Italy and in Sicily, food continued to arrive and, above all, there was never an interruption in grain supplies. That meant not only that the granary structure continued to operate but also that the food administration, along with transport from the harbour to the city, continued to function (cf. Coccia, 178 and 189). Furthermore, levels of employment survived and only entered a crisis between the second half of the ninth and the beginning of the tenth centuries. There are those who even cast doubt on this date since John VIII in the last quarter of the ninth century exhorted the people of Amalfi to enter the *Portus Urbis Romae* to return 10,000 silver mancuses. This means that the port was still highly active (cf. Coccia, 192 and 196).

**II.40** One "basically unknown" fact should be recalled: the circulation of locally produced ceramics during the same period, that is, between the late ancient period and the High Middle Ages. A study of this phenomenon brings out the fact that there were two major ports along the Roman shore: Ostia and Porto. The latter has practically been forgotten. The few excavations carried out have revealed items exchanged between the various Mediterranean routes (Ciarrocchi, Martin, 203 and 214-215). It would be advisable to continue excavating to shed light on a period that is still obscure as far as trade is concerned. The same might be said of the circulation of money in the entire region. This has already been examined (Rovelli, 1993, 333 ff.) but further surprises might come in the two ports themselves. Moreover, even at times considered to be periods of crisis, such as that between the sixth and seventh centuries, we have evidence that it was possible to be supplied with anything on the market of the city of Rome. Wine itself, which can be seen as the product of the "Remaining Roman assets in Africa", actually came from Gaza and Cyprus, thereby showing that "trade in high-quality goods" still existed. The aid magnanimously offered by Gregory the Great certainly demonstrates the sense of charity of the Pontiff, but it could certainly not have been enough to feed all of the city's population (cf. Delogu, 1993, 14 ff.). Much of the self-sufficient population continued to reside in Rome.

**II.41** In the background to this, a world of professions and workers gave a stimulus to daily life. Many of the jobs were performed by women. This may all seem hazardous speculation but "above and beyond literary stereotypes" inscriptions and linguistic studies and tradition have amply attested to the fact that erudite women had professions, for example obstetrics (cf. Malaspina, 363-364). This professional competence was being consolidated with Christianity on a spiritual level as well (cf. Lazzari). In other words, to use Richard Hodges' fortunate phrase, *"with all due respect* for Edward Gibbon" the Roman world was anything but the expression of a crisis even in the seventh and eighth centuries. Quite the contrary: it was filled with "remarkable activity". Churches, mosaics, paintings, coins, the restoration of civic buildings and walls confirm this belief (cf. Hodges, 363 and 360-361).

**II.42** Between the papacy of Hadrian I (772-795) and that of Leo IV (847-855), Rome was the scene of extraordinary activity, producing, for example, tapestry and drapery used to decorate presbyteries, ciboria altars, etc. Their origin, as shown in the *Liber Pontificalis*, brings to mind rather diversified commercial activities since the *Byzantine*, *Alexandrian* and *Tyrian* fabrics bear witness to various sources from various parts of the Mediterranean, especially the eastern ones (cf. Delogu, 1998, 123 and 126). The interruptions in some typical periods seem due to temporary bans on exportations imposed by the Byzantine authorities. This means that the diversification in supplies was not due merely to economic factors, costs in other words, but also political ones. It may, at times, have been that "the Popes no longer possessed adequate means of payment", but perhaps, too, conflicts with the Byzantine systems had made alternative sources of trade with Spain advisable. Perhaps, in addition, both factors had led to trade alternatives. It is no accident that, under Hadrian I, when the Council of Nicaea condemned iconoclasm and there was the consequent reconciliation of Rome and Constantinople, various importers were attracted to Rome (cf. Delogu, 1998, 134-135 and 137-138).

**II.43** These facts have been confirmed not only by archaeological research and the remains of precious fabrics but also by the discovery of exceptional numismatic objects, for example those found in the *Crypta Balbi* where even Arab and Byzantine coins have been brought to light. This all proves intense trade activity. From the 680s onwards, "singular anonymous coins are to be found that the mint of Rome began to produce towards the end of Constantine IV's reign (668-685) and the beginning of Justinian II's (685-695)". These specimens "bring up various questions". Anonymous coins are present that were such "because of the intentions of those who had issued them". Now this is believed to be the first "Pontifical interference in the activities of the mint". Some coins have monograms that C. Morrisson believes bring to mind names of Popes starting with Sergius I (687-701). Many of these are bronze coins (cf. Rovelli, 1998, 79 and 81). The ceramics found in the excavations, too, prove that many of their origins – 80% – are foreign, especially African, and are from the seventh century. Those of the subsequent century, however, come from Southern Italy, in particular Campania and the Straits of Messina. This suggests an increasing separation between the two capitals and the growing independence of the Popes from the Empire. To be sure, there was no immediate break, and this could mean that at the beginning the ability to mint money was "by Imperial authorization". It is certain, in any case, that this was not a question of the decadence of Rome since many of the objects of craftsmen that have come down to us are highly refined "in terms of techniques of craftsmanship and iconographic models". In fact, the objects show that there were Lombard as well as Byzantine influences (cf. Rovelli, 1998, 83 ff.).

**II.44** The launching of a mint is evidence of political rather than economic factors. Rome was, indeed, not a city left to its own devices. Considerable reconstruction work occurred. This took place on the initiative and under the direction of an efficient and ever-present bureaucracy. As Arnaldi maintains: "under Gregory the Great the Roman Church had now taken the place of the Imperial administration in managing food services" (cf. Lonardo, 63). *The events of that period are obscured by considerable ignorance.* "Few people" in fact "imagined that as late as 663 an emperor came to live in the imperial palace on the Palatine as a sovereign in his own home". This was a clear sign that the palace had to be kept up even during his absence. For this reason some believe that the administrative apparatus had not ceased to function before the Carolingian period. If anything, as the imperial bureaucracy gradually entered a situation of crisis the Popes "progressively became the points of reference and guarantors of this administration tout court". Even though the Popes had reached the point of increasing their civil authority later than other bishops, relatively speaking they kept it for a longer period. The election of the Bishop of Rome took place independently of the sovereign's indications, even though the latter had to ratify the result. The fact is that the long vacancy before consecration was of use to the civil power only to "verify the correctness of the procedure". That imperial ratification was never denied for the election of a Pope is evidence of the "authoritativeness of the Apostolic See". Ratification also confirms the fact that, for the Roman sources, the authoritativeness of the Empire "had not been interrupted" as far as Roman sources are concerned (cf. Lonardo, 5-6 and 21-23). In parallel fashion, it was the Holy See that allowed the Empire to maintain ties with the kingdoms of the West, as far away as Britain, since they were continually "visited by missionaries and their emissaries" (cf. Lonardo, 33 note 59). This says a great deal not only about the authoritativeness of the Roman Apostolic See but also about the difficulties of travelling during the High Middle Ages, making trade impossible. I shall return shortly to this subject.

**II.45** It is useful to point out that in 381, during the First Constantinople Council, "the seat of Rome was proclaimed to be the foremost of all the bishop's seats" and subsequently, when theological conflicts arose, Rome took care to observe that the condemnation always concerned the Bishop of Constantinople and not the Emperor at all (cf. Lonardo, 42-43). The *distinction* between temporal and religious power had already been established. When a Council had to be convened in the mid-seventh century to resolve the question of monotheletism, this was prepared by Rome in the Lateran Synod. Its major source of inspiration is the author who wrote the most significant passages – probably Maximus the Confessor. This arrests to the fact that, among other things, "the great ability of the Roman chancellery, in this circumstance, to operate in the two languages, Greek and Latin (...)[is] a clear indication that the ability to produce culture remained in the Rome of the mid-seventh century". That the Holy See had particular influence in Constantinople is shown by the fact that the voice of the Roman Curia was listened to in other areas as well. During the brief papacy of John V (685-686), the Emperor modified the legislation on taxation to make it less onerous, "probably upon specific request from the Pope" (cf. Lonardo, 112-113 and 192).

**II.46** Some scholars have noted that from the papacy of Benedict II onwards, the classic dual *Senatus Populusque Romanus* was gradually being replaced by the triple *Clerus-Exercitus-Populus*. This indicates not only a political turning point, when the city was decidedly on the side of the Apostolic See, as the events surrounding Martin I show, but also one of an economic character. In that period an increasing localization of the army took place with the specific purpose of reducing military expenditure due to continual transfers of troops and to "make the defence more efficacious *in loco*" (cf. Lonardo, 255 ff.). This all underscores the fact that there was continuity and, I would say, autonomy, in the management of the region's financial resources. The distribution of salaries for the bureaucracy and the military, but not only these, implied a tax system capable of acquiring revenue. In the *Liber Pontificalis*, the regularity of these payments was emphasized. The system of taxation was, moreover, rather diversified. This shows that the imperial authorities were fully aware of the diverse systems they had to govern. As far as Roman finances were concerned, account must also be taken – and the documents often bring this out – that the administration took care not only to pay salaries but also made charitable contributions, which, logically enough, were a decisive factor for the Church (cf. Lonardo, 264-265 and 276). Building and maintenance costs also became financial items. "The impressive list of the works carried out provides a view of Rome as a city which did not seem to be in ruins or in total chaos". As has already been said in relation to imported materials, attention was devoted not only to restoration and building but also to embellishments. This shows that the city now certainly had independent funds and management (cf. Lonardo, 280 ff.). In other words, civic and financial life developed hand in hand with religious life.

**II.47** The fact that the papacy now felt independent from Constantinople is also shown by another economic aspect – that of defence expenditure. We know for certain "that the *plurima pars murorum* was restructured". A threefold threat was being felt – "Lombard, Arab and Byzantine" – and it could come from many sides. This explains why, in addition to the city walls, thought was given to restoring those of *Centumcellae*, the Civitavecchia of today. Given that it was faced by the Lombard enemy demonstrates that Rome was confronting, and now on its own, the various populations from the North, and its moral reputation gave it a primary role in political matters and not just religious and pastoral ones (cf. Lonardo, 340-342 and 427). The events of the return of the Lombard King of Sutri is worthy of mention here. All of this "seems to have come about thanks to the simple request by Gregory II who, in his capacity as Bishop of Rome, addressed himself to the king, as one of the Church's faithful" (cf. Lonardo, 324). This shows that "Rome was not perceived as being exclusively tied to the Latin world" and not only as far as religious matters were concerned. The recurring expression "*toto in orbe terrarum*" shows this clearly. It was used several times by Pope Zacharias, as records of his life show. Furthermore, the settlement of the monothelitism question also conferred theological and spiritual superiority in the eyes of the Eastern world. The weakening of political ties, even genuine autonomy, had increased with the exarchate crisis of Ravenna. The consecration of Pope Zacharias a week after his election confirms this, further proving that there was no longer any need to wait as there had been in the past, "no *iussio* of the exarch" on the Emperor's behalf or by the Emperor himself (cf. Lonardo, 406-410 and 347).

**II.48** Whatever the case, the recurring delegations and trade associated with them show that the Lombards and the various peoples of the North did not hinder travel and trade, as was the case in the Mediterranean. To be sure, there were, as always, periods that were less or more advantageous for commerce and trade. Even when there were "time restrictions", administrative, military and commercial structures continued to function. All of this, naturally, "is not consonant with a Rome of the seventh century depressed and largely consisting of the indigent". The city was still full of construction, restoration and rebuilding and was thus also capable of offering jobs (cf. Lonardo, 473 and 486). Similar construction also went on in the eighth century when major works were engaged in, such as those for the *eccelesia Sancti Laurenti* and in particular for the basilica *beati Pauli apostoli* whose beams were brought in from *Calabria* for the work of restoration (cf. Lonardo, 304 and 306), proving the vitality of trade and transport.

**II.49** The monumental work *Origins of the European Economy. Communications and Commerce, A. D. 300-900* by Michael McCormick shows that there were a large number of people travelling, even during the most difficult moments of the High Middle Ages: ambassadors, pilgrims, refugees, slaves, pillagers, merchants, and, accompanying them, news, letters, illnesses, and all sorts of objects, coins, silk, spices and a not insignificant dose of relics of saints (as the collection kept in the *Sancta Santorum* of the Papal Lateran palace, which is "the most appealing and the least well known", demonstrates). Activity in Rome went on between 200 and 700, even if the economic trend was downwards, but it recovered in the two subsequent centuries in particular areas and under clearly defined political systems. In the central period, which McCormick deals with, a significant number of inscriptions bear witness to the attempt to restore part of the western road system. In the seventh century in Rome there was a prosperous and numerous Greek monastic community, but the Holy See was able to collect funds needed to assist the numerous pilgrims coming to visit the tombs of the apostles. There is considerable evidence on the food, but also the services, baths and assistance that the travellers received at the expense of the papacy, for example under Martin I and Leo III.

**II.50** This confirms the fact that between the eighth and ninth centuries there was a period of political and institutional stability that favoured commerce, trade and the resumption of civil life. One must start with what happened for at least two centuries, between the end of antiquity and the beginning of the Middle Ages. As has already been pointed out, the state had assumed responsibility for a significant number of economic activities. This took place in trade since ship owners were encouraged to transport food supplies at the lowest possible cost. To be sure, tax incentives were offered, but transporters could also carry other non-food merchandise tax-free. Moreover, *navicularii* could more easily obtain supplies of raw materials, such as wood for shipbuilding. All in all, they enjoyed a series of safeguards that encouraged them to back the statist view of trade because the state could always confiscate the fortunes of those ship owners who diverged sharply from the statist policy. Whatever the case, this policy of food transport reached the point of modifying the flow of long-distance communications. It was, in particular, the eastern Mediterranean and hence the Byzantine world that implemented this policy. However, the food administration system continued to operate, guaranteeing communications and transport that would otherwise have been unthinkable (cf. McCormick, ch. IV). In addition, if one really wants to opt for an era of crisis and war, it is impossible not to realize that the war industry also depended on mining – an activity that was not in fact affected by crisis.

**II.51** The movement of pilgrims itself implies that the activity of passenger transport may have experienced highs and lows but also periods of considerable development. If one considers that not all departure and arrival localities could be reached by sea, one must then suppose that overland movement developed with correlated economic and professional activities. One need only think of hotels or all the other activities related to hauling or horses. It is useful to recall that in the case of the trips studied by scholars, very few of these were interrupted by forms of violence (cf. McCormick, ch. VI), not to mention the travelling of monks and missionaries. For example, the movements of St. Cyril and St. Methodius, and their followers, certainly not few in number, show a relative ease of movement even in the interior. Their continued ties with Rome, where they stayed several times, settling various controversies that had arisen with local bishops as well, amply shows this. We know that the funeral of Methodius was celebrated in Latin, Greek and Slavonic – a demonstration of the variety of followers who had accompanied him (cf. McCormick, ch. VII).

**II.52** At the time of Charlemagne a veritable market "of international importance" grew up where merchants from a variety or linguistic and cultural backgrounds – Arabs included – came together. It was Arab merchants who were amazed at the roofs they saw at certain hours of the day, reflecting light like the sea. In fact, the Frankish king sent, as he had promised, lead and tin over the Alps and by mule for the conservation of various religious buildings. All of this is further confirmed by the ample presence of moneychangers and the flourishing fabrics market. This reawakening gave rise to various trade treaties just a few decades later which benefitted other economic realities such as Venetian trade. The fairs that were being developed in Western Europe, such as that of Saint-Denis, attracted markets that were even in contact with Iraq (cf. McCormick, ch. XXI).

## III. THE MIDDLE AGES
## AND LATE SCHOLASTICISM*

III.1 In the ancient world, a slave was considered to be an entirely normal thing, so much so, that among slaves themselves there is such acceptance of this status that it was not possible for class-consciousness to form, as it has been understood in the contemporary world; a consciousness capable of overturning the existing socio-political pattern. The slave was a thing which the freeman considered useful, but always a thing. He is useful because he does what the free man himself would never do, because to do what the slave does would mean putting himself on the same level. Thus, on the part of the free man, there is a certain contempt for the activities of the slave, because these are the things that define him; things that pertain specifically to him. But what *are* these

---

\* The text of this Chapter, except for a few additions, in points 1-13, 17-23, 35 and 36, is taken from the recording of a lecture of mine entitled *Work: from servitude to service* held at Caprarola (VT) in May 1985. It has not been possible for me to cite the precise sources used, although the principal reference texts are as follows: DENIS H., *Histoire de la pensée économique*, Presses Universitaires de France, Paris, 1965. JAMES É., *Histoire sommaire de la pensée économique*, Éditions Montchrestien, Paris, 1959. MIRA G., *Storia del movimento operaio*, vol. I, *Storia del lavoro nel Medio Evo e nell'età moderna (sec. XIII-XVIII)*, Edizioni dell'Ateneo, Roma, 1949. MIRA G., *Il lavoro nella storia economica medioevale e moderna*, (Lezioni tenute all'Università degli studi di Perugia), Roma, 1969. NUCCIO O., *Il pensiero economico italiano, 1. Le fonti (1050-1450). L'etica laica e la formazione dello spirito economico,* tomo secondo, Edizioni Gallizzi, Sassari, 1985. SCHUMPETER J. A., *History of Economic Analysis,* Oxford University Press, New York, 1954.

activities? They are essentially manual ones, never highly regarded in the ancient world, and indeed despised because they were thought to possess little dignity in comparison with others. This was true above all in the Greek world: manual labour in general was held to be practically advantageous (for the master), and was accepted as a reality, but was subordinate to those activities that were not only nobler but also more attractive.

**III.2** The Roman world seemed to be moving in the same direction, but in reality quite a few thinkers make a distinction, among manual works, of those which seem to be worthy of the free man. Cato, for instance, in his *De Rustica*, defines agriculture as worthy of the free man, not to mention the fact that Pliny the Elder was against the use of slaves in working the land. Furthermore, what Seneca says is surprising: "Do you not think that the man whom you call a slave traces his origins to the same seed, that he enjoys the same sky, that he breathes the same air, that he lives and dies like you? You can see him as free in the same way that he can see you as a slave". The same could be said of Marcus Aurelius, who actually made his slave Epictetus into his master. These considerations lead us to think that many of the manual labourers were already forming a conspicuous and economically important group. Certainly they took no part in the management of public affairs, but they reached the point of being so strong as to found corporations. Even though there were many restrictions on these corporations from the beginning, they gradually multiplied until they became a genuine social force. The corporation, which would then see a strong development in the Middle Ages, not only brought certain advantages to those who belonged to it, but stood out almost as a natural organism, responding to that almost instinctive desire which all those who carry on the same activity feel, to gather together, to support one another, and above all to defend themselves from hostile forces.

**III.3** The Latin language itself, in giving us two distinctive words which we still use in Italian form today – *artigianato* and *lavoro* – (craftsmanship and physical labour) provides us with an instance of civilisation. The word *arte*, which distinguishes all that is done with the hands, is for the Latins, what is done well, what is useful, what is beautiful. *It does not represent an ideal of beauty to be imitated, but an instrument to use.* *Lavoro*, labour, on the other hand, originally meant to slide or to fall, to be reduced to total exhaustion. The slave has slid down, he has lost his former condition; by this exhausting effort he carries on an activity useful to others. This sense of fatigue is still well-expressed by many Mediterranean dialects, and by one or two languages such as Spanish and French, where the expressions specifically refer, apart from tiredness, to the sense of travail, even psychological travail, which certain activities can bring on.

**III.4** The change wrought by Christianity in this field should be viewed in this perspective. Even the motto of St Benedict: *Ora et labora* – pray and labour – should be examined in this context, because the monastic saint is completely imbued with Latinity as well as with Christianity. It should not be forgotten that he studied law in Rome, and that his Rule constitutes one of the few fixed points in the most chaotic period of the early Middle Ages, thus succeeding in guaranteeing the basic elements of the rebirth. With the proclamation of the Gospel, work assumed characteristics that were not only new but such as to cause an upheaval in the whole story of humanity. We have only to think of one fact that is often passed over too lightly: Christ did not merely talk about work, he worked; he came from a family where work and exhaustion were the pattern of life. Jesus worked, he worked silently, he praised hard-working qualities – not the kind of work that was an end in itself, for that would even be condemned by some of the Fathers also, if it only generated fatigue and anxiety. But he praised hard work accompanied by the contemplation coming from service. To confirm this, it will be enough to summarise a page from a notable scholar: "Certainly he chose all the apostles from among working men; he subjected the aims to which material work is directed to aims of another nature, that of the spirit; he recommended constancy in work and faith in God (the miraculous draught of fishes); he wished that labour should be active and productive; he considered all form of labouring activity to be good; he considered work to be close to redemption".

**III.5** All these undeniably positive aspects of work should not, however, lead us to think that it does not meet up with limits. These are imposed for all, and especially for evangelists. While necessary, work must a) not be harmful to the soul; b) be undertaken without deception, dissimulation or lying; c) above all, not be undertaken with such intensity that it merely generates greed for riches. Clement of Alexandria stated: "work, but do not wear yourself out with work". Work must not constitute the sole reason for life. It should be noted that all this is in line with the considerations made on the subject of gain in the early centuries of Christianity. No particular distinction is made between those who gain little or much, between poor and rich. The latter, as long as they have not set the whole purpose of their lives on gain, are not cursed. What comes under discussion is the use that can be made of gain. There is a conviction that it is precisely from the use of goods and riches that the real understanding of the value and purpose of work is achieved. No judgment that is made on the nature of work, however, can ever be exhaustive. Only God can read in the hearts of men, and so can fully judge the effort, the commitment, the dedication, the seriousness, the intention and so on. God alone, therefore, will be able effectively to reward the Christian who works. The Christian worker knows that earthly remuneration is often an imperfect means of measuring, and he or she knows that only God will be able to give full recompense.

**III.6** This is perhaps the aspect that struck the pagan world more than any other. In fact, it failed to understand the industriousness of Christians, which scandalised the world of the "free men", based as it was on *otium*. For the Christian, true freedom is freedom from evil, and not from fatigue. To flee from tiring effort means abandoning oneself to vices, the most dangerous of which, in this field, is *accidie*, from which apathy, boredom and total lack of interest all derive. An individual who reaches this extreme point is devoid of biting power, of a reason for living, and seeks – often in illicit fields – for something, anything, which will momentarily satisfy him. Hence the dramatic nature of so many lives. Because of this, ancient Christianity on the one hand presented work as a means of human elevation, while on the other hand it warned against the dangers of an excessive activism, reminding people that even work itself, if it has no other-worldly perspective, makes no sense at all. To say that Christianity gave a new value to work remains a general statement. Quite a few crafts and professions caused some perplexity to the Fathers of the Church. We may think particularly of the military profession, but Christian artists – painters, sculptors, decorators, workers in marble – also met with difficulties; in working on commission, they would be forced to make images of misbelievers and sometimes actually of gods. There was thus the problem of finding work for those who, once converted, could not continue to exercise their ancient crafts.

**III.7** Among all activities, however, two in particular come in for praise. The first is teaching: the Church had an almost natural penchant for the problems of education, since this latter activity gave opportunities to presenting the new moral and religious vision of life. The second, mentioned especially by the earliest Christian writers, is the medical profession which, by its very nature, is alongside the brothers who suffer. It is not rare to find a doctor who is also a priest. The two functions are often brought together because all too often sickness is considered a consequence of sin. Jesus is seen as the physician who heals the whole human being. Alongside these two activities, many others were immediately held to be useful, but there were others which were viewed with a certain diffidence for a certain period of time. This is certainly true of political activities. The reason for this is simple: as several of the writers of the period reveal, political responsibility often placed Christians in the position of contradicting the principles of their faith. Christians did, however, very often have responsibilities of an administrative kind, in which, indeed, they were favoured because of their competence, precision and honesty. In short, not only the type of work but the way in which it was carried out characterised Christian activities. Furthermore, if we look at the person of the worker, it should be said that this can be found in every level of social extraction: every category has the possibility, and indeed the duty, to realise itself fully. Because of this, every kind of work is worthy of respect. Those who can, should also take thought for the moral and physical conditions under which the worker has to work. St Ambrose says explicitly: "How many meet with their deaths so that you can have what delights you!". And he lists the dangers which building workers run, and in general those who labour, whom the early Fathers of the Church themselves first felt the need to safeguard. Dangers of a no less serious kind were met with by those who carried on activities which led to the handling of huge sums of money, like bankers, for example. These dangers not only had a moral aspect, because it was possible to defend oneself from this by a more careful preparation, but also an economic aspect, such as the risk of bankruptcy. The human story of Pope Calixtus is symbolic, in view of the fact that his banking activities did in fact lead to failure, possibly because of the excessive favours he gave to clients of limited financial capacity. This was the source of his indulgence – of which he was accused after he became pope – towards certain human weaknesses which, according to a strict interpretation of the Gospel, should never be pardoned.

**III.8** When we mention defence and appreciation of the most humble and risky manual tasks (builders, unskilled labourers, peasants, etc.) the name of St Benedict springs immediately to mind. In him the best of the Latin tradition and the most profound and rigorous of the evangelical traditions are brought into synthesis and harmony, as in few other spirits of the western world. It has been said of his Rule: "The Roman simplicity of the provisions of which it is made up is paralleled by the consummate experience which informs it, gradually revealing the incomparable adherence to the ethical and social needs of an age of upheaval and decline in the old political and social world". In the course of close study of the legislation of Rome, Benedict had realised that by now it was not just a matter of renewing the general lines of a system which had grown old, but of promoting a new social ideal by the example of new and fruitful institutes. Benedict came to terms with the needs of western peoples, but without abandoning anything fundamental in the teaching of the Gospel. Indeed, the latter was presented in all its special points of finesse which struck, converted and often sanctified individuals in an era which was violent and brutal as few previous ones had been. It is in the motto of St Benedict that the real novel elements in his teaching emerge: work is no longer a just and blessed necessity, but becomes a duty which is common to all the faithful, whether clerical or lay, those who live in communities or in isolation. What distinguishes the former from the latter may be the way in which they approach work, but certainly not the way they understand it.

**III.9** *Ora et labora* is not merely a motto or an ideal of life. It is life itself which must be given flesh and blood in those two words held together by a conjunction which expresses the essential reciprocity between them. It is not two alternatives that we are faced with here, but two inseparable aspects, each of which in the end gives meaning to the other. As a man of a particular culture, Benedict uses the word *labor* to indicate a particular activity. *Labor* is for every man because every man is fallen, has lapsed into sin, has become a slave of sin. Because of this *labor* exhausts the individual, in *labor* one is sacrificed, one is sanctified, we might say today one is realised. But labour sanctifies only if it is linked to prayer and it has a value of restitution only if it is done in obedience. Certainly this is not obedience of the slave/master kind typical of the pagan world. But it is a matter of obedience to those who, by spiritual gift, represent an Other. Only thus does work have meaning and an element of redemption; otherwise it is pure self-exhaustion without any purpose. According to the Rule all the possible degenerations to which exaggerated individualism may lead must be eliminated. Moreover, there are no works with special privileges. The hours of the day are divided in such a way that each brother can carry out several types of work, from manual to intellectual and vice versa, without ever forgetting that prayer gives value to industriousness that otherwise remains sterile busy-ness. This is why not only work but also its fruits must be seen in the context of a community.

**III.10** The community of brothers, and also of all those who live around the Abbey, gives life to a community understood by Benedict as a family, disciplined by the Rule, which is interpreted by the Abbot. This singular figure also directs the monastic work, and confers dignity on it. He is capable, we would say today, of "getting the maximum productivity" out of the monks by guaranteeing the support of all in valuing the attitudes, capacities, conditions and needs, both physical and psychological, of all his monks. It is the presence of the Abbot which makes *Ora et labora* into a concrete reality. In the early Middle Ages, this ideal was soon to become a universal one, given value by undeniable historical evidence: around many monasteries there soon grew up settlements which allowed whole villages to share in the Benedictine ideal, developing that sense of work and economy which was to be at the basis of the revival of the communes. Those who lived around the

Abbey would have a life punctuated by new rhythms provided by the sound of the monastery bell, and later by that of the village, as Jacques Le Goff has shown in *La civilisation de l'Occident medieval*. No one should abstain from work. St Bernard of Clairvaux was to bear this particularly in mind; he caused even the rich to understand that they could not abstain from work and from the daily round of tasks, because in doing this the rich paid their debt to a society which had been so generous to them in benefits, and so kept at bay the dangers of idleness or *otium* which are so damaging to the human being.

**III.11** The Abbey, and everything that grew up around it, enjoyed greater security than could be found in other places. This security became more and more apparent after the year 1000, which could be described as a real divide between the first and second parts of the Middle Ages. Awareness grew that peace and security were crucial elements for any economic activity. This need can also be deduced from works which apparently do not have an economic theme, such as the *Chronicles of the Year One Thousand* by Rodolfo the Bald. Despite the dramatic character of the events described, which were part of the millenary fever of those times, and the character of some of the historic episodes which, as the title of the work suggests, display more of the spirit of the chronicler than that of the historian, there is no doubt that a number of economic activities are brought to light which mark the beginning of the revival which was to culminate in the civilisation of the communes. A vast number of churches were being rebuilt, and the reconstruction of civic buildings in the bigger cities followed. These operations involved a trade in more or less refined materials, and also the movement of manpower. Even the revival in pilgrimage showed the rise of a series of activities; we need only mention the lodging houses with the related availability of food supplies, which implied movement of wealth and need for security in the transportation of people and goods (cf. Rodolfo, III, 13 ff.).

**III.12** With the transformation of civil life after the millennium, the way in which work was understood also changed. This should not lead us to think that the wisely accumulated presuppositions of the patristic age and the Benedictine ideal were set aside. But these began to be integrated into a situation which was rapidly changing. It is clear that new responses were required, and these came from scholasticism, which would have the merit of ascribing to work the content which would carry it to the threshold of the modern age. Apart from theoretical formulations, we should also point to the birth of the new religious Orders, the Franciscans and Dominicans, which were to have no small influence on the transformation of the world of the communes. Thanks to them, the conception of work as intended to pursue the supernatural destiny of humankind in every activity, was reasserted. We may mention one of the crucial concepts of Thomist social thought: every time that man comes into contact with goods and riches, either to produce them or to trade them or, finally, to consume them, he must take care that the economic factors which are brought into being, and the way in which he carries out the transaction, do not contribute to prejudicing his ultimate goal, but rather help him to draw nearer to it.

**III.13** In this way, there gradually developed a concept of the legitimacy of wealth, as long as this was not an end in itself, but had a value for all, which today we would call a social value, and as long as it was the fruit of one's own labours. This in fact came to be seen as the best way that man possesses of expressing his own personality. Aquinas holds that all work can be considered valid as long as the love of money, important though money be, does not become the primary aim. In this light we can see the reservations which Aquinas, and others too, make against large-scale commerce, when this, having in view only the aim of enrichment, often even setting aside the rules, ends up by seeing life only in terms of riches, and one ends up being ready to do anything to acquire them. Some very clear words are written concerning this: "When the aim of the merchants is directed *uniquely* to gain, cupidity is rooted in the hearts of the citizens, and for this reason every town becomes venal, and lacking all faith, everyone seeks his own particular advantage, and love for virtue fails, and honour, which is the reward of virtue, is set aside by all". The word "uniquely" here speaks for itself.

**III.14** This reservation about large-scale commerce, however, should not be generalised; first and foremost because in concrete terms it was practised in the Christian world – for example by the marine republics, and also because the trade intended to provide the things that were needed for life, or indeed things of beauty, is held to be just and due, as long as it is honest in delivering to the purchaser goods that are genuine, and in establishing a just price for them. The latter, for the purposes of definition, must take account of the production of the market itself. This is Aquinas' idea, and on the subject of prices he cannot be accused of ingenuousness. He is well aware that, if prices are left to a purely economic logic, they will be fixed on the basis of the laws of demand and supply, laws which only favour a section of the sellers and consumers. On the contrary, a serious price policy must also permit the less well-off to procure the goods that are necessary. If no account is taken of these aspects, the logic followed will be a commonplace one, which will not permit us to understand the reality of mediaeval civilisation. The economy and the work of the latter cannot be understood by an exclusively economic "logic", because the economy, and even money itself, possessed a value that though it was undeniably important, was instrumental and contingent, subordinate to other ends. Thus, when certain thinkers took a stand against wealth, they did not do so to contest artisan or commercial activities, but solely to make it clear that these could not become ends in themselves, bypassing that sense of the social order which is guaranteed by very different means. The same could be said of property. Alongside many visions of holy poverty, we find (even among the Franciscans) careful reflections on the notion of property. We need only mention what Ockham states, when he says that "God has allowed man to appropriate to himself individual things (...) Property, therefore, is a historical institution: it has its date of birth, its designer and its social purpose" (Bazzichi, 46). As I have stressed elsewhere, Ockham deserves the credit for having shown the far from irrelevant difference between lay and ecclesiastical property (see ch.VII of my *The Open Society*). Here we are dealing with reflections that are by no means merely rhetorical which could have facilitated the solution of the "problems of the Third and even the Fourth Worlds" if we had not lost our way behind certain utopias which then led us to ignore the most concrete needs of development (cf. Lombardi, 8).

**III.15** With regard to the maritime republics, it should be remembered that they are a fundamental element in those juridical guarantees that are at the basis of their commercial activities. I shall have something to say later about Venice; here I will just mention the example of Amalfi. This city, like many others after the year 1000, owed its strength to the fact that it had codified a complex of civil customs or rules, on which it founded its commercial activity. The young Alfonso Falcone, in his study *Consuetudines Civitatis Amalfie: le norme consuetudinarie di una città marinara*, shows how the Amalfitani understood that it was necessary to draw the discipline of commercial traffic from the actual foreign laws of those cities with which Amalfi found itself, from time to time, engaged in trade. The citizens made a *professione juris*, declaring that the legal trade relationship brought into being would be bound and regulated by the law of the city in which they lived. This need had always been felt by a city such as Amalfi, which had for a long time preserved a copy of the *Digest*, ever since the Dark Ages, almost as if it were a relic.

This precious volume remained in Amalfi until the siege carried on by Pisa in 1135 or 1137, and it had no small influence on the transcription and composition of the city's *Consuetudines*. As can be seen, the impact of Roman law is at the basis of the revival of trade. There are numerous institutions which take the *Corpus Juris Civilis* as their historical reference-point. Again in connection with Amalfi, we have only to remember its provisions about dowries. This means that well before the academic revival in juridical studies, which took place above all at Bologna, it was the custom of many cities to take their inspiration from Roman law. Moreover, as Caravale points out in his well-known study, Amalfi is only one example among the many juridical systems which were inspired by Roman law in mediaeval Europe.

**III.16** To return to the problem of the just price: it should also be remembered that even before Aquinas, the question had been widely examined in quite a few pontifical Decretals. Innocent III, for instance, who certainly intended to defend the feudal landowning of which the Church was the first beneficiary, just as certainly had become aware of the great economic questions which had arisen over the question of ownership, the payment of tenths, the taxes, and so on, which were at that time arousing much discussion in the Christian world, forced to look at wealth with new eyes after the revival and establishment of a mercantile society. We have only to read the Italian short stories of the fourteenth and fifteenth centuries to find that commercial life is exalted in fulsome terms in all its manifestations. Not to mention the *Decameron* of Boccaccio, considered to be a "real Odyssey of trade" where the merchant appears as a new hero, who takes the place of, or is added to, the knight and the warrior (cf. Ja.Gurevič, 119). In short, as was already the case in the ancient world, at a certain point we can see a radical changeover in the way in which merchants and mercantile activity were considered. There are three characteristics in this change: "a) elements of appreciation of certain aspects of the mercantile function expressed by the dominant culture, and shared by the merchants themselves; b) overturning of the criticism of the behaviour of merchants expressed by the dominant culture, and c) special values of classes involved at various levels in commercial activity" (Giardina, 30). The way in which the entire mercantile society is seen thus becomes more and more specific. It is examined with rigorous mathematical rationality in all its aspects by Leonardo Fibonacci, who even concerns himself with the theme of company profits, *de societatibus factiis inter consocios*, and the division of the proceeds on the basis of the proportional quota of shares held by each shareholder. In the examination of concrete facts, and thus in a real world, the first exercises in accountancy are undertaken, and there is even the beginning of a discussion of money and the problems relative to metals (Nuccio, PEI, 1159 ff, 1181).

**III.17** After almost a millennium, there is a new consideration of the different forms of loans with the hope of obtaining some gain through them: *propter spem lucri pecuniari*. Quite a few scholars considered this hope to be legitimate (we only have to read the numerous *disputae* published in the period); for example when someone makes a capital of a hundred "soldi" available in the hope, if the venture of a merchant proves successful, of receiving some benefit from it. This is justified by the risks run by someone who may see the capital diminished or lost, as Raymond de Peñafort had shown in his *Summa*, especially if the mercantile venture were conducted by sea and thus, as the ancient Roman jurists had already pointed out (cf. point II.2), would prove to be more risky. It was specifically from the recovery of Roman law that certain canonists found the justification for the creditor receiving interest. A further justification was derived from classical jurisdiction; if the money were given for vague ends, certainly not illicit but risky and difficult for the creditor to control.

Interest varied by law according to the risky nature of the venture, and, we might add, also the character of the merchant (Nuccio, PEI, 1194 ff). It is truly curious to see what Marx transcribes in *Das Kapital* citing a statement by a certain Büsch: The Church had prohibited the taking of interest; but not the sale of property to relieve oneself of need; nor of letting it, for a certain time or even until the repayment, to someone who lent money, not only so that this person should have some sort of guarantee, but also so that during the period of ownership he could make use of something which took the place of the money of which he had been deprived (cf. Marx, K, vol. III, 612-3).

**III.18** In any case, it is a certain fact that the lay mediaeval jurists took up again from Roman law the basic principle according to which no one could enrich himself by causing harm to others. But also from Roman law, and from Papinianus in particular, there came the legitimisation, "in clear and modern terms, of the payment of interest *(usurae)* in relation both to the use which the holder might make of the capital provided on loan, and to the gains which he might draw from it if he had used it made use of it himself". This was something which arose long before the scholastics and before St Antonino of Florence. Nuccio rightly reminds us that it has been thought for too long that Aquinas himself only dealt with economic problems after reading Aristotle. In this way the far more ancient contribution made by the canonists and the civil lawyers tends to be forgotten. If confirmation is needed it can be sought in the juridical writings of Enrico da Susa (cf. Nuccio, CI, 67). But, as I have tried to show, the Roman jurists and the thought of Cicero exercised a wide influence on scholasticism (see ch. V of my *The Open Society*). The rediscovery of Roman law gave to the material which it regulated, and in particular economic activity, that necessary autonomy with regard to the rules laid down by theology, which favoured the revival and development of the economy.

"If we do not understand and accept the role played by the 'rediscovered' Roman law, the historical analysis of the origins of economic thought (...) will never be set free from the partial and misleading representations which dominate at present" (Nuccio, CI, 78).

**III.19** The same is true of property seen as the fruit of one's own work. Private property is logically safeguarded, but its use may not be for selfish ends. It will never be possible to attain to a system of collective property, which would be unnatural; however, the individual must understand himself as a trustee, or as the Fathers had already said, an administrator of goods. Obviously, he must gain, but he cannot become the slave of the *superfluous*, which, even though rarely, can also become an obligatory *quantum* which varies in relation to the social situation in which the individual finds himself operating. Again according to Aquinas, we must praise, and require, that the destination of the superfluous is directed towards other works, avoiding the excuse of being excessively cautious so as not to fall into the most dangerous forms of selfishness. Aquinas, therefore, is not opposed to commercial profit, which indeed is permitted for a series of motives: the need to acquire means of living and performing works of charity; for a due remuneration for services rendered, and for the improvements brought to the goods sold, for the difference of prices in time and in space, and finally, for the risks run. Moreover the legitimacy of moderate profit is also justified (see *Summa Theologica*, II-II, q. 77, a. 4) for the maintenance of the family, the helping of the needy but also for the generation of public utility, and it constitutes a due recompense for labour (cf. Hop, 17).

**III.20** In the Middle Ages, and especially during the rise of the communes and the period in which they flourished, a structure developed which had in any case already been present in ancient Rome: the corporation, or guild. An examination of the *Corporazioni delle arti e dei misteri* is basic if we want to understand the religious spirit which animates everything – even legislation – in those times, a spirit based on the conception of work viewed as service. Anyone seeking proof of this should take an analytical look at the statutes on which the communes and corporations were founded. These statutes were deliberated in the name of divine authority, and in conformity with its perceived laws. Apart from the general rules which established the criteria whereby the activity of an individual must not damage the community, there were some rules which were truly unusual and more specific. For example, there were some initiatives of a charitable kind which must be undertaken by members of the corporation. In certain periods, in much the same way as applied to the Jewish tenth, every work contract or mercantile contract had to provide for a certain sum of money to be destined to charitable uses. With the rise of the corporations, every statute began with the same invocation: *"In nomine Domini"*; the invocation of the Virgin Mary followed, then the patron saints of the city, and finally the patron saint of the Guild itself. The illuminated miniature image of these saints is often found placed among the first phrases of the statute. This is not just a matter of custom or formality; in fact solemn feasts and religious celebrations were provided for every corporation. Confraternities to carry out actions of assistance and benevolence were often added to the corporation, *almost always taking the place of the political authorities.*

**III.21** If we examine the corporations more closely, the Christian significance of work becomes even clearer. The corporations arose specifically with the intention of permitting those who carried on the same profession to give mutual help to one another. In addition, they were also conceived as more restricted institutions than those of the communes, and they claimed that *principle of autonomy* with respect to the political power and that spirit of association which would always be a characteristic of the Church. It is important to note that in the early days, the corporations all had equal importance. Then gradually, as the society of the communes became secularised, work, the various crafts, and hence the corporations themselves, assumed a different degree of importance according to the economic weight which the various "crafts" took on. Thus there would be corporations of major, medium and minor "arts", and these, starting out from different levels of importance in economic terms, would gradually come to have different juridical status as well. Those who belonged to the different corporations built the headquarters of their guild with their own funds, as well as the attached church or chapel. Here they carried on their own festivals and meetings, and also kept the archives of the guild itself. Examples of this kind can be found in any city. The festivals were respected in the true sense of the word, and this reminds us that the guilds also took on teaching and social functions, and not only those connected with work.

**III.22** Many of the functions of the guilds are quite overlooked today. We should remember that one aim of the guilds was the distribution of raw materials needed for work, in order to avoid the creation of inequalities – we might term them monopoly situations today – in which a certain number of artisans would find themselves in conditions of difficulty in relation to others. It was necessary to seek to guarantee a possibility of work and gain to all; creativity and personal capacity would then make for differentials. If one of the guild members were to break the rules, he would be punished, not only by the public authorities, but also by the guilds themselves, which had a kind of court of their own. Because of this, we find advice from some experts in certain institutes on how to assess the genuine nature of the goods, and even a committee to establish the just price. The various members of the corporation had to contribute by annual subscription and by special offerings to any difficulties which the corporation might meet with, and also to the state of need of any of the other members. In short, the spirit of solidarity was already present, and to manage it, specific reference was made to the divinity. We could cite for example certain merchant companies of Florence in the fourteenth century, such as those of the Bardi and the Peruzzi, which set up an account in the name of Messer Domineddio. This meant that, in the act of constitution, it had been decided to pay over from time to time two parts of the capital, of which one was for the Lord, actually opening an account in the name of God in the actual books of this merchant company, as if He was a simply one of the guild members; making Him a participant in the annual division of profits. These funds obviously served for works of charity which the company exercised in favour of the poor. It should also be noted that the sums of this account, even when they were not spent in their entirety, were never spent for other causes which were not religious in character. What was left over, however little or much it might be, was credited to the account for the following year, as no member would ever have dreamed of taking part of it for his own needs.

**III.23** These and other reasons combined to produce a real transformation in economic life. For example, manufacturing activity, which until that time had developed along artisan lines, slowly became industrialised. The merchant entrepreneur no longer limited himself to the mere exchange of goods, but began to think also about their transformation, and then about the production of different goods as well. And labouring activities, too, underwent a real transformation. In agriculture, not only were new techniques of production introduced, but there was a marked development in the relations between town and country, which previously had encountered many difficulties. In the world of craftsmanship, there was more and more development of the notion of a workshop, and of apprenticeship no longer confined to family members but also open to outsiders who wished to learn. Perhaps we should also mention that it was precisely from these workshops that the greatest artists of the modern world emerged. As trade became more and more widespread, the worker could no longer produce the goods as a craftsman and sell them as a merchant at one and the same time; he had to opt for one activity or the other. If he chose to go in for salesmanship, then he would need some other element of the family to help him in the art of commerce, on condition, however, that he took on someone else who took his place in the workshop. *And this is the point at which the category of wage-earner makes its first appearance.* Such a category had, in a sense, always existed, but it is the growth of its dimensions that marks the transition from mediaeval to modern times. From a series of historical testimonies, we can in fact draw some important conclusions: the *first* is that in the first decades of the phenomenon, and in general throughout the era of the Renaissance, wages had good purchasing power, and employment – at least in certain zones of Italy – never met with interruption, as long as there was a readiness for a certain mobility (one might mention Renzo, one of the characters in *I promessi sposi*, who thanks to the help of a cousin, succeeds in finding work in the textile sector by crossing over the boundary). The *second element* is that, with the decline and failure of the religious spirit which had animated work in the Middle Ages, many kinds of work went back to being considered a form of slavery, something which would, not unjustly, spark off many of the social conflicts of the modern world. The *third factor* is that work tends to be considered almost exclusively as a means of satisfying earthly needs, with a solely economic purpose. This is shown by the fact that certain characteristic aspects of the Middle Ages, like beneficence, are no longer linked to economic activity in direct fashion, but their putting into effect now depends more and more on the good will of the individual. And as this is always insufficient, policies of intervention arise: i.e. those fiscal policies by which the public authorities obtain the means to carry out the activities which no one, perhaps, would otherwise undertake any longer. In this way they also facilitated the redistribution of incomes.

**III.24** This is the reason that one can claim that well before the centuries which Weber examined, certain preliminary preconditions developed, such as the principle of legality, and a bureaucracy to resolve controversies in a rational way; a mobile and specialised workforce, the institutional system that keeps in mind trans-generational investment, and the notable physical and intellectual efforts that were made, together with the accumulation of long-term capital; an enthusiasm for discovery, adventure and the creation of wealth and new enterprises. However, this was not enough in itself. All this was made possible thanks to freedom of enterprise, the markets, and competition (cf. Novak, HC). But I would add, thanks also to many other elements which had already signified the development of the ancient Church which, as it had been able to adopt certain characteristics of classical culture, was now presenting them anew in order to back the revival after centuries of uncertainty which had accompanied the end of the ancient world.

**III.25** The development of economic activity was accompanied by the birth of new professions, not only those directly linked to economic activity, but also those in some ways connected to it. To the administrative bureaucracy at local level, there were added arbiters, jurists, negotiators and judges, as well as a single jargon for the international language, Latin (cf. Novak, HC). Nor did this mean the suffocation of local cultures. This is witnessed by the fact that the contracts which had limited juridical value and significance, were written in the vulgar tongue, so that modern European languages find many of their first signs of life in contracts written between private individuals. This explains why although at an early stage in the high Middle Ages, the Church became the first bureaucracy, more rational than ever at world level, capable of forming the normative context necessary for supplying a freely and predictably orderly economic development (cf. Novak, HC). As time went on, as

John of Salisbury for one maintained, all this favoured the birth of lay professional classes dedicated to the development of liberal arts. They were laymen, but not secularists, because they were in all cases inspired by the values of Catholicism. All this explains that the reborn economy took place in a context not only capable of favouring it, but also of giving it backing and guarantees. The famous 'spontaneous order' of the market does not operate in the absence of laws or in the presence of chaos, but only in conditions of rationality, controlled by the laws. It thus allows the individual representatives to act in the presence of predictable economic rules. Moreover the legal appearance of this new European situation effectively moved the target of the various economic activities towards common objectives, bringing order among the diversified individual initiatives (cf. Novak, HC). All this contributed to providing the juridical and economic security without which no type of development is possible. This may seem to be a banal consideration, but it is hard to understand for many people, and above all for politicians. It should also not be forgotten that the new emphasis given to clerical celibacy played an important role in the development of capitalism. It gave Europe an extraordinarily motivated workforce: well-educated, specialist and mobile (cf. Novak, HC). From them, and from the need that they felt to organise themselves, there arose the earliest labour organisations blessed by the Church, so that – as Collins remarks, Pope Innocent IV (1243-54) was for this reason described as 'the father of modern corporate culture' (cf. Novak, HC).

**III.26** Among the new professions, special attention should be paid to those which sought to rationalise economic activity, going so far as to devise new systems of calculation, registers of economic operations, accounting practices such as the double entry, and so on. These were largely scholars of the fifteenth and sixteenth centuries, who, however, in the end only rationalised and conceptualised practices which in a more rudimentary way were already present in the high Middle Ages. The classic study by Alfieri, mentioned in my first chapter, provides useful information on this matter. Among other things, the important conclusion emerges that already before the year 1000, and anyway long before the crusades, Venice was a mercantile power in the Adriatic and all the way to Constantinople, where the Doge was represented by a *podestà*, which means that the city had developed a series of industries, building vessels, ships and all that served for their production. This is also witnessed by the great flourishing of merchant companies. Trade was an activity supported more and more by the Venetian Republic, by the hard work and genius of the Venetian merchants, by the development of a maritime law of customs and public revenues, by a scientifically designed economic and commercial policy, which enabled the Serenissima, as Venice was called, to reach commercial routes ranging from the Far East to the North Sea, and from Africa to Flanders. Colonies and free ports were founded in every angle of the Mediterranean, and as far as Persia, and everywhere there was a flowering of lay and religious foundations which recalled the Republic of St Mark. Venice was even in intimate relations with the distant commercial port of London, and was authorised by the Popes to trade with the Sultan of Egypt; it established offices in Alexandria for stable commercial activity. The ships never travelled empty: where they carried spices, jewels, wool and materials, they returned with copper, pitch, hemp and much else. Many of these products were sold along the trade route, as for example in Flanders, where the "raw wools" then purchased in London were sold (cf. Alfieri, 2-7 and 10-1). Other refined products, derived from glass, had, on the other hand, been produced in Venice itself since remote times; certainly since late Roman times since, perhaps as a result of the turbulence due to the barbarian invasions, many artisans from the hinterland of Venice moved into the lagoon, where their glass-making art revived.

**III.27** What had in the past been the fairs and markets of the villages or small towns, were transformed into meeting points of great importance for business. This happened in many cities; in Venice and its surrounding area these markets gained great renown, frequented by Armenian, Greek, Turkish, Syrian, German merchants apart, obviously, from those who came from all parts of Italy. The reason for all this may perhaps be found in the fact that in Venice, the Republic had made itself the guarantor of the commercial rules, to such an extent that no one could fail to observe them with impunity, and all knew that the legality of the "traffic" was the first concern of the Venetian State (cf. Alfieri, 12-13). This is clear proof that the political structure can favour economic development, and is far from being the mere result of the latter, even if it may find the reason for its constant updating in the economy. But it can also act as a stimulus. Because of this, foreign merchants hastened to Venice where they found, for themselves too, special legislative dispositions. Something similar had happened in antiquity in Rome, during the period of economic growth. As long as the legislative dispositions favoured private initiative, Venice expanded; when, on the other hand, the public spirit took over, there was the same result as had occurred in the crisis of the Roman world; the nobles abandoned the "marketplace", corruption (and not only public corruption) increased, and a very slow decay set in.

**III.28** One of the ways which permitted the state to restore the Treasury or meet the expenses for greatly needed public works was the game of *Lotto* – which was to become a national lottery. This expedient had a notable development and also became a way for private individuals to speculate. This meant a further intervention of the state, in order to regulate the Lotteries. Slowly the state became more and more intrusive, and no longer limited itself to seeing that the rules were respected – making sure that times for payment of agreed terms were observed or judging the protests of some of the merchants, as in the past (cf. Alfieri, 24 and 29). Previously the administration of a company was a purely private matter. This is proved by the registers of accounts, which were progressively evolving into genuine double-entry account books, with legal value. They were deemed worthy of trust and commonly recognised. In short there was no need of public written records in order to manage business affairs. They started with the assumption that one cannot administer anything that one does not know well, and they arrived at the conclusion that no one could have better regular knowledge of what was being done than the person directly interested. Certainly, private matters were managed in an atmosphere of generally accepted morality. This is shown by the invocations which we meet with at the beginning of the "journals" which register business affairs: "In the name of God and of good gain". This shows that the state was only supporting element for the activity of private individuals, who managed their affairs in the context of a well-defined and commonly accepted morality. The idea of the religious formulae at the beginning of the registers lasted for a long time in the Venetian Republic, especially in the period of its greatest splendour. Certainly, we should not be viewing it in terms of an idyllic situation in which counterfeiting and dishonesty were absent (and it was in these cases that the public authorities intervened) because the private operators themselves had available to them a series of checks to evade easy abuses in the registration of affairs. For example, in some registrations, Roman numerals were used instead of Arabic ones, because they were harder to alter. Those who did not respect the rules or the prescribed times were entered in a register as "defaulters", and this judgment certainly did not favour their future businesses. The formula *In the name of God* with which the accounts registers opened cannot certainly be described as a meaningless ritual. We only need consider that the various accounts always began with the month of March precisely because it was sought to honour the announcement of the incarnation of Christ. When, for convenience' sake, there was a demand to change to the solar year, the beginning of the registers still continued to be marked by a religious feast, i.e. Christmas. One can find further evidence by reading the summary of the text *Della Mercartura e del Mercante perfetto*, by Benedetto Cotrugli. The work printed in Venice and written in 1458, apart from, obviously, dealing with technical matters, devotes a specific book to the religious practices of the merchant, and his moral and political virtues (cf. Alfieri, 45-8 and 117)

**III.29** These registers make further use of the so-called double entry, and they developed because of the need for economic control. The master volume of the *Fraternity of Soranzo* (Fraterna dei Soranzo), maintained in irreproachable fashion from the point of view of double entries, dates from 1406, and thus everything leads us to suppose that similar formulae had taken shape a good deal earlier and were in a state of progressive development. Luca Paciolo considers this way of registering business affairs by the companies to be well-known and highly regarded in the Venice of the time. It was later also admired abroad, so that almost everywhere «the method was by consensus known as the *modo veneziano*». But what purpose did this double-entry register serve? Was it perhaps to facilitate business and assist economic development? Again, Luca Paciolo, says that among the needs of the true merchant, "the first and foremost reason is the numbering of money exchanges and every other substantial faculty", and the second "that it is well reasoned and readily calculated", and the third "that in good order, it shows all his affairs in due manner, and makes it possible for every one to take note of them in brief time". If there is no good rational account of economic transactions, "his affairs will feel their way along like a blind man" (cf. Alfieri, 63-4 and 104). We could add many other conclusions to these by Paciolo, and even though this is not the place for spending too much time on the Renaissance scholar, it is certainly worth recording that as distinguished a historian as Braudel stresses that Spengler places Luca Paciolo, among the spirits of his times, at the same level as Christopher Columbus and Copernicus (cf. Braudel, CM, 2, 692).

**III.30** In any case, commercial techniques and techniques in general received a notable boost in Venice. As was to be the case for Holland in the seventeenth century or England in the eighteenth, in the Venetian Republic of the fifteenth-century science, within the limits of the times, did not prove to be lacking as a support for commercial and economic activity. The Arsenal of Venice is just one proof of this. But all this is certainly not the product of mere chance. There is a kind of "pre-history" of these great centres of economic activity. This is a matter of centuries-old structures of everyday life, which over the years made it possible to create and accumulate wealth, to the extent that one can assert that the grand character and supremacy of certain cities and their monetary strength were the consequence of choices which had their origins far back (cf. Braudel, DC, 19-21). From the wandering craftsman, as Braudel calls him, to the great merchant and ship-owner, there is a link which passes through the centuries and which unites, in one identical thread, men and activities from different centuries. Those who dominate the commercial routes of one period always owe recognition to those who first opened them up, and with these predecessors, they have in common the need to guarantee peaceful passage. This is because the sea routes of the whole world and their control have always guaranteed trade and riches (cf. Braudel, CM, 1, 456 ff). The same goes for the land, once goods are conveyed into the hinterland. The confirmation that the relation between sea and land is a very close connection can be found everywhere, for example in the Mediterranean. The ancient basin between the three continents never seems to have lost this aspect, not even today despite the fact that economic and military techniques are no longer territorially based, thanks to the use of satellites. As Braudel has shown, an effective role has also been played in

Mediterranean civilisations by climatic and geographical factors, which at times, together with other components, risked dragging the whole area down towards anarchy (cf. Troiani, 29-32 and 47). Another proof can be found here that where there are no institutions which can guarantee rules, and are capable of adapting to the changing of circumstances, there is no economic development.

**III.31** Venice is a symbolic element of the history spanning the fifteenth and sixteenth centuries: what could be defined as the renaissance of the urban market. But in fact, this is a phenomenon which had assured economic revival even in the ancient world, and then in that of the Middle Ages. Without wishing to enter too deeply into this, how could we fail to mention the role of the city-communes, and that of the Hanseatic League? And how could we omit to point out that this was to be the destiny of Antwerp, Genoa, Amsterdam and even London? Nor should it be forgotten that the manner of making economic activity more scientific would lead to the passage from what Braudel calls the *régistre inférieur* to the *régistre supérieur*, i.e. from the daily records or journals of the early merchants to what in the future to become proper Stock Exchanges (cf. Braudel, DC, 28). It is these technical and legal factors, together with the technical-scientific ones, all contained within a specific institutional framework of reference, that permits the economy to develop and to guarantee (as was the case for Europe – see Braudel, DC, 38) a supremacy of one element over the other. These elements begin from a local context, but go on to become national, international, and in the end global. The extension of the zone of influence of one economic element gives to that area a certain stability, indispensable for the guaranteeing of further economic development. I think the idea of the *mano invisibile*, dreamed up by Adam Smith, should be related to this capacity that a certain society possesses – when it lives in certain conditions – sooner or later to resolve all the controversies and "turbulences" of the economy. Perhaps it is from this that the idea of *laissez-faire* or *laissez-passer* comes. In short, it is the great Mediterranean and European institutional tradition that has guaranteed that supremacy that a few modern cities have been able to exercise in the modern world, even in far distant lands.

**III.32** The city is the real pride of Europe. But when we think of the city, we should not always think of those who have been capable of developing a fundamental role in history. On the contrary, it means stating that after the revival of the communes and the maritime trade, even the most humble village of the West partook, even if indirectly, in the changed economic climate. Even the medium-sized cities are proud of their tradition, which grew up around their market-place – something which led to the word *campanilismo* – ("parochialism") in Italian, not always positive in its connotations, and perhaps more typical of Italy than of any other country. In every city, or even small town, the local fairs, markets, small and great economies grew up. From this, perhaps, comes the deleterious aspect of the market, or in general of that which was to be defined as *capitalism* – the rise of those who are known as *the friends of the prince* (cf. Braudel, DC, 60). Those, in other words, who by making themselves friends of the governing class and, in the broad sense, of the rulers – not always in reputable ways – seek to change the rules to their own advantage. This is the origin of the idea that the political situation is a superstructure of the economy, but the latter usually begins its phase of decline precisely from this point. From the decline of the political organisms begins the irresistible decline, even of the greatest political powers, and the collapse of their economies. What happened to the communist regimes should lead us to reflect.

**III.33** The cities which first set off trade, production, exchange and the expansion of markets in Europe are those of the Mediterranean, together with the states which revolve around them, and this seems to me to be a definitive refutation of Weber's theories on the birth of capitalism. When the cities of northern Europe replaced those of the south, this was due first and foremost to the *changed geopolitical conditions of the world, and also to the new relationships of strength between the rising states*. Moreover the ease of finding certain goods in new lands would also determine the invasion of products which were already produced in traditional areas, and the rise of new economic operators. What remains basic, wherever certain economic transformations are found, is that they change certain social privileges. An emerging class breaks down some of the bastions conquered by the old class and high society, to construct others to its own advantage. Thus new rights emerge, from which a far wider range of individuals are able to benefit, especially among those who live in highly developed economic centres (cf. Braudel, DC, 74 and 94). At that point begins the search for political support which, in its first stages, causes an innovative moment in the social context, only to become rigid again at the moment when the victorious class seeks to maintain its newly-won privileges. This operation is hard to achieve because it is typical of a truly open economy to ensure an alternation in those who occupy certain roles.

**III.34** We owe to Braudel the expression *économie-monde* which describes a universe all to itself, an economically autonomous entity. In reality, this expression recalls the *world-economy* of Wallerstein, which is usually taken to indicate a part of the world which represents a quite precise economic ambit made up of a central and restricted zone (the heart) a fairly broad *internal surrounding area* and *peripheral zone* of vast proportions (cf. Braudel, Intr.). As a world economy, it would be possible to think of the Mediterranean somewhat as it has been understood over a long period in the last millennium. The Mediterranean area, in fact, although politically, culturally, sociologically and religiously divided, nevertheless constitutes an economic unity which goes quite beyond the boundaries between Christians and Moslems, usually considered insurmountable (cf. Braudel, CM, 3, 14-15). It should be remembered that the Venetians obtained (and from the Pope himself) the authorisation to trade with Egypt (cf. Alfieri, 10), as a proof of how commercial activity could overcome every kind of prejudice. According to Braudel, one can speak of a species of typology for the *économie-monde*. The limits of its area of influence are easily identifiable, because they become modified in slow motion. A city, a dominant centre, constitutes the starting point. When these centres tend to multiply, they can either indicate the ferments of a young society in expansion, or forms of degeneration or mutation. The new centres can never surpass the basic one without modifying the balances of the *économie-monde*. This element tends towards a hierarchical pattern, because it is made up of an ensemble of particular economies, some of them poor, others modest, and so on right up to the rich one which lies at the centre. This explains why the real motor centres of this *économie-monde* become actual "supercities", where there is a strong social diversification. There is a risk here that at some moments it becomes radicalised to the point where it explodes in moments of crisis when the poor become poorer and poorer, and the rich constantly richer. This is the moment at which the cost of living constantly rises more and more until it becomes insupportable for many. This spatial model of development and sub-development is opposed to that of humanity divided into two camps, spatially confused, as Marx held (cf. Braudel, CM, 3, 25-6 and 18). Much literature of the time clearly illustrates this intuition of Braudel's. We need only mention the Venetian comedies of the greatest period of La Serenissima, or so much English narrative writing, like that of Dickens, on the conditions in which people lived on the margins of the great cities or in the life of the ports.

**III.35** This problem of costs, together with that of the loans or consumer goods is to be found present in the peak of the economic analysis undertaken by the so-called representatives of the Third Scholastic Age. These recovered texts from the classical age and reinterpreted them in the light of the novelties of the modern world. Eventually they came to the point, as Schumpeter says, of giving definitive birth to the science of economics, to such an extent that if one could talk of "founders" of such a science, this title would belong to these scholars – most of them unknown today. The bases and the analytical tools shaped by them were more solid than those of many of the thinkers who came after them. If they were to be studied seriously – again according to Schumpeter – a large part of the science of economics of the twentieth century could have been developed more rapidly, with less difficulty and with notable savings in time and effort. Among their basic perceptions we may mention: *first*, that the cost of an item, even if it plays a part in determining the value of exchange or price, does not represent its cause; *secondly*, they perceived the theory of utility which they considered as a cause of value; *thirdly*, when speaking of utility, they did not refer it to abstract goods but to the quantity of goods available, and *fourthly*, they listed all the factors which determine prices in such a way that for the authors of the twentieth century there was nothing to do except add the technical apparatus of "marginal" concepts. In short, still in the view of Schumpeter, these later scholastics were the forerunners of the liberalistic theories of the twentieth century.

**III.36** One of the presuppositions of their analysis, expressed in the clearest possible way by Mariana in the footsteps of the ancient jurists, is that society comes before government, from which it may be deduced that governments cannot take decisions without the consent of those who operate and animate civil society. As Chafuen rightly says, in several parts of his study *Christians for Freedom, Late Scholastic Economics,* the best economic policy for governments is that of allowing individuals to enrich themselves because by so doing the state becomes richer, since the citizens are capable of exploiting the riches more than the governing classes, which close them up in the state coffers. The latter are filled with the taxes which the governing classes take from the private individuals to provide for the needs of the community. It is obvious that this way of doing things can be turned into a form of robbery, not only if certain funds fail to achieve their purpose or only fulfil it poorly, but also if tax laws do not respond to certain criteria of justice and equity. Taking up the teaching of the Fathers and the early scholastics, these first modern authors are impartial in the face of economic activity. Like other things, from a moral point of view it may be good or evil, according to aims and circumstances. Taking up once more certain of Aquinas' positions, these authors, apart from applying them to economic activities in general, also apply them to international trade which must, like any other economic activity, be subject to the laws. This is the reason why without an ensemble of guarantees and laws, which must be as broad and universal as possible, the economy has no facility for development. On the contrary to many liberal spirits, and in a mirror fashion also socialists, these scholastics considered the political situation as contemporary to the economic one, and certainly not a consequence of it, or as was to be said in the second half of the eighteenth century, a superstructure. Without wanting to force the issue, I believe that this is also an implicit conviction of Weber, expressed in his famous *Wirtschaft und Gesellschaft* (cf. *Die rationale Staatsanstalt und die modernen politichen parteien und Parlamente – Staatssoziologie –*, vol. IV, ch. IX, sec. VIII). What I have suggested in this and the preceding chapter finds confirmation in the fact that a difference of proceeding had already been noted in Rome between the political process and that of civil society, in a law which in any case expressed its own rationality. The latter was typical of the modern western state, and was applied by a professionally trained bureaucracy (I shall be returning to this point in ch. VIII); it derives, at least from a formal point of view, from Roman law. Even the Church itself came to refer to this mode of conceiving law, when it sought to intervene in economic life – once again according to Weber – in order to infuse it with a minimum of ethics and justice – aspects which could be best pursued in a pacific social context.

**III.37** In conclusion, it should be remembered that the pacific social context has always aided the tranquillity of transport, favouring trade of various types, and also stimulating the search for new land or sea routes in order to discover new markets. Certain synergies between the world of enterprise and that of modern science – certainly not to be seen as a discovery of our own times – can be explained in this way. And this is how it has always been. We need only recall the role played by certain Italian businessmen during the period of the great geographical discoveries. The part played by some of the rich Florentine families in financing the voyages of Giovanni da Verrazzano has already been documented (but other major Italian cities were also engaged in other enterprises). All this points to a very real entrepreneurial role, so that such financiers "were able to appreciate (...) the possibilities and the validity of an undertaking, even in unexplored territory, with all that it would demand in personal and real terms, and in the context of the risks which would surround it" (Melis, MI, 295). Obviously here we are confronted with figures who carry on "the function of the merchant venturer" with companies which fulfil almost multi-national roles. Clearly, the expansion of business involved a diversification of roles, so that the figure of the "maestro" began to emerge. This person "interposed between the merchant-venturer and the artisans (...) and is the person who organises the project on behalf of the entrepreneur, keeping close contact with the artisans who carry out its various phases, and at the same time, making use of several firms" (Melis, MI, 312). The degree to which the Italian firms were punctilious in examining minutely all aspects relating to the voyages is witnessed by what has now become a very considerable array of research, so that we can say that every movement "was not only a voyage of transfer, but an occasion – a well exploited occasion, also – for gathering interesting economic information". This goes also for brief and normal voyages, such as that between Florence and Perugia (cf. Frangioni, MV, 4).

**III.38** Not only the fruitful initiative by private individuals, but also the role played by the state such as that of the Roman state on the threshold of the modern age (cf. Mollat, XIII). What happened during the Jubilee of the year 1400, for example, is truly odd. There is no doubt that a widespread movement of renewal and penitence was making itself felt from the extremities of the Christian world, and that among other things, it was these very manifestations which "must have convinced the Pope to proclaim the Jubilee" (Melis, TCM, 246). But what is surprising, despite the fact that the provision to hold the Jubilee had arrived very late, is the readiness of many firms to invent new means of transport and sea-travel. We need only mention that "even on 31 December 1399, the relative Bull was still awaited" (Melis, TCM, 249). Given the uncertainty of certain maritime havens pinpointed by the pirates, whose viciousness "since they are Saracens, was naturally greater when it was a matter of fighting Christians" (Melis, TCM, 251), safer routes and means of transport were sought. Ports such as Livorno and Gaeta on the one side, and Ancona on the other, received pilgrims coming from the remotest parts, thus avoiding very long journeys overland which, for that reason, remained limited. "In previous Jubilees, the movement of peoples was notable; but the 1400 event was certainly more abundant in riches (…) The high number of participants can be attributed to the greatly increased capacities of the ships (and their number), which constituted one of the major factors – not only in technical and economic terms – of the end of the fourteenth century, due to the driving thrust of commercial exchanges under the aegis of the powerful companies of the era. These had completely revolutionised the economy of transported goods, creating the modern structure of related tariffs" (Melis, TCM, 257). Furthermore private enterprise met with collaboration from the authorities. Ships from specific geographical areas berthed in the above-mentioned ports, (in Gaeta from Barcelona, in Livorno from France), and from there they set out again, carrying the pilgrims returning from Rome back to their places of origin. Here they could congregate together by various routes, from the south, the north and the east, according to the port of origin, and this made the traffic flow easier and more manageable. All this was certainly not due merely to improvisation. It was possible because "certain ports had strictly specialised both in the import and the export of well-defined goods" (Melis, TCM, 70). For many ship-owners, this meant frequenting and knowing their special routes. In short, by land and sea, there had been for some time a revival of familiarity with certain transit routes that had been abandoned after the crisis of the Roman Empire. The example of the Alpine passes may be illuminating in this context (cf. Frangioni, MSS, 57 ff.).

# IV. INSTITUTIONAL PRECONDITIONS FOR THE ENGLISH ECONOMIC TAKE-OFF

**IV.1** In the first chapter of the third volume of his monumental analysis of the modern economy, Wallerstein gives us a series of suggestions which enable us to penetrate further into the basic works of the political and economic thought which developed over the span of the eighteenth and early nineteenth centuries. One of the first aspects analysed is the overall transformation of the social structure of the agrarian world, where a rapid increase of the proletariat was taking place in the country in addition to its more obvious rise in the cities. But there was also a series of other motives which conditioned the take-off and development of the British economy. These motives are closely connected, even though Wallerstein places them in chronological order: the growth in demand, the availability of capital (which made mechanisation possible), the demographic growth (which facilitated the phenomenon of "proletarianisation"), an agrarian "revolution" (a factor which made the demographic growth possible), and finally the evolution and change of landed property. Moreover, we must also seek the basic rationale for the movement of so much manpower from agriculture to industry. Apart from the many causes considered so far, Wallerstein also reminds us that there must also have been an increase in the yield from the seed used, which also meant more intensive cultivation and permitted the transfer of part of the labour force from the countryside to the city. There were, however, also juridical and social changes; enclosure became a key element in the whole process. This caused the elimination of open spaces, land formerly used for common grazing, turning the land into individual and cultivable units. This meant the abolition of common rights on the land which *de facto*, precisely because it was the property of no one in particular, had lain abandoned from the standpoint of cultivation (this is one of the many elements in common between the history of Rome and that of England: cf. what I said in chapter II concerning agrarian property, and the sense of ownership and boundaries, even seen in sacred terms in the feasts of the *terminalia* in ancient Latin civilisation). With enclosure, the work of those who sowed seed was protected by the intervention of those who sought to make free use of it. Because of this, enclosure made cultivation more fruitful, and favoured the joining together of scattered units of land. If this consideration is true, it is once more clear that a real economic growth needs juridical and institutional conditions which ease its path or at least do not stand in its way.

**IV.2** If this is true, it is not possible to maintain that the Industrial Revolution in Britain took place spontaneously and without any political or juridical backing. On the contrary – and it seems to me that Wallerstein himself thinks this way also: it is *only the existence of a more free state, juridical conditions which provide better safeguards both for property and for individual initiative, and finally particular geographical contingencies*, that favoured the process of what we call the "Industrial Revolution". The phenomenon may explode at any moment, but in reality it always has behind it a preparation stretching back quite a long way. I certainly do not want to say that the state played a direct role in the take-off of industry and trade in Great Britain, but it did, even so, have an important and even decisive indirect role because it had the capacity to express all those guarantees of which modern *homo oeconomicus* had need in order to achieve the best of his activities. Braudel maintains that the tendency to consider the Industrial Revolution as a total phenomenon and at the same time a slow one which involved distant and deep-rooted origins, is now to be taken for granted. To this should be added the transformation of the relations between city and country. This makes it clear that all the sectors of the British economy mutually influenced each other, and all profited from a favourable historical phase from the socio-political viewpoint. It was not only the great city of London which would take advantage of this, and in fact it only seized control of British capitalism around 1830; much of the territory of Great Britain also benefited (cf. Braudel, DC, 111-13).

**IV.3** I know that I may be raising a hornets' nest, but it would certainly seem to me that in *The Wealth of Nations* Adam Smith does not grant a clear temporal pre-eminence to natural society as opposed to artificial or civil society. The Scots philosopher takes up a series of reflections which, from the time of Hobbes and Locke, had animated British philosophical debate, and implicitly he seems to state that without any guarantee no economic development is possible. In fact, to say that freedom is the necessary and sufficient condition to ensure progress leads us on to ask who it is that should secure that freedom. His reflection is thus the product of a mentality typical of the British citizen of that period, who lived in a context of legal right, and who took for granted some secure conquests of the previous century. It is clear that the economic and industrial revolution was to change civil society and the political institutions, but it is equally clear that these were the indispensable preconditions – however rudimentary in character – for the revolution itself to take place. Henri Denis, in examining the chapter on landed income, makes an interesting observation. The interests of the landed proprietors and that of the wage-earners seem to be linked to the general interest of society, in that their income increases with the increase of national wealth. Those of the merchants and manufacturers on the other hand are in conflict with that of society in overall terms; their wealth in fact diminishes when the wealth of the nation increases. Smith perceives here not only the diversification of the different social classes, but also the suspicions which will sooner or later grow up between them. What also emerges is the desperation of some of the workers, who often suffer the alternative choices of dying of hunger or wrenching their demands from their employers by force (cf. Denis, part II, ch. IV, § 6). Despite this, Smith is optimistic about the outcome of these conflicts; one has only to think of the overworked image of the invisible hand which puts everything to rights. In reality, such optimism comes to him from a socio-political context which has successfully assimilated certain rules, and which is disposed to update them, but never to suppress them completely.

**IV.4** In the third book of *The Wealth of Nations,* and especially in chapter 2, Smith confirms the foregoing conclusion. He tells us that in the ancient world, agriculture was the most profitable of all occupations (an idea, moreover, which he had entertained since his youth, showing considerable influence from the Physiocrats). But he also tells us that at a certain point agriculture reached a moment of crisis, in part because feudal regulation impeded the free investment of capital. Still earlier, the invasions of the Roman provinces and the disorders that followed provoked rapine and violence, and even interrupted the conditions for free trade between cities and the countryside. The crisis that arose out of this lasted for several centuries. It is important to note that Smith gives a realistic image to the Middle Ages. As long as the disorder endured (and it endured for several centuries), the economy was a matter of pure survival, and the period witnessed the effort, very slow because it was so enormous, to recover a minimum of security. When a measure of security of law was recovered, thanks to the institutions and to the re-appearance of the figure of the merchant, then the economic recovery began. Again, in relation to Roman agriculture, and also in confirmation of what I have said in chapter II about economic and institutional development in the ancient world, it is worth mentioning that Smith was astonished at the modernity of the laws which regulated land ownership in the Latin world. When precarious conditions did not prevail – i.e. before the invasions began – the law of land succession did not distinguish between primo- and secondo-geniture, nor between male and female, distinctions that were introduced in the precarious conditions of the early Middle Ages.

**IV.5** In the same context, there is another consideration on the socio-political plane, which contradicts one of the commonplaces about ancient history: the use of slaves in agrarian activity and many other forms of work. Apart from the fact that in the working world, the employment of slaves was quite limited in the West, because it pertained to those who were less wealthy but free, who, like the plebeians, carried substantial weight in the institutions. It should be pointed out that agriculture in particular was considered by the Latins (there are many witnesses to this) as an activity of a free man. It is certainly no coincidence that slavery exploded in dramatic fashion both at the end of the Republic, and at the end of the Empire: always when the barycentre of the Mediterranean was moving eastward. In the Orient, slavery was an established practice, and for many unfortunates it was merely a matter of changing masters rather than changing social conditions. In keeping with these considerations, there is also a reflection by Smith which states that when slaves work the land they do not benefit from any real improvements. The experience of all times has shown that work done by slaves, even "though it appears to cost only their maintenance, is in the end the dearest of any" (Smith, WN, 418).

**IV.6** Agriculture develops at an even pace with the juridical notion of property, because security of possession and the possibility of redressing wrongs derive from the laws. This is one of the basic conditions of English political thought in the eighteenth century. We can find it expressed in various authors, ranging from Hume to Ferguson – even though the latter, perhaps because he is a liberal-conservative, sees it more on the level of security, which seems to favour the present moment in positive relation to the past. This, however, is seemingly one of the basic requirements of the liberal movement, which justifies the Industrial Revolution and which is distinguished by this very fact from the radical Enlightenment thought that in contrast sees the past as a completely negative influence against which it is necessary to make a clean sweep. In short, in England the liberals of the second half of the eighteenth century are more on the side of Montesquieu than of Rousseau, and "assign the leading role to civil society, whose movements can be for the most part regulated by the state, but in no case permitting any act of coercion" (Merolle, 111). Every economic operation must be guaranteed and protected; this is the role of government, which cannot, however, go beyond the functions of a guarantor. Man has within himself the capacities which drive him towards progress, and he feels himself fulfilled only in putting his intelligence to work. In this, Ferguson maintains, *his happiness consists* (Ferguson, vol. I, 250, quoted in Merolle, 27). Thanks to this, he emerges from ignorance, and matures towards knowledge; from poverty he heads towards wealth, from the primitive state to political organisation (cf. Merolle, 30). This passage *from disorder to Political Establishment* sums up the history of England, which emerges from the Glorious Revolution and heads towards affirmation as an economic power. Such a passage is only made possible (and here all thinkers of the time are agreed), because the system of *limited monarchy* which so fascinated Montesquieu has become an established fact.

**IV.7** We can understand from this that, when Smith states that the right of property is the most sacred and inviolable, he is able to do so because society, which Smith describes as "natural", and which pursues this right as a main aim, is guaranteed by institutions which protect property. Such institutions may also be seen as superstructure, as artificial society, because they change with the mutation of natural society; but in order for this mutation to take place, they are also indispensable premises. The attempt to establish a priority between the "economic element" and the "political element" is a chicken – and – egg question: a fascinating subject, perhaps, but quite devoid of meaning. This explains why not only Smith, but the English progressives of his day in general, feel a sort of love/hate relationship to the state and the government. On the one hand, if they claim to carry out direct interventions in civil society, they find them incapable of guaranteeing real and effective change; on the other hand they know that without political authorities, changes become empty dreams – and even dangerous ones. In short, the entire work of Smith should be seen as the search for the limits which both elements must impose on themselves in order to allow the other to operate for the good of all, rather than being seen as the primacy of "natural" over "artificial" society.

**IV.8** Limitation also makes it possible to safeguard the diversities which, for the true liberal, are a source of riches. For this reason many English liberals criticise the French Enlightenment, which claims to manufacture *ex novo* the criteria for perfect equality. *Impossible planning is a symbol of poverty, like every operation which claims to realise uniformity by mortifying creativity.* Certainly all this does not mean ignoring injustice and perpetuating it; apart from anything else, there can be no peace if justice is lacking. The dynamic vision of society implies improvement for all, and perfection of the criteria for justice. But it is only the dynamic tension between political reality and economic reality which makes such an objective possible. *When one of the two takes precedence over the other and surpasses its own limits, a process of involution is always set into motion.* To cite one of Ferguson's statements, which anyone in that situation would subscribe to, the merchant can be helped and supported in his activity, but he cannot be stimulated to direct it in one way rather than another (cf. Merolle, 118). In the introduction to Book IV, Smith presents his conclusion: "Political economy, considered as a branch of the science of a statesman or legislator, proposes two distinct objects: first, to provide a plentiful revenue or subsistence for the people, or more properly to enable them to provide such a revenue or subsistence for themselves; and secondly to supply the state or commonwealth with a revenue sufficient for the public services" (Smith, WN, 455). As can be seen, here political economy is taken to be a branch which grows concomitantly with the others.

**IV.9** Seeing the economy as a branch of the science of the statesman and legislator, however, does not mean that it must be subordinated to politics. Smith, anticipating some of von Hayek's thoughts in a more balanced fashion (in my view) maintains that the possibilities of judgment which the economic operator possesses are in certain sectors more appropriate and well-calibrated than those of the political operator: "every individual, it is evident, can, in his local situation, judge much better than any statesman or lawgiver can do for him. The statesman, who should attempt to direct private people in what manner they ought to employ their capitals, would not only load himself a most unnecessary attention, but assume an authority (...) which would nowhere be so dangerous" (Smith, WN, 485). In other words, distinctions of competence are to guarantee social well-being. As this gradually develops and spreads, the relationships seem to interweave more and more, and it becomes more and more necessary, therefore, to make distinctions, because rich and complex societies see rapid change in all the other aspects of social life – even those aspects which are not merely economic and political. We may consider some of these as having a physical nature: the taxes on certain kinds of goods can be acceptable at one moment and intolerable at another. Smith is speaking explicitly of the taxes on goods of prime necessity; these can be tolerated only in rich countries already possessed of a certain level of well-being. Poor countries would not be in a position to bear them (cf. Smith, WN, 496). The same must be said for the economic premiums and/or incentives which a government may study in order to encourage certain economic activities which it would otherwise not be convenient to undertake. The Scots philosopher's words on this subject are very clear: "The effect of bounties, like that of all the other expedients of the mercantile system, can only be to force the trade of a country into a channel much less advantageous than that in which it would naturally run of its own accord" (Smith, WN, 541). From these lines two fundamental conclusions emerge: First, that Smith confirms that if politics do not create the right conditions, the economy cannot take off; and second, that spontaneous economic development may be corrected and in some cases should be.

**IV.10** In a further reference to premiums, it is Smith himself who stresses how far-sighted the political world needs to be in understanding the times and modes of their extension. In contrast to what might be supposed, it is, for instance, less absurd to give rewards in time of prosperity than in times of poverty, because when the public enjoys a greater income, it learns how to diversify the ways of using it. Even less absurd is it to give rewards to successful artists or manufacturers, because these people know better than others how to direct the resources towards the most advantageous channels (cf. Smith, WN, 560). This suggests that for prosperity a certain culture is necessary which knows how to harmonise the economic and political factors, and both of these with the arts and various kinds of knowledge. Smith finds a counter-proof to this in his examination of colonies: "The colonies carry with them a knowledge of agriculture and of the other useful arts, superior to what can grow up of its own accord in the course of many centuries among savage and barbarous nations" (Smith, WN,

609). To this may be added the favourable environmental conditions and the abundance of land and natural resources. But all this is not enough in itself; why have certain colonies developed more quickly than others? In Smith's opinion this has depended on the fact that although they have a combination of favourable environmental conditions common to every colonial expansion, it is the British colonies alone which possessed an institutional background favourable to progress (cf. Smith, WN, 616-17). This is confirmation that for Smith too there is no real economic development if the political preconditions and institutions capable of ensuring it are not firmly in place.

**IV.11** At a date much earlier than the appearance of the classic which made him internationally famous, Smith had already tackled the above problems in a cycle of lectures in the early 1760s, entitled *Lectures on Jurisprudence*. In these pages Smith seems to have virtually followed a plan suggested by Montesquieu. He attempted to trace the gradual process of jurisprudence from its primordial origins to his own times. The important thing is that this concerned not only public but private jurisprudence, to show how both have combined to the creation, the accumulation and the improvement of property. In the last part of his lectures, he also examined those political regulations which took into account the principle of expediency rather more than that of justice, in order to understand how these can increase the wealth, power and property of the state. He thus shows how he considered the political institutions to be in close relationship to trade, and finance and generally to the various problems of the establishment. It should perhaps be mentioned that the word "jurisprudence" is used by Smith in a fairly broad sense. At times it is even defined as "the theory of the rules by which civil governments must be governed", or also "the theories of the general principles of law and government". However, the main aspects of jurisprudence are the maintenance of justice, provision for security with the aim of promoting wealth, the growth of income, and the constitution of an army for defence (cf. Meek, Raphael, Stein, 3-4). It is easy to see that political and economic factors are closely interconnected.

**IV.12** In relation to what I am seeking to show, it is interesting to find that in these pages there is also some discussion about the aims of government, and about the limits of power. A sort of collaboration arises between the political and economic elements, even though each remains within its own limits, which alone can guarantee their development. Where the economic and legislative elements interweave more is in the manner of acquiring and defending property. However we wish to judge this question, it remains virtually the basic reason for jurisprudence. Property, which is not a given fact of natural society except in a confused sense, matures and develops, as Latin juridical tradition foresaw, throughout the history of humankind. This explains why Smith goes so far as to defend the idea that institutions which are today seen as damaging to society may have been necessary and useful at other times (cf. Meek, Raphael, Stein, 33). The only policy which is never damaging to economic development and the prosperity of a state is that of peace and internal security. Such a policy is considered by Smith, right from the opening words of his work, to be the pre-condition for promoting wealth and increasing incomes (cf. Smith, LJ, 5). Justice itself, if it seeks to avoid compromising such a policy, must make sure that no one is deprived of anything of which they are legitimately possessed. These "preconditions" have allowed society to improve, and such improvements have allowed the various crafts and trades and professions practised at the outset by each individual only in relation and proportion to his own need and well-being, to become distinguished and increasingly specialised on the basis of the natural inclinations of each, or of the natural and social conditions in which people are living (cf. Smith, LJ, 15). But this division of labour continued to improve with the maturing of society, and with the development of the concept of property, which is such only once it acquires stability. In principle, property was identified with strict and continuing possession. It was held that a thing could no longer be "ours" in any real sense once we had lost immediate possession of it. A wild animal captured by us, as soon as it escapes from our control, is just as if it had never been "ours". As time passes, in order to render the links of property stronger, it came to be argued that it also extended beyond simple possession. This means that in the case of the wild animal captured and then escaped, it remains our own property, even if for the moment it is beyond our control, provided that not only do we seek it but there is a real possibility of its being found. (cf. Smith, LJ, 18-9).

**IV.13** With regard to the reference to Roman Law and the history from which it emerged and declined, Smith is quite explicit: "When the barbarian nations of the north overran the Roman Empire, and settled in the western parts of Europe, property came to be very unequally divided. At the same time all arts were entirely neglected. This threw a great share of power into the hands of those who possessed the greatest property. It will be evident also that the balance of property will make those who are possessed of it have a far greater superiority in power, than the same share of property will give one in a more refind and cultivated age" (Smith, LJ. 49-50). The spread of property which had characterised a slow historical "itinerary" previously, had come to a halt because of the disappearance of that sense of limitations, of boundaries considered sacred (cf. what I have already said in connection with *terminalia*). The very security created not only by laws and institutions but also by moral convictions, which characterises a society based on freedom, had broken down. But there had also been a breakdown in a whole way of understanding life which the distribution of property had guaranteed – one has only to think of the rules of succession, for example (cf. Smith, LJ, 28 and 39). The conviction that moral and political sciences were closely linked to economic science – far more so than to mathematics, for instance – was a fairly widespread one during the latter half of the eighteenth and the early part of the nineteenth centuries. It was to be seen before long in Ricardo, but perhaps it is worth noting here the first lines of Malthus' famous essay *The Principles of Political Economy considered with a view to their Practical Application*. That economic science is more akin to moral and political science is demonstrated by a simple consideration: if it were more akin to mathematics, economics would not partake of that difference of opinion which in fact characterises the political and moral world.

**IV.14** But let us return to the acknowledged father of political economy. To say that *"the will of the proprietor and tradition are both absolutely requisite"* (Smith, LJ, 71) means that they can never break down completely, on pain of the loss of liberty and a certain way of understanding society. It is certainly not mere chance that the feudal system, which was gradually replacing the Latin one, forbade vassals the opportunity to renounce certain goods, thus conferring on them a role which is some ways was inferior to that of freedmen. In this, Smith sees not only an involution of society, but a real danger to civil and economic development. To impede the diffusion of property favours the establishment of monopolies, and "all monopolies evidently tend to promote poverty" (Smith, LJ, 83). In the end, industries are discouraged, as are the development of the arts and everything which is consequent upon these things, beginning with trade, and going on from there to the exchange of both goods and ideas. But this is not everything; the development of personal rights is also impeded; those *jura personalia,* which progress in human relations regulated by tradition and constantly enriched (cf. Smith, LJ, 85-86). The development of personal rights and their safeguarding traces the journey along the path of civilisation, and of the governments which it has succeeded in producing. The first level of civil life is in fact characterised by governments which do not have the authority to punish crimes. Then, there is slow progress towards obtaining the possibility of punishing in exemplary fashion, but in a way which is excessively severe and often unbalanced (cf. Smith, LJ, 129-30). Society, however, can only call itself civilised when everything is related to the rules and a criterion of equity exists. The breakdown of such a criterion makes even a civil society intolerable, and it ends up by representing, though with various connotations, the phenomenon of slavery. With regard to this "we may observe here that the state of slavery is a much more tolerable one in a poor and barbarous people than in a rich and polished one" (Smith, LJ, 182). Here we find introduced a problem which would be further developed by Marx, who (as Smith had already perceived), was to hold that in the more highly developed societies, those who live in poverty find themselves in fact in a condition of slavery.

**IV.15** There is a point at which Smith, anticipating what he will later say in his more famous work, shows that the development of wealth has accompanied as "I have tried to explain to you, in the most complete way possible, the forms of government which emerge naturally from humanity". This same development also shows how such forms of government "advance in society, and in what way they gradually proceed". At the beginning there was always a head *(chieftain)* in charge of the government, who had a superior power to that of all others, and in all matters, thanks to his family descent and his wealth. All this allowed him influence and authority over others. From then onward, it should be said that the actuation of the arts and trade must in any case be related to the strength of the power or the institutions; it will be just the same in a republic (cf. Smith, LJ, 215 and 231). This means that the capacity of a government to ensure progress is measured by its manner of understanding and supporting or tolerating the arts and commerce. Another element which ensures economic activity and its development is that creditors, in lending their money, must possess some security. This happened in the United Kingdom well before the industrial revolution. The surety of creditors was accompanied by the broad liberty of British subjects, as guaranteed by the limited power of the judiciary (cf. Smith, LJ, 268 and 275-6).

**IV.16** The problem of the power of the judiciary, and that of the possibility of maintaining a civil order that is more than apparent are two issues which Smith is keenly aware of. The *first*, in the conviction that in Britain the liberty of subjects was ensured by the precision of the laws, and also by the way in which that fact was accepted that the judges (the reference is to the judges of the *Common Law*, not to the *Chancellor*) should have less power than anyone else to amplify and correct the laws. The *second* issue, concerning the maintenance of civil order, leads him to a concern with the numerous penalties directed at those who undertake to encourage the papal religion. These may, by his time, be considered useless, since the zeal for that faith has been strongly reduced, and could be further discouraged by imposing double taxation on its adherents (cf. Smith, LJ, 282 and 299). Quite apart from the problem in itself, this concern of Smith's shows how any sort of social upheaval, even though far distant from economic problems, could have a bearing on these unwelcome consequences. Smith is concerned that differences can be composed in order to guarantee the development and well-being of the state, as took place in ancient Rome in the reconciling of the clashes between patricians and plebs, and in the England of his times between the Whigs and the Tories, whose basic principles held English society together. The principle of the Tories was that of authority, which was in harmony with that of utility as adopted by the Whigs (cf. Smith, LJ, 319). Such well- articulated institutions favour the activity of individuals, and allow them the tranquillity to operate and show the different qualities of their genius. It is very problematic for this to emerge in a society of savages, because there, even if they existed, the different manifestations of genius could not possess the ease and security to express themselves (cf. Smith, LJ, 348).

**IV.17** The relationship between politics and economics was also a crucial aspect for Ricardo. As the two scholars Sraffa and Dobb warn us (in the famous introduction to the first volume of the complete works of Ricardo), the principal problem of political economy was that of putting into effect the distribution of the national product among the classes, a problem over which the British economist found himself at times in difficulties because the dimensions of this product seemed to change with the varying of the division. Today one might also ask who in fact puts this distribution into effect – a question which already caused Marx some perplexity. However, it may be that Ricardo was concerned with the repercussions that such distribution might have produced within the social context. Such a supposition can be deduced from a series of other considerations made by Ricardo, for whom the importance of safety, or indeed certainty, of possessions such as goods was, it seems an indispensable presupposition. In the second chapter of his *On the Principles of Political Economy and Taxation*, the one dealing with income, certain problems are raised which recur here and there throughout the whole work. In speaking of the different remuneration which may be paid for two neighbouring estates of the same size and natural fertility, Ricardo stresses that, apart from having different commodities and being sufficiently reclaimed, the one which obtains the greater remuneration may also be provided with better fencing, hedges and surrounding walls (cf. Ricardo, PPET, 67-8). This brings us back at once to the certainty of property, and the safety of goods, aspects which have an underlying assumption of legislation and institutions capable of guaranteeing them.

**IV.18** The laws which regulate the bases of civil life cannot, however, claim to regulate everything, otherwise that which is a just expectation of certainty would be transformed into an oppressive constriction. In short, even as far as the law is concerned, a sense of limit exists. We may take the example of the wage issue, which apart from certain principles, should be left to the free and equal competition of the market, and never subjected to legislative interference. When the state intervenes in economic matters, for example in order to improve the conditions of a class, it risks worsening the conditions, along with those of the other classes because it ends up by absorbing all the resources in order to satisfy the inexhaustible needs of public expenditure (cf. Ricardo, PPET, 105-6). In an important note, Ricardo maintains, agreeing with Buchanan, the usefulness of knowing the limits of the law in order to avoid, while seeking to achieve the impossible, not doing what is really useful and practically possible. Because of this the laws, especially in matters of economics, must innovate with extreme caution, and the same goes for the abolition of certain dispositions (cf. Ricardo, PPET, 105-6). It is certainly true that the laws may also play a positive role in the increase of the perception of profits, and thus of wealth; they can do so, however, in an indirect and no less effective way. In fact, apart from the advantages deriving from economic action, it is possible, given real skill, to encourage others. Industriousness must be stimulated in various ways, for example by recompensing genius and seeking by different forms of encouragement and prizes, to stimulate it (cf. Ricardo, PPET, 133-4) Thus the task of politics is to put in place a series of facilitations which will make economic development easier, conditions which must also take account of the suspicion, laziness and fear of those who should be taking the risks. These people seek tranquil relations, long-established habits and everything that proves to be most advantageous to their wealth (cf. Ricardo, PPET, 136-7).

**IV.19** Governments should seek never to impose taxes which weigh inevitably on wealth and capital, because by doing so, on the one hand the state feels itself to be authorised to increase its own expenditures, and on the other hand, by causing future production to diminish, it does not favour development and employment. The same may be said for taxes on the transfer of property, which result in impeding national capital from being distributed in the most advantageous way. Fur the purposes of general prosperity, the advantages conceded will never be too great. It must be kept in mind, in fact, that it is by means of these exchanges of capital that encouragement is given to the acquisition of capital itself on the part of those who will know how best to use it to increase national productivity, to the advantage and prosperity of all. Taking up a statement of Smith's, Ricardo reminds us that every tax on the transfer of property tends in fact to diminish the funds destined for productive work (cf. Ricardo, PPET, 154-5). It thus becomes pointless to lament the poverty of the work-force. No legislative procedure is capable of rectifying this if the previous barriers which have obstructed the progress of the economy are not removed.

**IV.20** Recalling the specific statements of Smith, Ricardo also maintains that every citizen should contribute to maintaining the government in the best possible way proportional to his capacity; that taxes should be certain and not arbitrary; that such taxes must be collected in the time and the manner most suited to those who pay them, and finally that the taxes must be conceived in such a way as to make the contributor delve as little as possible into his resources (cf. Ricardo, PPET, 181-2). The system of taxation provokes many other reflections on the relation between politics and economics. Most importantly, this system must not be improvised, because – should it prove to be defective – much more may be extracted from the citizens than effectively ends up in the state's coffers. It also happens, almost always when taxes are unjust, that the advantage falls to those who should collect them, because, perhaps, they suggest the way to get round them. In order to avoid all this, it would be better, as Say suggests, that financial plans provide for spending little, and at any rate, for spending what it is practicable to spend. It should also be remembered that, as Smith insists, the taxes, since they cannot fall to any appreciable extent on the working classes, always end up by putting the heaviest burdens on the same people and the same goods. For this reason it is essential not to go to excess in their use. It should also be added, as Say reminds us, that those who are deprived of part of their revenue are usually forced to reduce their consumption. The contributor will thus lose part of his own satisfaction and the producer part of his profit, and in future, the Treasury part of its revenue (cf. Ricardo PPET, 234-6). It could thus be said that not only must taxes be justified, but the way in which they are spent must be made concretely evident, so that citizens are placed in a position to assess their use and are also rendered more ready to bear further necessary tax burdens. The control of expenses thus becomes a fundamental of any democratic economy.

**IV.21** It may be that in certain given moments, in order to deal with unexpected necessities, for example natural disasters, or to maintain unproductive workers in certain difficult situations, some forms of taxes have to be raised, or the state incurs debts to resolve the problems of this type. But Ricardo warns that justice and good faith demand that the interest on public debt must then be paid, so that those who have advanced their own capital for the general advantage are not compelled to do without their just returns. Neither is it just that a national difficulty should be transferred to the shoulders of a part of the community only. In this way, public debt comes to be considered the best system for dealing with the expenses and needs of the state, and the point is reached of considering it normal to be less parsimonious, until the real situation in which the country is placed becomes completely hidden.

Sacrifices must be salutary for nations as well as for individuals. This will be possible only as long as the systems of recovery do not become too artificial, ending by causing counterproductive results (cf. Ricardo, PPET, 245-8). Moreover it should be remembered that even unforeseen necessities should be handled with farsightedness, and above all without increasing the fear of instability which certain situations already bring with them. After a moment of crisis, it must be kept in mind that the way of employing capital cannot change too violently without generating further turbulence. This is obviously even more the case in the richer countries than in the poorer ones. For this reason, as Marx himself observes, the former feel the effects of economic crises more severely. We can easily understand why the working class has an interest in understanding how the country's wealth is spent (cf. Ricardo, PPET, 392-3).

**IV.22** Ricardo states several times that the value of every kind of merchandise increases or diminishes according to the ease or difficulty of its production (cf. Ricardo, PPET, 273). The difficulties do not depend only on the type and quantity of labour employed, but also on the social and political contingencies of the moment. It is these which cause foreign capital to flow in or out. It is the policies of free trade and those which show negligible or minimal risks which cause capital to flow in, apart, obviously, from the costs and productiveness of work (cf. Ricardo, PPET, 348-9). This means that there is a necessity for a serious economic policy in which the political element can certainly not be considered secondary. Ricardo points to this necessity when speaking of monetary policy, holding that there exists an interest on the part of the public that it should be the state and not a society of merchants or bankers which issues currency. However, in a free state, with enlightened legislators, the faculty of issuing paper currency, regulated by the limits of convertibility on presentation, can be entrusted to appropriate independent commissions not under the control of the ministers, but controlled by appropriate regulations (cf. Ricardo, PPET, 362-3). This is certainly not the policy of a despotic state, but one which provides guarantees of respect for the rules.

## A note on economic thought in Italy in the eighteenth century

**IV.23** What was stated in point 2 of the present chapter (i.e. that it is not possible to maintain that economic development can take place spontaneously and without any political or juridical support) finds a confirmation in the reflections of some of the Italian economists of the eighteenth century, who on a number of occasions anticipate certain themes of the classics of British economics. This is the case with the treatise *Della Moneta* by Ferdinando Galiani, which appeared about half way through the century. Some years later, in 1768, Galiani went to live in England, and according to some, met personally with Adam Smith (cf. Caracciolo, XXII). In a context in which wealth was still seen as lying in precious metals or other goods, Galiani maintains that "the true wealth is humankind (…) Man alone (…) makes a state prosper" (Galiani, 134). In this he anticipated the theme of the resources of human labour and inventiveness. This is true to such an extent that when "men depart or allow themselves to be overtaken by death without creating any further progeny, the manufactures fall into ruin and the earth returns to its wild state" (Galiani, 112) Other themes, too, such as, for example, those of inflation or those of the forced intervention of governments in the economy, must be examined with great farsightedness. With regard to the latter themes, while not denying the importance of a serious economic policy, Galiani holds that the laws of economics and finance are such that no government can modify them at its own pleasure. The task of governments, on the other hand, is "the concern for peace and tranquillity" (Galiani, 3), without which economic activity cannot be carried on in the best way.

This is what history itself has shown since the ancient Roman world "when, as the barbarians had flooded and smashed the empire, in the overturning of cities and their sacking (…) it was not possible to revive, even with trade, which was interrupted and extinguished (…) From this poverty that the governmental orders of those centuries arose" (Galiani, 29).

**IV.24** This insecurity became evident in all the political activities of the time, and even in the structure of governments, as also in the way of collecting and managing resources. The hierarchical structure of the early middle ages gave life to vassalage and laws which caused a growing tax-collecting structure; monetary scarcity did the rest. The collection of taxes itself followed this custom; in fact "sovereigns and masters were unable to collect dues in other ways than by personal services or fruits of the soil" (Galiani, 29). In these cases human 'greed', which under civil regulation causes the enrichment of the state, when it is not subject to rules is an element of disorder and turbulence. These are the difficult situations in which individuals, searching first and foremost for security, end by retiring into themselves and causing the conditions for development and enrichment to fail. In fact, "since trade is the favoured child of the mutual need that everyone has, and could be defined as a communication, which many carry on among themselves by their own efforts to meet common necessities" (Galiani 87), it is clear that where the conditions for realising exchanges and communications are not present, a real economic take-off is not possible. These conditions also have a bearing on the stability of currency, which has a need for "its measurements to be stable" (Galiani, 80). This stability makes the consumption and the industriousness of producers easier, even if at times this proves to be a matter of goods considered pointless and according to some, mere luxuries. "Cursed be that *luxury*, that *idleness*, those *ignoble arts*, which ought to be termed *opulence, mildness, industry* (…) sumptuous expenditure, which is the offshoot of opulence and of the overfast circulation of money" (Galiani, 104 and 107), even if all this may create other problems.

**IV.25** Considerations regarding duties are also of some interest. He begins with the definition of duties as "a portion of the possessions of private individuals which the prince takes and then renders back (...) Thus the duty by nature neither harms nor benefits; but if the duty is not returned to those who paid it, it harms some and benefits others" (Galiani, 110). To render back to those who paid means, in the language of today, to provide services in return for the taxes paid. It may also happen that certain revenues are employed "to reward the kings, the un-meritworthy and the idle; or again, for these to give themselves exemptions while honest folk are forced to pay" (Galiani, 111). This is almost equivalent to spending the resources of a country abroad without any benefit for the citizens who pay. In these circumstances, many people think of emigrating, "and the first are those who leave least, i.e. the merchants and artists" (Galiani, 113); this produces a drain of wealth and intelligence. What can be done to avoid all of this happening? Order and justice must be safeguarded. "Duties and taxes, the remuneration of magistrates, then, are just, when they are so ordered as to increase our tranquillity, providing sustenance to the wisest and most virtuous people, who are capable of maintaining peace and regulated freedom. Tyranny is nothing else than that same evil order, in which he who is either not useful to others or merely pernicious acquires wealth" (Galiani, 159). That regulated freedom is witnessed to by what the thought of Vico and Montesquieu introduced into the European mind. Here *regulated freedom* also bears witness to how the certainty of law is important for economic life, and in every day commercial life also. "The laws are necessary in these contracts only to render the agreement true, banishing fraud and trickery, which by falsifying ideas make esteem and consensus false also" (Galiani, 160).

**IV.26** Where this regulated liberty exists, prosperity is assured, in part because no one would want to abandon such a state and those who do not live there would wish to do so. "Happy is that government, where the upbringing of offspring is not costly, where to come and live is desirable, where to find oneself living is happy, and to leave is sorrowful!" (Galiani, 249). Such conditions are to be found very rarely in history, but they have always made the fortune of those states in which, sooner or later, arts, manufactures and trade of all kinds have established themselves. Here money has a reliable and not fictitious value, and those who carry out economic and commercial activities are reassured by "the certainty of debts, the punctuality of the debtor and the true value of the pledge that one has in hand" (Galiani, 265). Development is assured, in such conditions, by an order which guarantees the recognition of merit and the just recompense for sacrifices. "Nor can there be a greater disorder in a state than that the taxes (…) are destined to benefit the well-off without any kind of thought or effort" (Galiani, 297). In this way, not only are initiative, inventiveness and risk discouraged, but encouragement is given to laziness, dishonesty and the contempt of the capable and honest.

**IV.27** Among the other reflections of the Italian eighteenth century which contribute to the European cultural context, we may also mention here the thoughts of Pietro Verri in his essay *Della economia politica*, which appeared for the first time in 1771 under the title *Meditazioni sulla economia politica*. From the opening words, when he analyses commercial activity, political and social motives interweave with economic analyses: "The easier transport is made, the greater communication extends, the more ideas multiply, the more needs increase, and the more commerce grows" (Verri, 133). This not only has an economic value in itself, but it has a notable importance on the psychological plane and that of relations, and in the broader sense on the political and social level. Entering into relationship with others, making contracts, carrying out any form of economic activity, changes our way of thinking and of being. "Isolated man is timid, savage and inept; infrequently as he may be united to a few, he knows little or nothing; but a union of many men gathered together, condensed and restricted in a small space becomes animated and ferments and improves, and all around there is an expansion of activity, reproduction and life" (Verri, 205).

**IV.28** Along with a far-sighted analysis of monopolies, duopolies and competition (cf. Verri, 144-5) consideration is given to the relations between political and economic entities, and he reaches the conclusion that the former, with its dispositions, may exercise an indirect influence, but must not intervene directly. "Direct laws may drive away crimes, but they will never animate industry" (Verri, 151). Interventions in property, which at times may even be sources of injustice, can never be direct "since this would be an assault on *property*, which is at the basis of all justice in all civil society. This can be obtained indirectly" (Verri, 152). It should obviously be remembered that the historic moment saw in private property the possibility of removing certain spheres from absolute power, and these guaranteed a certain freedom of action. Thus it was a question of eliminating certain restraints which denied freedom, and also prosperity, "because the effect of restrictions is to accumulate goods in a few hands" (Verri, 163). The sole effect of this would be to raise prices and render availability and distribution difficult. The tasks of government are very different. To define the *optimum government* is not difficult, because it is "that, in other words, in which the highest security and internal stability for the laws and for the civil liberty of the citizens are found at the same time" (Verri, 168).

**IV.29** One of the most absurd claims of politics is that of believing that it can "by law level out internal prices" (Verri, 171). In this field politics can only invite, and at times guide, because it is very hard for it to succeed in enforcing prescription, as often suggested, by means of the law. What politics can do is to reconfirm that sense of confidence which must animate civil life if it is sought to avoid creating a growing sense of insecurity. In these cases faith in the public administration is also lost, and corruption is encouraged, even without willing it to be (cf. Verri, 185-6). Politics can, then, create the confidence so that the industriousness of individuals is encouraged, for example by carrying out a series of public works, of infrastructures as we would say today, capable of assisting economic activity. These works must not simply pursue a sense of sterile grandiosity, but must "be limited solely to utility". Because of this, the first aim of public works must be that of facilitating exchanges through the construction of means and routes for transport, which in those days might be canals, in order to "reach the remote populations": moreover, to guarantee "public safety on the roads, the convenient placing of hotels and similar other means". Finally, an international reputation which excites credibility: "A maritime power, whose flag is respected, may say for that reason that it has borders with every port in the world" (Verri, 213). It may in fact trade with all, because it enjoys the maximum of trust.

**IV.30** His observations on the tax system are acute. Taxation will be an element of disruption when "it exceeds the strength of the nation and is not proportionate to its wealth", or when it is "viciously distributed" (Verri, 223). It should be added, and here many of the reflections of classic economists are anticipated, that even collecting taxes may be a cause of trouble for the state. The agents of the gabelle *(i.e. a special tax)*, skilled in the collection of taxes, are "a class of men who neither being reproducers nor mediators *(i.e. who neither produce or trade)* but mere consumers, and consumers who possess no funds, who do not defend the state, are thus purely a burden" (Verri, 229). Here we find what was also to be

Smith's reflection on the difference between productive and unproductive work, and the fact that the latter is maintained by the former. Hence, in collecting taxes, it is necessary "to choose that form which involves the least possible expenditure in its collection" (Verri, 229). Public expenditure must therefore be carefully watched, because it is carried out with the money of everyone, and above all, of those who work and produce. Because of this, it is essential to make sure that the "offices" handling the taxes do not multiply, and that they reach the purpose for which they are collected as soon as possible. "Taxes will always be less harmful in the degree to which they pass swiftly from the hands of the contributor to the fiscal office and from there to wage-earners or to public works" (Verri, 253). The laws themselves must make these operations easier, as they must also stipulate contracts and multiply them. If the laws fail in this task, economic activity will certainly not be helped. "Every time that in any society a man may do more than the law, let industry never have any hope. Industry does not reign if the security of the nation and its goods is not dispersed generally over the whole face of the nation" (Verri, 230-1). These laws, however, must not go beyond their task, because otherwise they would create useless limits, and would be an embarrassment and it would be easier for "the boundaries of the country which doesn't have any trade to be instituted – whose *economic boundaries* are the whole world, provided that it is in freedom" (Verri, 245). Because of this, growing agreements between states are to be welcomed, beginning with those of Europe, to facilitate trade, the stipulation of contracts, and the development of industry. The well-being of the Old Continent would be assured, Verri maintains, as long as it does not fall into the error of a demographic crisis as grave as its contrary, i.e. uncontrolled growth. All these elements together with "never leaving fraud unpunished" (Verri, 259), favour economic development in every way, and thus the happiness of humankind.

# V. A SPOTLIGHT ON ECONOMIC DEVELOPMENT
## An analysis of *Das Kapital*

**V.1** Even in the preface to the first edition of *Das Kapital*, Marx was already unequivocally pointing out the path along which all his research would proceed. "My standpoint, from which *the evolution of the economic formation of society is viewed as a process of natural history*, can less than any other make the individual responsible for relations whose creature he socially remains, however much he may subjectively raise himself above them" (Marx, K, vol. I, 21). I do not want at this point to take up the criticisms which have been formulated in abundance, and at times over-repetitively, by methodological individualists. What I feel it is vital to point out is the independence of the process of the formation of a political superstructure from the economic structure. Only in this way can we escape not only from the rigid determinism of Hegel, but also from Marxian fatalism. In fact, at the end of the Preface to the second edition, Marx – coherently developing what he has stated in the foregoing quotation, says: "The contradictions inherent in the movement of capitalist society impress themselves upon the practical bourgeois most strikingly in the changes of the periodic cycle, through which modern industry runs, and whose crowning point is the universal crisis. That crisis is once again approaching, although as yet but in its preliminary stage" (Marx, K, vol. I, 29). Now it is evident that for Marx capitalism was heading towards a final crisis; in fact "the universal crisis", to which the bourgeoisie, that "creature" of the process of economic history, was bound to succumb. But for those who never acknowledge the crises to be final, however profound and irreversible they may be, it must be remembered that in order to restart economic development, the individuals, the bourgeoisie – I would even say society (understanding the word in its etymological sense) – realise the need to recreate those guarantees, those juridical realities, without which the risk (which I shall deal with in the final chapter) becomes too high.

**V.2** Probably Marx himself sensed the need to re-examine the whole *"development of the economic evolution of society as a process of natural history"*. But he never succeeded in freeing himself from the Hegelian dialectic, even though in a revised form, on to which he grafted certain categories from Smith. An important note helps us to understand that Marx was aware of this need, though he never managed to return to it. After having reiterated the insufficiency of abstract economics to explain the phenomenon of social evolution, given that "from the economic standpoint this explanation is worth nothing, because the historical element is wanting" (Marx, K, vol. I, 352), in a note he makes an interesting digression on historical research, which unfortunately had no follow-up, that would perhaps have enabled him to free himself from rigid dialectical determinism. Speaking of natural history, of the history of technology and then also of the history of religion, he asks himself: "And would not such history be easier to compile, since, as Vico says, human history differs from natural history in this, that we have made the former, but not the latter?" (Marx, K, vol. I, 352). Dialectical materialism seems for a moment to reserve its rigidity to nature alone, while humanity seems capable (and this is the real doctrine of Vico, which no one seems to want to understand) of emerging from its perpetual crises thanks to its imagination, and hence to its creativity and freedom. But for Marx, this was just a momentary suggestion – also because, as far as I know, he had never had an opportunity to read Vico.

**V.3** Humanity emerges from its crises specifically because in certain individuals there is a drive towards betterment, and certainly also towards enrichment, which must be regularised. From this tension there emerges that creativity and that spirit of initiative which can produce benefits for an entire civilisation. Marx himself was convinced of this, and he knew that not all individuals are, in this field, equally endowed. The criticisms which he often directs against the bourgeoisie should be read in counter-light; they would then sound more like eulogies: "This boundless greed after riches, this passionate chase after exchange-value, is common to the capitalist and the miser; but while the miser is merely a capitalist gone mad, the capitalist is a rational miser. The never-ending augmentation of exchange-value, which the miser strives after, by seeking to save his money from circulation, is attained by the more acute capitalist, by constantly throwing it afresh into circulation" (Marx, K, vol. I, 151). This statement seems to be saying that as in various fields there are those who excel over others, the same is true for those who operate in the economic field: the important thing is that these two are subject to rules which, in the time of Marx, were often non-existent: we need only think of the regulation of working conditions. This could be the real precondition for development. It seems to me that here Marx did not wish to let pass what he himself had previously asserted, because it was animated by other intentions. To say: "Value therefore now becomes *value in process, money in process, and, as such, capital* (…) Let us now return to our would-be capitalist (…) With the keen eye of an expert, he has selected the means of production and the kind of labour-power best adapted to his particular trade, be it spinning, boot-making, or any other kind" (Marx, K, vol. I, 153 and 179-180), may possibly mean that without that "keen eye" the economic process could never have been put in motion. If for Marx labour and its exploitation is the real motive force of development, can it not also be said equally well of those "intuitions" and initial choices? The real problem of the economy is that of safeguarding this creativity, this imagination – in a word, Rosmini would have said, the speculative intelligence. I will be returning to this in the next chapter. It should not be forgotten that, at times, real economic crises actually arise from this. Marx too senses this concern when he speaks of "some crippling of body and mind" (Marx, K, vol. I, 342), typical not only of the division of labour but also of society in general.

**V.4** That certain phenomena of an economic kind cannot be summed up in the context of economic theory alone has been shown abundantly by quite a number of those who have studied Marxism. One well-known editor of *Das Kapital* went so far as to say: "Every relationship connected with the right of property, every distinction between proprietors and those who own nothing, is regulated in the category of social or sociological factors". Moreover there are some, like Joan Robinson, who consider "the notions of exploitation and added value as moral judgments disguised as simple economic factors". But in any case why should we be surprised, since Marx himself does not seem to relegate everything to simple economic factors? "The qualitative characteristic of relationships was equally important as the quantitative solution of the problem of value and the derivation of the price of exchanges" (Dobb, 8-9). This qualitative characteristic also affects the world of labour, with its reflections on everyday existence. It is really curious that after having recognised the merits of the mobility of labour and a whole body of other circumstances such as the liberation from corporate and geographical links which allow the workers to move from one job to another (cf. Giddens, ch. 4, § 1) Marx reaches the point where he says that all of this, even though it has been a determining factor in capitalist production, ends up by failing in the final phase of capitalism, unless it is recovered, in an almost transfigured form, in the future classless society.

**V.5** Furthermore, *Das Kapital* produces quite a number of reflections which lend themselves to an existential analysis. Among them we find: "It must be acknowledged that our labourer comes out of the process of production other than he entered (...) In place of the pompous catalogue of the 'inalienable rights of man' comes the modest *Magna Charta* of a legally limited working day" (Marx, K, vol. I, 285-6) We could multiply the quotations, but for the moment it will be enough to reflect on that creation of the party for the realisation of which it is necessary to acquire a particular consciousness. Here we should stress that over-production itself is not simply part of a sort of purely economic analysis, even though obviously the latter not only cannot be excluded but retains its undeniable importance. With regard to certain goods, recognising "something purely social, namely, their value" (Marx, K, vol. I, 63) one may surmise that over-production itself changes the social value of goods, partly because once these have been distributed and made available to all, these cause a sense of surfeit and change of desires, and hence needs for different consumer goods, giving rise to what can be defined as "tendential fall". This phenomenon is of important significance for economic history, and much depends on whether one considers it the endemic evil of capitalism, and thus incurable and fatal, or, on the other hand, the reason for constant renewal which operates in the economic context. It is this "tendential fall" which makes the capitalist, with his "keen eye of an expert", turn to production of other goods to satisfy the new needs, obviously in search of what, if we wish to term it thus, is a new added value, without which no producer would feel himself motivated to produce. Perhaps because of this Marx says, with reference to Ricardo, that he "never concerns himself about the origin of surplus-value. He treats it as a thing inherent in the capitalist mode of production, which mode, in his eyes, is the natural form of social production" (Marx, K, vol. I, 483).

**V.6** This constant factor in the development of capitalism naturally comes into collision with Marx's own reflections. This is also due to the fact that his theory of the development of capitalism is founded on the formation of surplus value which capitalism itself brings; based originally on the free market in which the goods, produced by individual initiative, come to find their own value, and move further and further away from the conditions which determined the birth of the capitalist economy (cf. Giddens, ch. 4, § 1). We have only to think of the competition which capitalistic development renders more and more difficult by projecting itself into monopoly situations. In short, the mania for profit becomes the absolute objective of capital, which even loses sight of the necessity to satisfy needs. The trouble is, as Giddens neatly summarises, that capital does not take any account of the "law of the tendential decline of profit", which as soon as it makes itself felt, forces capitalists to take up positions setting off antagonistic causes against the tendency for the profit to diminish. There are many possibilities which can be tried. One of the simplest is that of importing goods at low prices in order to increase the rate of surplus value and to satisfy the demand for subsistence goods from the working class. However, it may also happen that the latter are exploited still more, by increasing the working day or by lowering wages (cf. Giddens, ch. 4, § 2). What is surprising is that *these crises of capitalism*, even if they are not seen as final but periodic and capable of repeating themselves regularly, *are never seen as capable of insuring capitalism a new dynamism and new possibilities of adjustment.* Capitalism and its market system appear to be anarchical, but the anarchy hides from the eyes of the critics its intrinsic characteristic: freedom. Certainly this anarchy can also prove fatal, above all where the political conditions too become such as to provide no assurance for the dynamism of development, within the real guarantees of various kinds – not least cultural ones. In fact development does not only require ductility, but also awareness that the socio-political reality is not an unchangeable metaphysical structure, but an environment which must guarantee social ascent, equality of rights and as far as possible, of possibilities, etc.

V.7 It is well-known that in the opinion of Marx, this anarchy will in fact become fatal. It will cause the phenomenon of over-production in a gradually growing number of sectors, and will set off a series of chain reactions. The first effect will be unemployment, which will increase out of control, reducing the level of wages. The effects of the crisis will be multiple, and will tend to favour the concentration of capital. But the real effect of the crisis is that of favouring the birth and growth of revolutionary consciousness. This latter is considered an ineluctable aspect, even though Marx's exposition seems anything but clear and obvious on the way in which it will be achieved. An equally difficult element is the organisation of that work-force which on the one hand appears to be subject to growing unemployment and under-employment, and on the other hand seems like a constant reservoir from which capitalism can draw during new periods of prosperity. We may well ask why *Marx mistakes chronic instability for what is the natural dynamic quality of capitalism,* while presenting on this matter a series of justifications for what were the conditions of capitalism in his own day. At a certain point, in fact, a "concentration of capitals already formed" is reached "Capital grows in one place to a huge mass in a single hand, because it has in another place been lost by many (...) Here competition rages in direct proportion to the number, and in inverse proportion to the magnitudes, of the antagonistic capitals. It always ends in the ruin of many small capitalists, whose capitals partly pass into the hands of their conquerors, partly vanish" (Marx, K, vol. I, 586-7). For Marx this is the mortal virus of capitalism. Not only can competition not be regulated and corrected (an aim for which any civil society worthy of the name must aspire), but the idea of the fatal crisis also leads him to ignore the possibility that the "capitals", apart from swelling in a single hand or being lost altogether, may also, at certain moments, be moved into other fields of production, in certain new circumstances, with enormous possibilities of development.

**V.8** Summing up, one could say, as Giddens puts it, that capitalism shows its antagonistic character, in Marx's sense, by accumulating wealth on the one hand and poverty and wretchedness on the other (cf. Giddens, ch. 4, § 3). This is a debatable, and typically Manichean dichotomy, which was to provoke some reflection by Bernstein. But what remains fundamental is that, according to Marx, in order to emerge from this situation of perennial crisis, the political "moment" must take priority over the economic one, without disappearing – or rather dissolving – when a situation of justice is re-established. I would say metaphysical justice, because it is located outside space and time. This metaphysical aspect did not escape contemporaries of Marx, who often point it out. Marx himself felt the need to respond to such critics, for the fact is that in the *Postscript to the Second Edition* he stressed that "the Paris *Revue Positiviste* reproaches me in that, on the one hand, I treat economics metaphysically" (Marx K, vol. I, 26).

**V.9** Again, if in order to change the world, or if in simpler terms, to make revolution, it is necessary to create a party, and also to acquire a class consciousness whose modes of realisation are all to be explained, a further question arises. Is the creation of a party not the *obvious admission* that without a political situation (one might say without a superstructure) revolution cannot be brought about, and thus the structural conditions of society cannot be changed? In short, we are again faced with the basic theme of this work: while I remain convinced of the autonomy of the political sphere with respect to the economic sphere and vice versa, not only are such spheres often forced to interact, but the political one, held to be artificial and superstructural by Smith and by Marx, also constitutes the precondition for the changes. This is not an immutable and statically *a priori* precondition, but even so a condition for being able to operate in a certain way. Among other things, it should be remembered that Machiavelli warns us, and history has fully borne him out, that the dissolution of power never comes about in a spontaneous way, if one is not in a genuine democracy, but always costs blood and tears. But there is another curious fact: according to the most extreme Marxist theories, it ought to be the political structures which reorder and establish certain of the characteristics of mature capitalism such as mobility of labour and suitability of the various social functions in a new way. It is a question therefore of overcoming capitalism while holding that it is capable of overcoming itself and improving, as if it were a closed society.

**V.10** Also in the *Postscript to the second edition*, Marx seems to admit, involuntarily, not only that his dependence on Hegelian dialectic confined him within a methodological rigidity of the classical metaphysical type, but he seems even to foresee certain criticisms which would be directed at him, specifically on the dialectical plain, by future exponents of the Left, such as Mao Tse-tung and Merleau-Ponty. He in fact maintains that "Ricardo, in the end, consciously makes the antagonism of class-interests, of wages and profits, of profits and rent, the starting-point of his investigations, naïvely taking this antagonism for a social law of Nature" (Marx, K, vol. I, 24). *This passage is important*, because naturally for Marx, all this could not constitute a "social law of nature", otherwise it could not be suppressed and the dialectic opposition could not have an end, just as the contradictions between the various classes would never have an end either. But as Mao clearly tells us in his essay *On contradiction,* (unfortunately neglected by the Left), passively accepting the dialectical method in the footsteps of Marxism-Leninism means putting a barrier in front of the natural need to renew which is implanted in humankind, and hence in history. Merleau-Ponty is even more specific. If dialectic is the expression of liberty and change, the end of dialectic means the end of liberty, and the end of any possibility of opposition. Is it a mere coincidence that all known revolutions have degenerated? The seizure of power by a revolutionary class is often the eclipse of the revolution itself, which can be regarded as progress when it is compared with the past, but only a source of disillusionment if it is linked to a future which it has only conceived as a dream and then suffocated (cf. Merleau-Ponty, 278-81).

**V.11** As we have already noted, it can certainly be debated whether certain Marxian conceptions are or are not of a metaphysical nature, but it is certain that quite a number, especially in *Das Kapital,* have a moral character. We have only to think of his reflections on working activity: "labour, whether previously embodied in the means of production, or incorporated in them for the first time during the process by the action of labour power, *counts* in either case only according to its duration; it amounts to so many hours or days, as the case may be" (Marx, K, vol. I, 190). This seems to be the destiny of a society which seeks to quantify everything and relate everything to numbers. Marx views this with a certain distaste, which he makes apparent on every occasion, such as when he considers aspects which are even strictly economic: "Assuming that the price of the product is the same as its value, we here find the surplus-value distributed under the heads of profit, interest, rent, & c." (Marx, K, vol. I, 211). It seems that here certain forms of modern practice, regarded as immoral and therefore illegitimate, are being rejected. Rather than correcting matters, as would be right and dutiful, it seems almost as if there is a desire to depart from history. The same may be said for the *capitalist use of machinery*, which creates anxieties not only because it prolongs the working day immeasurably, and revolutionises the actual manner of working, but because it breaks down the resistance to modifying this tendency and furthermore comes close to "new strata of the working class, previously inaccessible" (to the capitalist) because they were not yet attracted to modern industry (cf. Marx, K, vol. I, 384-5). The tendency to become operators of the capitalist system, even though remaining wage-earning workers, should thus be broken when there has been a constant desire to become part of such a system on the part of the workers themselves. A *desire*, not just a need, as witness the constant migrations of the work-force in the course of the whole of history, and as witness also the events of recent years, after the fall of the Berlin Wall. In an interesting study by John Mickletwait and Adrian Wooldridge, recently published, there is an examination of the expectations aroused in those who crowd the international migration scene by the economic opportunities to be found in the richer countries. The phenomenon is viewed in a different way, thanks to the various forms of globalisation operating at the level of the planet, but it is also an ancient phenomenon, and always determined by the natural need for ever-increasing well-being on the part of humanity. It could certainly be objected that Marx had, basically, foreseen the problem when he stated: "The development of capitalist production and accumulation lifts labour-processes to an increasingly enlarged scale and thus imparts to them ever greater dimensions (…) It is, then, natural for the individual capitalists to command increasingly large armies of labourers" (Marx, K, vol. III, 219). But as my friend Juan Avella, sadly now departed, pointed out to me, the conviction is already to be found in Smith and Ricardo and other classic writers that an effective development needs a constant increase in the population, even if it be a contained one. With Mill the idea was first mooted that the growth of the proletarian population could, for various reasons, come to a halt. It is from this that the problems of the migration of the labour force arise.

**V.12** We might well say with Marx that "the labourer sells his labour, that is, the function of his labour-power, and our assumption is that he sells it at its value, determined by its cost of reproduction" (Marx, K, vol. II, 119). But the fact remains that here, *the work changes* existentially, in the sense that *life itself* changes. Thus, *it creates an entity which cannot be evaluated*, like the hours of work granted to capital. Work opens up new cognitions, prospects, needs, expectations and so on. If he did not sell his labour-power, would the life of the hypothetical wage-earner be the same? We would need to ask those desperate individuals who compete with each other in a search for employment. It would be possible, *today at least*, to have a sort of *alienation deriving from non-work*. Basically even those *who do work obtain something more* than mere wages; a sort of *plus-wage* constituted by opportunity, by social relations, by possible gratifications, etc., which those who do not work do not possess. If it is true that the capitalist is proving more and more to be a social power (cf. Marx, K, vol. III, 264), it is also true that *work confers on everyone a different social dimension*.

**V.13** Possibly it may be appropriate to make another observation at this point. Marx maintains that "all costs of circulation which arise only from changes in the forms of commodities do not add to their value. They are merely expenses incurred in the realisation of the value or in its conversion from one form into another" (Marx, K, vol. II, 152). But if they do not add value, and hence do not create *surplus value*, this means that there are labourers who do not produce surplus value. Does this, then, imply that *those who are employed, for example, in the circulation of goods which do not produce surplus value are themselves not subject to surplus value?* It must be said that in reality for Marx this is not how things are. "Just as the labourer's unpaid labour directly creates surplus-value for productive capital, so the unpaid labour of the commercial wage-worker secures a share of this surplus-value for merchant's capital" (Marx, K, vol. III, 294). Even if the commercial wage worker does not produce surplus value directly, given that he costs the capitalist what he produces for him, we must keep in mind that there are different sized entities on the plane of economic evaluation, because although they are not the cause, they are nevertheless the consequence of the surplus value increase (cf. Marx, K, vol. III, 299-300). These are, in any case, reflections which leave room for more than a few doubts, especially today with the proliferation of new professions.

**V.14** Another aspect of economics with obvious moral implications in what today we may term "mobility of labour", which has led to various kinds of delusions. Here, too, technology, which undeniably helps progress, may also bring about frustrations: "the sufferings of the workmen displaced by machinery are therefore as transient as are the riches of this world (...) So soon as machinery sets free a part of the workmen employed in a given branch of industry, the reserve men are also diverted into new channels of employment, and become absorbed in other branches; meanwhile, the original victims, during the period of transition, for the most part starve and perish" (Marx, K, vol. I, 414-5). That this is *one of the saddest existential consequences of capitalist society* is undoubtedly beyond discussion, as is also the need to *combat all the more extreme forms of that social Darwinism* which today has moulded in its own image much of what happens in the economic world. This is what a free society can and must do. But to claim that it is possible to renew everything at once *ex novo*, as many maximalists have claimed, wiping the slate clean of what already exists, may provoke the cancellation of the most elementary rights and the suppression of that well-being from which many benefit, and also the chance for it to be corrected as it should be in order to allow all to gain access to the rights and benefits.

**V.15** Access to rights and benefits not only improves the conditions of life, but also the moral conditions which were truly appalling for workers in the time of Marx. He actually quotes Montalembert to show how "ignorance and vice abound in a population so brought up". And all this depends on working conditions which, it is true, have drawn men forth "above the rank of animals", enabling them to become "to some extent socialised", and so on, permitting the development of productive forces. "The productiveness of labour that serves as its foundation and starting-point, is a gift, not of Nature, but of a history embracing thousands of centuries" (Marx, K, vol. I, 441 and 479-80). Marx's conviction is similar here to that of : certainly accept economic and technological progress, but also admit that it is necessary to change its profound underlying contradictions. These contradictions make themselves felt from the outset of the economic process, *ab imis*, almost as if to seem like a kind of original sin. The statement that finds its broadest demonstration in Rousseau's two famous *Discourses* should not seem strange, for Marx himself makes use of it: "This primitive accumulation plays in Political Economy about the same part as original sin in theology. Adam bit the apple, and thereupon sin fell on the human race (...) but the history of economic original sin reveals to us that there are people to whom this is by no means essential. Never mind! Thus it came to pass that the former sort accumulated wealth, and the latter sort had at last nothing to sell except their own skins" (Marx, K, vol. I, 667). Hence the criticism of the concept of capitalism understood as *power to dispose of labour*, according to Smith's definition, substituted by the conviction that capital is "essentially the command over unpaid labour" – obviously, the labour of others (cf. Marx, K, vol. I, 500).

**V.16** At the origins of the economic process, "the exchange between capital and labour at first presents itself to the mind in the same guise as the buying and selling of all other commodities" (Marx, K, vol. I, 506). But then avoiding this first moment means blocking the economic process at its birth.

Certainly it is also necessary to regulate it because, as he remarks sarcastically, "legal limitation of the working-day puts an end to these amenities". The same may be said for other forms of labour, such as piecework (cf. Marx, K, vol. I, 512 and 519). The rules of labour are rightly those of an open and free society where the contrary parties can discuss on the basis of a plan of mutual equality. Certainly, without regulation, one of the parties – and it is almost always that of the wage-earners – lives in a position of subordination to the other. In these cases, "let us consider (…) the capitalist. He wishes to receive as much labour as possible for as little money as possible" (Marx, K, vol. I, 506-7). The important thing which emerges at this point in *Das Kapital* is that work is a complex phenomenon, and that therefore the rules which deal with it cannot be abstract and unchangeable. "Wages themselves again take many forms, a fact not recognisable in the ordinary economic treatises which, exclusively interested in the material side of the question, neglect every difference of form" (Marx, K, vol. I, 508). Marx himself took into account "changes of wages with the changing length of the working-day (…) the individual difference in the wages of different labourers who do the same kind of work" (Marx, K, vol. I, 507). To this may be added, among other things, the changing of wages in relation to time and place by means of what is today called *local contracting*. All this backs the argument of those who consider the economic phenomenon an ever-open chapter in comparison with which, even in legal terms, it is important to retain a substantial degree of flexibility. Moreover Marx himself seems to take account of this, when he states that, in determining the variation of the size of national wages, account must be taken of all the elements which may condition its changes; from natural vital needs to historically developed ones, etc. (cf. Marx, K, vol. I, 524).

**V.17** What is strange is that the same measure of judgment is not used to consider the needs of the contrary party. Here we are told that the capitalist, "and his ideological representative, the political economist", in any case confuse the cards, and in the end "the cup of surplus value would be drained to the very dregs, and nothing but simple reproduction would ever take place" (Marx, K, vol. I, 537 and 544). That *shrewd eye* which put the economic process into motion is reduced to enjoying life on the backs of others, and loses that impetus of moral and civil improvement that determined the first phase of its entrepreneurial activity. We seem to be hearing a pre-echo here of what were to be the assertions of Sorel in the future! Marx here seems to be anti-modern, and it is certainly not a mere chance that he takes up once again the affirmations of those who had accused people who sought to enrich themselves of worldliness and certain structures of the past of departing from their original character. "Taking the usurer, that old-fashioned but ever-renewed specimen of the capitalist for his text, Luther shows very aptly that the love of power is an element in the desire to get rich"; the usurer sucks the fruits of rapine and robs the food of others. In the history of capitalist production "avarice and the desire to get rich are the ruling passions", and then waste, luxury, instincts of self-indulgence, hoarding up of treasure (cf. Marx, K, vol. I, 555-6). The same can be said for the merchants who are even reproved for hurling their complaints against the nobility. They want to achieve, in complete freedom, "such great wrong and unchristian thievery and robbery (which) are committed all over the world by merchants, and even among themselves (...) God employs knights and robbers, and punishes the merchants through them for the wrongs they committed, and uses them as his devils" (Marx, K, vol. III, 331, where he is directly quoting Luther's words).

**V.18** Where have those praises previously sounded in the Manifesto vanished? Praises for the bourgeoisie which has surpassed national boundaries, opened up markets, accelerated technological development and, last but not least, carried out the revolution which the proletariat has so far not been able to achieve? What would human history have been without that instinct for enrichment which, in a less restrictive way, could be defined as an instinct for betterment? To maintain that the "starting-point of the development that gave rise to the wage-labourer as well as to the capitalist, was the *servitude of the labourer*" (Marx, K, vol. I, 669) means really to have a crudely metaphysical conception of history: to have identified the original sin which only the blood of revolution would be able to wipe out. But it also means claiming to operate a *total moral reform in history*. Otherwise, who will assure us that after the revolution, other immoral individuals, even though perhaps in different sectors from the economic one, will seize ascendancy over others and reduce them to slavery? Moreover, history – not distant history but very recent history – has amply proved this. Claims of divine inspiration! Certainly this does not mean that we have merely to surrender before injustices, as a stupid kind of conservatism demands, but rather to reform and keep constant watch on a society on which no one can print the stamp of perfection. To claim a *total moral reform* as a unique panacea for humanity means, after a mammoth effort at analysis, simplifying every kind of reflection beyond due measure To place on the same plane in the moments of *original accumulation* such different countries as Spain, Portugal, Holland, France and Britain, for example, obviously leads to not asking why, subsequently, the take-off of capitalism is observable in some of these and not in others. Just as seeing only atrocity in some periods of history means barring the analysis of far from irrelevant cultural factors such as, e.g. what in really reductive terms is referred to as the Age of the Schoolmen (cf. Marx, K, vol. I, 703-7).

**V.19** A fact which is overlooked in the historical tendency of capitalist accumulation, is the analysis of individual property. Possibly taking up some suggestions made by Fichte, Marx considered the *dissolution of private property based on* *personal work*. Personal private property is seen as an antithesis of social property, and these two extremes contain within themselves an infinite number of shades which are no more than a reflection of the intermediate states which really exist. "The private property of the labourer in his means of production is the foundation of petty industry (...) the peasant of the land which he cultivates, the artisan of the tool which he handles as a virtuoso. This mode of production pre-supposes parcelling of the soil, and scattering of the other means of production (...) To perpetuate it would be, as Pecqueur rightly says, 'to decree universal mediocrity'" (Marx, K, vol. I, 713-4). But what, then!? we feel like exclaiming: if economic development has brought us out of universal mediocrity, why think of abolishing it, while considering the instincts on which it is founded to be deleterious. Why not rather regulate the actual instincts behind which a great number of capacities are hidden, as the democratic states have done?

**V.20** But another serious problem arises at the end of the dialectic process, or perhaps better, at the end of capitalism. As the centralisation of capital proceeds, so "grows the mass of misery, oppression, slavery, degradation, exploitation; but with this too grows the revolt of the working class". But, and this counts for more, the struggle between capitalists is also intensified, to the point that "one capitalist always kills many others" (Marx, K, vol. I, 715 and 714). There is a kind of struggle for survival of a Darwinian kind, stirred up, however, by the "original sin" which has split society in two. A "sin" which, once eliminated, should generate a kind of second birth of humanity, its total transformation, which should lead it to set aside all idea of struggle. This possibility had already begun to arouse quite a few doubts even a century ago, but they were set aside. The motives for human contention were reduced to simple economic conflicts. An exemplification which certainly inflates problems which may in fact be less important, but even so not devoid of meaning.

**V.21** In his Preface to the second volume of *Das Kapital,* Engels, referring to Adam Smith's *Wealth of Nations*, mentions how some individuals *naturally* employ capital to give work to diligent labourers, etc. (cf. Engels, 16). This naturally seems to be taken from some of Marx's reflections; in the two volumes to be published posthumously later, he seems here and there to continue to admire the action of the bourgeois entrepreneur. Suffice to mention that the latter "must begin by buying means of production such as buildings, machinery, etc., before he buys any labour-power" (Marx, K, vol. II, 31). But even before this he must devise projects which not every one is capable of inventing, projects which are fitted to particular contingencies and not to others. The means of production themselves "acquire this specific social character only under definite, historically developed conditions" (Marx, K, vol. II, 37), conditions of which it is essential to have a good knowledge in order to assess them carefully. There are always some individuals who must *naturally* evaluate "the rapidity of sales", and how "the degree of efficiency of any given capital is conditional on the potentialities of the productive process, which to a certain extent are independent of the magnitude of its own value" (i.e. the value of the capital itself). There are always certain individuals who must *naturally* evaluate how "the process of circulation sets in motion new forces independent of the capital's magnitude of value and determining its degree of efficiency, its expansion and contraction" (Marx, K, vol. II, 40-1). To this it should be added that the economic operator, examining the different stages of the passages of capital, must even ask himself whether moments of "stagnation" exist or not (cf. Marx, K, vol. II, 50), and if it is possible to avoid them. Moreover, to the calculations of production must be added those of prevision, without which all economic activity is doomed to failure. The time in which the changes in the form of capital take place – and it is Marx himself who maintains this – is directed subjectively by the capitalist. He dedicates a substantial part of his affairs to such judgments. Then we may also say that if the "compelling motive of capitalist production is always the creation of surplus-value by means of the advanced value", then there is always a need for the intuition of the entrepreneur, which causes investment to be preferred to hoarding (cf. Marx, K, vol. II, 132 and 156). Investment is seen as a possibility of further gain. It follows that the «rate of profit is the motive power of capitalist production. Things are produced only so long as they can be produced with a profit» (Marx, K, vol. III, 259). This conviction accompanies all economic activity, as it also accompanies every reflection of Marx, to such an extent that even in the final lines of *Das Kapital* he states: "Profit, then, appears here as the main factor, not of the distribution of products, but of their production itself" (Marx, K, vol. III, 882).

**V.22** Without anticipation, which the capitalist, to paraphrase Marx, has "thrown into circulation to satisfy his personal wants" (Marx, K, vol. II, 424), there would in fact be no economic development. How could a collective entity, such as the state, evaluate those intuitions which are first and foremost personal needs? Many people may object that it can, but the examples which occurred in the twentieth century demonstrate that it is not only impossible, with a few rare exceptions, but that all this is paid at a high price on the plane of public morality, in that the choices are always conditioned by a combination of factors which are only rarely economic. What we have said on the level of initial motivations for economic action is also valid for its crises. As Marx seems to suggest – every year is the year of death for some fixed capital which must be substituted in this or that individual company, or in this or that branch of industry. But these are cyclic crises of capitalism, which cannot be mistaken for epochal crises. The latter, to return to our basic theme, depend first and foremost on political crises which, as the revolutions of our century have well illustrated, take place at moments of great conflict, as for example during wars. This takes us back to the fact that not only can the superstructures constitute a precondition of development, but they can also be the causes of its crises. Marx himself seems to be saying that the superstructure may be a precondition, when he states that "usury, like commerce, exploits a given mode of production; it does not create it" (Marx, K, vol. III, 609).

**V.23** The decisions of those individuals who have a shrewd eye for distinguishing and prospecting all the above-mentioned conditions, make it possible for us to return for a moment to the basic theme of this essay. There is a paradigm of Marx which is really interesting: "A place of production which once had a special advantage by being located on some highway or canal may now find itself relegated to a single side-track, which runs trains only at relatively long intervals, while another place, which formerly was remote from the main arteries of traffic, may now be situated at the junction of several railways. This second locality is on the upgrade, the former on the downgrade" (Marx, K, vol. II, 254). This is how the activities of the superstructure favour those of the economic structure. For example, in Italy when we speak of the problem of the South, we should remember that a train running from Rome to Pescara or Campobasso* requires four hours, a time which in other cases is required to cover distances almost three times as far, such as Rome-Milan or vice versa. It is worth noting that the trains between the two major cities are always full, and thus are more profitable, because, if they had the same average speed as the others, and if, in proportion, they took twelve hours, they would travel

---

* For some time, since a new tunnel came into operation, it has been possible to reach Campobasso in three hours and fifteen minutes. Certainly this is not a competitive time with what it takes by road vehicle, even though some of those involved in the works tell me it may well eventually take less than three hours. We shall see.

half-empty and would have the function of local trains. We could further add that fast communication can provide the prospect of development, unthought of today, for a series of professions, and hence to the workers linked to them, which today tend to think of moving towards certain "markets". When Marx observes that, thanks to the process of hoarding, there exists a capital *in spe*, which "represents (...) nothing but additional and reserved legal titles of capitalists to future additional social production" (Marx, K, vol. II, 326), this should lead us to understand two things. The *first* is that here too the motivations of the individual economic operator for beginning an activity prove to be of importance. The *second* is that such motivations must be incited to make capital "move", remembering that "the hoard is merely the creation of money-capital existing temporarily in latent form and intended to function as productive capital" (Marx, K, vol. II, 353).

**V.24** The above discussion introduces another item in the modern economy almost unknown until a few decades ago. When, with regard to communications or other types of machinery, Marx says that "the degree of their effectiveness depends on methods and scientific developments which cost the capitalist nothing" (cf. Marx, K, vol. II, 360), he forgets that research is one of the additional costs of modern industry which, without such investment, risks falling out of the market. In fact, it is precisely the far-sightedness of large-scale capital which makes research possible. The so-called "popular democracies" knew this quite well, since to hold their own against the hated world of capitalism, they were constrained to spend heavily on very productive industrial espionage, since they had no capacity to compete on the level of research. Furthermore, only capitalism can invest to obtain "articles of *luxury*, which enter into the consumption of only the capitalist class and can therefore be exchanged only for spent surplus-value, which never falls to the share of the labourer" (cf. Marx, K, vol. II, 407). Von Hayek would say that all this permits a real development, because the goods consumed today by the rich arouse the envy of the poor, and the market, in order to have additional forms of gain, produces such goods at more and more advantageous prices. But it is also true, as Marx maintained, that every "crisis at once lessens the consumption of luxuries (…) The reverse takes place in periods of prosperity, particularly during the times of bogus prosperity, in which the relative value of money, expressed in commodities, decreases (…) so that the prices of commodities rise independently of their own values" (Marx, K, vol. II, 414). Here the close link between history and economics is very clear; it makes of the latter a science which cannot be analysed in merely abstract terms – something which Marx did not always take account of.

**V.25** It is truly interesting that Marx on several occasions indulges in considerations about how extra-economic realities may influence the capitalist world. At times a series of facts operate "against the foresight and calculation of the individual capitalist" (Marx, K, vol. II, 109). These are moments in which certain events interfere more than they should and certain fundamental presuppositions of economics, e.g. competition, stand in the way of exact assessment. In this way, we exist constantly in a state of approximation, from which it is only possible to escape by perfecting the capitalist system. The words of Marx leave no doubt about this. In similar circumstances, even if in theory it is possible to suppose that the processes of production may develop without interference, this does not in fact happen in real life. In the latter "there exists only an approximation: but, this approximation is the greater, the more developed capitalist mode of production and the less it is adulterated and amalgamated with survivals of former economic conditions" (Marx, K, vol. III, 175). With an iron economic logic, Marx, speaking of prices, for example, adds: "the different individual values must be equalised at *one* social value, the above-named market-value, and this implies competition among producers of the same kind of commodities, and, likewise, the existence of a common market in which they offer their articles for sale; (...) it is necessary that the pressure exerted by different sellers upon one another be sufficient to bring enough commodities to market to fill the social requirements" (Marx, K, vol. III, 180-1). But to say this is equivalent to admitting implicitly that *first* if the market does not exist, all possibility of establishing a "just price" vanishes in fact; *secondly*: where there is no regular market, there is a tendency to a shortage of goods placed on the market, as the real situation of the "peoples' democracies" amply demonstrated.

**V.26** What I have said so far has been demonstrated by history itself, and for one who believes in dialectical materialism, it becomes an *irrefutable datum*: when certain goods "are first produced capitalistically and enter capitalist commerce, they compete with commodities of the same nature produced by pre-capitalist methods and hence dearer" (Marx, K, vol. III, 907). *This means that* they are available only to a few, and those few are very rich. Commodities, then, available to classes which certainly do not fully express a genuinely democratic society. This is amply proved by the course of events in the mediaeval maritime cities up to the beginning of the modern era. Until a certain moment, as Marx himself notes, Venetians, Genovese, Dutch, Hanseatic merchants, etc., had a special rate of profit, initially more or less great, which changed with time. "Equalisation of these different company profit rates took place in the opposite way through competition" (Marx, K, vol. III, 902). To sum up: *competition causes the emergence from a situation of political and economic privilege*, to which there is an immediate return as soon as it (competition) is abolished. It should be added that lasting competition not only becomes part of the social structure of a civilisation, but reaches the point of rendering the citizens more mature, since otherwise they remain permanent consumers to whom every type of goods can be offered, even the most worthless. Being unable to choose, we find the establishment of a basic criterion: "People will surely appreciate if we send them good samples at first, and then inferior goods afterward" (Marx, K, vol. III, 83). All this cannot happen if people have the possibility of comparison, and hence of choice.

## VI. NEEDS AND LIMITATIONS
### Connections between politics, economics, morality and other matters

**VI.1** Schumpeter paid particular attention to tracing the characteristics of the entrepreneur. Thanks to the great innovative capacity without which he or she would soon be out of the market, this figure is one of the driving forces of economic development, even though he may also constitute a cause of crisis. What distinguishes the entrepreneur is a special mentality, which leads him (or her) to transform the organisation of his company. It follows from this that to innovate does not only mean to invent, nor even to bring about technical changes. It is, rather, a question of considering the aspects of a new productive proposal, Schumpeter lists five in all: production of new goods, introduction of a new method of production, opening of a new market, search for and acquisition of new sources of provision, and reorganisation of the industry (cf. Schumpeter, TED, 66). We can understand why the entrepreneur constitutes a dynamic element, seeking to go beyond the existing economic mechanism, looking for new "combinations" which, if they are intended to bear real fruit, must be innovative. It is clear that the entrepreneur, as J. B. Say stressed in his day, is a historical category in its own right, which has been increasingly differentiated from that of the capitalist, and which, on the level of social relationships, has basically antagonistic relations with those who are pursuing the same interests. The entrepreneur has a crucial importance for modern capitalism because he is capable of taking on the leadership role, while accepting the duties which such a role imposes. It is hardly worth mentioning that for Schumpeter, one of the reasons which will enable socialism to assert itself, overcoming the capitalist phase, is precisely the lack of entrepreneurial figures who will almost always be absorbed by the growing bureaucratisation of industry.

**VI.2** A true entrepreneur cannot merely adopt productive combinations which have already been tried, because in this case he knows that at most he would end up by obtaining remunerations which could be described as of a "bureaucratic" type, for activities of coordination and control of traditional production. In short, he would be a "traditional" producer, who undertakes economic actions of a repetitive type. Only the entrepreneur who, to use one of Rosmini's expressions, shows a sharp practical intelligence, realises the need to change the real state of things, and for this reason needs to know the situation in detail, with regard to the availability of resources and the work-force, the stability or otherwise of prices, the effective state of the demand and the possibility of supplying it and even creating new demands, etc. I will return later to the problem of the creation of new expectations, and the difficulties and contradictions which all this can involve. What I want to stress here is that the innovating entrepreneur must seek to arouse new expectations in the market which he will then seek to satisfy (cf. Schumpeter, TED, 84-7). I believe that it is specifically on this question that the issue turns of whether or not there can be an opportunity to guarantee to every society a genuine possibility of economic development; one which, however, will not, in time, damage other aspects of civil life – aspects which in the long run could in fact compromise economic development itself.

**VI.3** One of the qualities of the entrepreneur is that of understanding the psychology of the individual who approaches the market; alternatively he may be stimulated by this individual, to undertake a task of persuasion with regard to him. It could be said that the entrepreneur, as Rosmini had foreseen and as I shall demonstrate shortly, plays on the faculty of abstraction. The aim is that of making the consumer change certain models (it might be more accurate to say products) of behaviour which have become virtually habitual, or to arouse the demand for other models before it is even perceived. The more the psychological resistance of the market weakens, and a constantly growing number of individuals begin to feel the same need, the more the innovation of the entrepreneur finds room for application. The actual credit policy supporting certain innovations becomes more convinced. In short, credit supports innovative entrepreneurial investments because it sees a better chance of profit. In this case the entrepreneur mobilises a whole social situation which would otherwise remain static and incapable of shifting the existing state of affairs. The true entrepreneur is characterised by never resting on his laurels, and by possessing an intensity of desire which is not diminished even by a successful operation, but indeed increases and drives him on to further innovative actions (Sylos Labini, 16).

**VI.4** The problem of the task of persuasion undertaken by the entrepreneur has aroused quite a few perplexities. There are those, like Kirzner, who do not see it as a problem, but indeed define it as *alertness*, in perceiving before others do the unsatisfied needs of the individuals present in the market, and offering them satisfactory solutions – again before anyone else does so. In other words, (as we find in his well-known study, *Competition and Entrepreneurship*), through greater or lesser profit, the entrepreneur can demonstrate that he has understood and satisfied, more or less than others, elements of imbalance due to situations of non-satisfaction. Things being so, in contrast to what Schumpeter maintains (seeing the entrepreneurial spirit as aroused in particular contingent circumstances) Kirzner considers the entrepreneur a figure who cannot be eliminated. This conviction rests on the fact that, considering the market in a perfect state of balance to be an impossibility – since it would, of course, render the entrepreneur unnecessary – it is in fact from the conditions of imbalance that entrepreneurial activity draws new and constant stimuli which support capacity and innovative efforts. As I have stressed in one of my previous works of an epistemological kind, I think we should speak of dynamic balance, rather than imbalance (cf. my work on *Dynamic Order*). I believe in any case that to be ready to discover new demands which are not always latent and which can also be provoked, causes problems of another kind on the part of the consumers, and these are not easy to solve (I shall return to this question later).

**VI.5** Returning to the question of credit, basic for any form of economic development, it could be said that it tends to show that all possibilities of development, and indeed of change in the productive systems, are founded on the double nature of decisions: individual and institutional. The former belong properly to the individual entrepreneur, the latter to the credit structures and the policies which regulate them. Once again, the relationship between politics and economics, between individual and structural matters, becomes very close. Between the monetary and credit policy of the various institutions and the expectations of profit on the part of the entrepreneurs, there is in fact constant interaction. We have only to remember that the various credit institutions, in deciding the amount of the price of credit, must evaluate the nature of the investments and the real impact of the productive innovation, in order to be certain that the return of the sum loaned will be repaid, with the relative interest involved in the agreement, within the times agreed. This means that no one, whether it be individuals or structures, can take decisions autonomously. Every decision derives from a context in which various intelligences provide novelty, but also security and basic stability. Classical capitalism, in which the individual entrepreneur decided each phase of the economy in his own interest, no longer finds a place even in the most romanticised notions. It is true that the entrepreneur can still possess the ownership of the means of production, or obtain the authority to administer them; he can certainly decide the way that certain tasks shall be carried out within the company, and also the type of a certain product or the way of producing it, and the amount of the investments necessary. But at that point he becomes aware that he is just one of many agents of economic activity. All of this is extremely important since economic development appears on the one hand to be a process open to every possible innovation, the product of creative intelligence and the desire for improvement and dominance on the part of the individual entrepreneurs; on the other hand, however, it appears to be generated by a condition of stability, of juridical certainty and of a real capacity on the part of certain institutions, among which are the credit banks, to guarantee real and flexible instruments for perceiving the real nature of emerging novelties. The institutions must not only provide credit instruments, but they must be in a position to govern the sources of instability which otherwise may cause certain variables, notably prices, to fluctuate until they run out of control. In conclusion, while the economic sphere can be a source of continuous novelty, the political one must be aware of how to guide the processes of change.

**VI.6** The matter of individual intuition does not find a welcome in the "institutional" field, unless it succeeds in demonstrating that the future product will succeed in establishing an effective usefulness in the market: in other words, consumption that will be sufficient to justify the efforts of production. It is here that the phenomena of information and persuasion enter the fray. Today, a great part of the effort of the economic and financial world is concentrated on these things. I certainly do not seek to claim to judge the world of advertising, however useful or controversial it may be; in any case it remains fundamental. I would simply like to examine some of Schumpeter's notions in parallel with others of Rosmini, to show how even here a different relationship of collaboration between the political and economic spheres could avoid some problems of considerable dimensions. In what has become a classic, *Capitalism, Socialism and Democracy*, Schumpeter examines the problems relating to advertising. This could also be described as an evolutionary phenomenon of an economic situation which tends to become depersonalised and reduced to an automatic process – a situation in which the work of offices and committees of experts tends to supplant the personal action of the entrepreneurs (cf. Schumpeter, CSD, 133). He takes up a certain position from this with regard to the relation between demand and supply, which cannot be considered as perfectly independent factors, as classical economics considered them. Above all, demand is always more influenced by a series of mechanisms which by now have become part of the economic system itself. Who could maintain today that advertising is simply an element of information and not rather a means of persuasion? Is there really a consuming public capable of exercising genuinely free choices? I know that methodological individualists maintain that the market always executes justice on those who cheat, but is it not equally true, as Rosmini had previously pointed out, that once certain needs have been triggered off, they go on to alter the psychological structure of the individual if they are not sufficiently satisfied? It is beyond dispute that advertising is a means of persuasion, but it is equally true that in order to win concrete success it must first create the necessity and the urgent desire to satisfy certain needs. In short, the problem moves into the delicate context of needs.

**VI.7** Companies which do not become players in the sector of needs sooner or later exit from the market. This is also because they are not capable of producing innovation. It should be very clear, *I am not criticising the latter*, but rather stressing certain dangers which in the end will rebound back against the credibility of innovation itself, and more generally against the whole of economic growth. It cannot be denied, in fact, that long before the time for advertising comes, real innovation leads the entrepreneur to go deeply into the real or presumed needs of the consumers; it leads in fact to a new enquiry into the market. This is a basic step towards determining readiness to consume the new product. It is true, then, that the consumer possesses a certain liberty in the choice of the product to be consumed, but it is also obvious that this choice has in fact been preconditioned. The consumer thus has a rather limited autonomy. His action needs to be rendered more free and responsible by increasing his effective degree of autonomy. This is yet another indication that the economic sphere is closely linked to the political one. The rules here cannot come from the market alone, which could otherwise decide upon conditions of scarce autonomy for the consumer: take, for example, the concentrations of monopolies which, in the USA at least, are strongly contested. That the problem is not simply economic is demonstrated by the fact that the choices of persuasive advertising, even though they may have the immediate objective of convincing people to consume, go on to influence the relationships between individuals, their opinions and evaluations, but also their cognitive schemes. In short social criteria are brought into play, and moral rules, and even the authority of certain social roles with respect to others. In conclusion, the economic problem is not only closely connected with the political one, but together they prove to be correlated to those of a social, psychological, moral and even religious character.

**VI.8** To create the need, and hence the restless desire to satisfy it, develops what Rosmini described as the "faculty of abstraction". It is certainly no mere chance that advertising techniques seek to work on the unconscious or irrational aspects which in the end determine the choices made by individuals. If this were not so, there would not be, in the consumer, that desire to change his purchases, and it would remain fossilised in what someone has described as his natural "cognitive idleness". For their part, producers do not always, over and beyond the surface information aimed at exciting desire, completely fulfil their productive action. In this way, the bases of the economic responsibility of the entrepreneurs seems to come to nothing, but so too does the civic responsibility of the individual citizen, who abdicates in this way from the primary political duty of active and knowledgeable participation. This means that politics itself has lost the reason for its existence, and that it must seek again for its true foundations, which cannot rest on the contingent and the accidental. This is the source of the critique that Rosmini among others makes of the concept of progress which exalts the primacy of the accidental. Such a primacy foments revolutionary ideals, which taking their inspiration from Enlightenment reason seek to make a clean sweep of the ancient institutions and laws (cf. D'Addio, LA, 73), in the conviction that it is possible to re-found society while setting aside tradition altogether.

**VI.9** For Rosmini, this attempt is a true folly, because in order to take political action, it is first necessary to identify its essential premises. It is for this reason that politics is so closely connected with philosophy, as a great part of the western tradition has amply demonstrated. While the political field in fact possesses the awareness of the problems which it has to resolve, philosophy looks into the knowledge of the "ultimate aim towards which the government of public matters must be directed. If philosophy is the doctrine of the ultimate reasons, then the philosophy of politics is by implication, the science (in the classical sense of the term: a systematic conception founded on a single principle), of the ultimate reasons of politics. These serve to give a secure orientation to special political sciences, which deal with the political means which governments use to pursue specific aims" (D'Addio, LA, 71). This means that no political sphere can ever set aside what constitutes the essence or substance of a society. This claim should not lead us to class Rosmini as a conservative thinker, as he has unfortunately been branded by certain over-hasty – and I would say superficial – critics, because in his thinking, returning to the substance of politics does not mean remaining anchored in antique institutional forms, frightened of the novelties which the modern world presents. In other words, "it does not mean remaining faithful to the closed traditionalism of the Restoration, and bound to the preconceived rejection of all innovation; respect for ancient institutions, for what belongs to the substance of society, 'does not oblige us to be enemies of useful innovations', but to work for their modernisation and perfecting, which calls us back to the validity of the inspiring principles" (D'Addio, LA, 74). This consideration is of crucial importance for Rosminian political thought, because that appeal to the process of improvement places the stress on the distrust that the philosopher of Rovereto showed towards all those political notions which appeal to absurd and utopian ideals of perfection that would mean the end of every ideal of improvement and the atrophying of all the best aspirations of man and humanity.

**VI.10** The ideal of the improvement of man and of humanity in general introduces one of the most important themes of Rosmini's thinking: that of the speculative reasoning of individuals and the practical reasoning of the masses. This is a matter of two different types of rationality. But we should remember that reason is also expressed in a global human dimension, because, as we have mentioned, it is ontologically based. In this reasoning, distinction must be made between two different faculties: that of thought and that of abstraction. With the former, real entities and the order in which they must be disposed and the ends for which they are destined are dealt with, while with the latter ideas and the relations between them are formulated, and above all, the means are identified which make it possible to attain the ends. However, when the relationship between the two faculties is broken, there is a breakdown in the harmonisation of intelligence which consists simply in relating the abstract to the concrete. In this way, human reason is satisfied and also asserts itself as a principle capable of organising political society. If, on the other hand, the faculty of abstraction is lost behind the irregular proliferation of needs, many of which can be termed "artificial", we find a concentration of intellectual forces exclusively in the faculties of abstraction, and their growing predominance over those of thought. Reason ends up by losing its own autonomy, being reduced to the level of pure and simple sensations. And in this way a regressive process is brought into play, because (to put it in terms of Vico's thought) the "quantity of intelligence" is reduced and hence the creative capacity of a society. What counts most is that such a process generates what amounts to a loss of vital energy, which causes a break up of society, a gradual disintegration which really results in its slow decomposition (cf. D'Addio, I, 32-33).

**VI.11** In the light of what has been said here, it is clear that the practical reasoning of the masses "is a sort of *social instinct* that suggests to the masses goods which can be enjoyed immediately, and which come within the context of the common good: in this case it has a positive effect on society" (D'Addio, LA, 74-5). The true problem is that this "mass instinct" is easily led into corruption, because single individuals are driven, as they are in all the other instincts, to give selfish preference to certain special goods at the expense of the common good. This means that the accidental is once again privileged at the expense of the substantial, to the point of generating those disintegrating elements which can lead to a crisis in the context of civil society and its institutions. Because of this, stress should be laid on the speculative reasoning of individuals which forms "the basis of politics at the rational level", and which can lead to a rebirth in the institutions and in society itself, even though with considerable difficulty. This is what happened already, in the ancient world: "Rosmini's conviction is that one of the historical merits of Christianity is that of having regenerated speculative reasoning – the reasoning of the individual – after the crisis of the ancient world" (D'Addio, LA, 75). But this possibility of saving society from possible dissolution has always been one of the inspirational motives that Christianity has displayed towards every kind of civilisation. One may say that in a certain sense, even governments seeking to prevent the dissolution of the body politic have a real mission to perform, in that they protect the very essence of civil life as represented by the unity of the body politic. "A society to which we attribute the title of 'political' or 'the state' is characterised by the unity of decision and command, by the unity of power and force which it exercises over a specific territory, and by the constant convergence of the activities of a large number of individuals towards a common aim" (D'Addio, LA, 79). The identification and attainment of the aim witnesses once again that politics, for Rosmini, is activity, and thus a dynamism assured of an order which, however, cannot be static but converges towards the aim to be attained. What ensures movement is the *spirit*, which here is certainly not to be understood in the sense that idealism gave to it. "Spirit, in conclusion, is the intelligent and rational subject. His activity, made possible by the presence in him of the most general idea of being, which presides over the intellect's perception of things, begins with reflection, thanks to which it 'produces' new ideas and carries on all the other intellectual operations which allow it to give added depth to knowledge" (D'Addio, LA, 81). In short, it is an activity which we might call eminently social, with reflections and perspectives of a gnoseological character. This too goes to show that the development of a society is also a development of intelligence, and vice versa.

**VI.12** From what has been said so far, some important conclusions emerge. Since society is made by human beings for the pursuit of specific aims, it is the result of the actual human beings who work with these aims in view within a system of relations expressed by laws and institutions. Society is thus an artificial entity, and cannot have its own, autonomous reason for existing, nor, even less, can it be the foundation of the morality of its associated members, as certain thinkers, notably Rousseau, would have it (cf. Rosmini, FP, 67 and ff.). Moreover, society as we ourselves see it, is the expression of a process of interiorisation. What appears is generated by the interior life of the associates. "The relationship between external society and internal life must be borne in mind in order to understand the dynamic of society: according to Rosminian theory the great political and social transformations mature in the invisible society, in the souls of the associates, to be manifested later and realised in the visible society" (D'Addio, LA, 91). Politics, therefore, cannot set aside interior problems. The satisfaction of the citizens is a problem which must concern governments, perhaps before all others. Just as the pursuit of its aim cannot be alien to any society, so the contentedness of human souls cannot be a problem which concerns individuals and no one else. Governments must not only not put obstacles in the way of all those who seek to pursue their true good, but they must work positively to make sure that everyone can, within the context of legality and morality, pursue what he holds to be necessary for his own satisfaction. Because of this, it must also be said that governments meet up with very precise limits in their work. In fact, in forming society, individuals have reserved the right to adopt the means of pursuing their own aims in full autonomy and liberty. This means rejecting all those conceptions, unjust and utopian in many ways, which claim the omnipotence of society in relation to individuals or minorities. This is a modern form of despotism which, moreover, makes use of a legality wrongly considered to be legitimate (cf. D'Addio, LA, 93-4).

**VI.13** Obviously, in this overall context Rosmini is disputing all those theories which, while claiming to put democratic systems in place, as Rousseau himself sought to do, in reality end up by eliminating the most elementary forms of freedom. And these basic freedoms constitute the "maximum subjective good of mankind", from which spring all a person's activities; they find their expression in competition. "And for Rosmini, freedom means freedom of conscience, religious freedom, freedom of thought, freedom of opinion, of discussion, and thus recognition of pluralism" (D'Addio, LA, 96). It is from these freedoms that the political parties arise, and contribute to the ongoing debate. The parties may also express negative aspects of political life, and everything must be done to reduce these, but nevertheless they are vehicles of interest and opinion, which justify political action. Here his analysis would really merit a deeper examination, not possible in this present context. It is enough to remember that often the action of parties is based on these popular passions, intense but short-lived, which may be susceptible to very different consequences. What needs to be emphasised is that Rosmini was concerned with an ordered and rational change which was detached from any kind of emotional outburst or improvisation.

**VI.14** At this point a question becomes unavoidable: how can the proximate end of a society be determined? According to Rosmini this "is determined by the practical reasoning of the masses and the speculative reasoning of individuals, who sometimes move forward in concord and at other times disagree. The end is always the result of the two counterpoised forces" (D'Addio, LA, 105). This is a vital relationship, which in Vico's way of thinking determines the "civilising process" of humanity. The masses, with their practical reasoning and with the conflicts which this causes in society, determine the proximate end of society, which changes according to the eras which mark the different stages of development of society itself. It is within these stages of development that we find the stimuli and the opportunities which allow human intelligence to grow and to find expression. The problem is that this practical reasoning of the masses is apt to be re-dimensioned and even corrupted. This happens when it is moved exclusively by sensations of pleasure, because in this case "it expresses a minimal amount – in effect no amount at all – of intelligence". This is the age in which the "unrestrained yearning for pleasures" alone prevails. Everything is directed towards the immediate, to the pre-determined, and reason, following passions in an almost passive way, ends up by becoming sterile and thus inoperative. The forces of the intellect are diminished, and even cognitive capacity is re-dimensioned. Intelligence becomes the instrument for making the quest for pleasure ever more and more refined, with the result that it loses its own autonomy and arouses the passions of the masses even to the point of paroxysm. Intelligence no longer has social activity in view, and in the end it becomes closed up in its own self-centredness (cf. D'Addio, LA, 109). Religion itself, which is the only means capable of restoring objectives and hence of regenerating social life, risks being overthrown if it does not hold firm to its genuine values, and fails to place them in their right dimension which is above and beyond the temporal and the political. Only in this way, even though only indirectly, can it exercise an effective influence on society. It is obvious that here Rosmini is referring in polemical terms to all those who, on the contrary, tend to take from the Christian religion its intrinsic tendency to go beyond history, and seek instead to render it immanent while annulling its huge innovative potential (cf. D'Addio, LA, 114). One might also say its evaluative potential, because it is in fact religion which makes it possible to evaluate the meaning of life fully, and consequently define the criteria for happiness.

**VI.15** Very appropriately, Rosmini distinguishes between satisfaction, the pleasurable state, and happiness. He reminds us that "the second is a property of mere sensation, while the first and third are linked to the intelligence, since in order to be satisfied or happy, it is necessary to have a judgment by which we recognise ourselves as satisfied or happy. Satisfaction is a 'satisfying state', while happiness corresponds to 'perfect satisfaction', such as to bring an end to all possible desire" (D'Addio, LA, 115). That these problems have an interior nature and are in very close relationship to intelligence is demonstrated by the fact that dissatisfaction or unhappiness can go so far as to cause suicide, but only in intelligent beings. It is not found in beings devoid of intelligence, and thus is not in fact a property "either of the animals or of the savage". It is on this interior quality that freedom rests and this leads Rosmini to be strongly critical of those egalitarian and equalising notions which are unable to understand that wellbeing itself, seen as the sum total of the goods at the disposal of a society, is determined by the free activity of single individuals, of their capacities, their expectations and their choices. On this matter there are expressions which leave us in no doubt: "this favourable *position* of the individual is the work in part of fortune (i.e. of the complex of circumstances which do not depend on man), and in part of the virtues and the industry of individuals themselves. It can never be the work of governments" (Rosmini, FP, 382). The latter have only the task of not putting obstacles in the way of the free activities of individuals and of assisting the development of their capacities.

**VI.16** Nevertheless, Rosmini allies himself with a widespread opinion of the theorists of utilitarianism, according to which in societies, only forward-moving urges would be recognised – almost as if they had inherited an abstract optimism from the Enlightenment, these theorists consider every impulse exercised upon the social body to be useful to progress. This is certainly a risky notion, in part because it may induce governments to hold that the actual increase in unsatisfied needs drives individuals and society to act in the right direction to satisfy them. This may cause an uncontrolled multiplication of artificial needs, without any limit at all (cf. D'Addio, LA, 126-7). Apart from the dispute with Melchiorre Gioia, this matter of needs is a problem which has social and political repercussions of notable importance, because of the imbalances which can derive from it. In this case too, it must be regretted that, even during the so-called epoch of decolonisation, no one was able to take on board Rosmini's surprising notion, to suggest a possible solution for so many problems which derived from that often chaotic and certainly confused process of development. In taking up some considerations from Tocqueville, Rosmini held that "to have proposed to the Indians the needs of a far more advanced society has had the opposite effect to the one predicted by the theorists of incentive and acceleration of economic development: in fact it has not aroused new working and intellectual energies, but has dispersed and dissolved the existing ones (…) the industrial economy with its system of needs cannot be proposed as a model of economic and social development for communities and nations organised on a tribal and village basis, characterised by a subsistence economy" (D'Addio, LA, 129).

**VI.17** Apart from the risks of the disintegration of the social fabric, a policy based on utilitarian criteria is also dangerous for the single individual, since he is led to confuse pleasurable sensations with happiness, which in this case can only increase the need for abstraction. The outcome can not be other than "to pass from one passion to another as soon as the first is exhausted: happiness is a fleeting illusion, but one in which we must even so believe for the little which lasts to renew expectation, the illusion that rekindles hope in our heart" (D'Addio, LA, 137). Then, Rosmini reminds us, we come up against that dangerous sophism which not only holds happiness to be fleeting, but impossible to attain other than in the incessant pursuit of different suggestions. In order to obtain these, life is transformed into constant agitation (cf. Rosmini, FP, 450-4) From this, two different sensations of individuals are derived, both of them unsatisfying. On the one hand, one lives in the indefinite hope of attaining complete satisfaction with means which, given their inconclusive character, prove to be absurd; on the other hand, a growing indignation is created, which often becomes anger, at seeing the emptiness of our efforts and the delusions which derive from them. In short, the improvement of material life does not raise the quality of life itself, and a general dissatisfaction is bred, accompanied by discontent, annoyance, irritation and resentment against everything and everyone. It is from this basis that utopias, including revolutionary ones, are born. They bring the hope that in changing everything radically, it may be possible to return to pursuing a viable satisfaction (cf. D'Addio, LA, 138). This is why market criteria themselves, today hailed as though they were absolute, must submit to other considerations. It is worth recording that "free competition itself does not express the criterion of justice; on the contrary it is justice which legitimises and regulates it" (D'Addio, LA, 140). Only in this way can the problems related to satisfaction be restored to their proper dimensions.

**VI.18** It is from this the analysis of the relationship between law and politics arises. In this context, it should be said that Rosmini tends to emphasise the intimate link existing between law and liberty. This relationship is, in fact, "the essential condition for the carrying out of the activities of individuals, from which come the benefits necessary to improve the conditions of life, above all in the less well-off classes" (D'Addio, LA, 177-8). It is not an abstract notion of liberty that derives from this, but an extremely realistic perspective, which tends to show an indissoluble link between civil and political liberty. This link provides Rosminian liberalism, also in the light of the philosophical and metaphysical presuppositions which we have mentioned, with contents completely different from those of his contemporaries, who nevertheless may also be termed liberals. It is a liberalism which "in substance, refers back to the conclusions which the philosopher had reached on the plains of theology and religion, philosophy, morals and law, which are systematically connected in the concept of the individual-person, on which politics is founded" (D'Addio, LA, 176-7, note 48). This conception is of fundamental importance for understanding the whole of Rosmini's political reflection. If the primacy of the person is not recognised, the "legislative power supposes itself to be infallible, and thus attributes omnipotence to itself" (D'Addio, LA, 191). The individual person, on the other hand, as conceived in Rosmini's theological-philosophical scheme, rises to limits that cannot be surpassed by the activity of the legislature, because he has inalienable rights which do not derive from that source of power. Otherwise there is the risk that what is described in Rosminian terms as "legal despotism" will arise.

**VI.19** From what has been said comes Rosmini's profound conviction – in accordance with what Tocqueville had already maintained – that religion is the basic fulcrum of any system which respects human dignity. Freedom of conscience remains the fundamental criterion which any political system should defend at all costs. These statements show the concern of Rosmini at the spread not only of philosophical atheism, but also of the political thinking which would result eventually in the collapse of morality as a basis for respect of the laws and for the survival of society as a whole (cf. D'Addio, LA, 197). These considerations find a reflection in the political situation of the times which were heading towards causing a confusion between political and ecclesiastical decisions that was certainly not devoid of consequences, in that it "eliminated the essential distinction between justice and beneficence (characterised by spontaneity) and transformed beneficence into an act or a duty of justice which creates rights and obligations, to be imposed where necessary by force" (D'Addio, LA, 212). Thus the state even claims to exercise coercion in activities which have always been carried on by private individuals and organisations created for the purpose. It should be stressed: Rosmini does not hold that the state should take no responsibility for the poor and needy, but in this boisterous substituting of itself for the free initiatives of individuals, who usually do things better and with less wastage of energy, he sees one of those expressions of "perfectionism" which characterise the political life of his age. What results is "a constant widening of the public sphere, and the related bureaucratic organisation, with a corresponding expansion of public spending, which feeds on itself because of the lack of effective control, and which provokes in turn a considerable increase in the public debt" (Rosmini, SC, 300). We have mentioned that Rosmini is not contrary to the state providing for the extreme necessities of needy citizens, but this most be done in a carefully regulated fashion, and taking account that public expenditure must be deliberated by those who have to pay. Given these presuppositions, it follows that "there must be no exclusion de jure, or even more, de facto, of the poor and dispossessed, who must instead be put in a position of power to share in the goods which society as a whole offers" (D'Addio, LA, 216).

**VI.20** A very important conclusion may be drawn from the foregoing considerations "on the relationship between the formation of the institutions which represent political choices, especially in the economic and social fields, and the system of taxation". The letter must be based on the principles of justice and equity rather than on the primacy of a state which considers its citizens simply as subjects. This means that the financial needs of the state, like the determination of what its tasks should be, cannot be divorced from the effective wealth of society and from its real productive capacity. Only thus can we hope to contain the public debt and avoid all those problems which will affect the welfare state (cf. D'Addio, LA, 219). Such a state, for a variety of motives, tends to limit the freedom of the individual even to the point of compromising it altogether in its more radical manifestations, which become an expression of pure state-worship. Thus there is a need, as Tocqueville in fact pointed out, to defend religion, the true presupposition for freedom of conscience, in order to limit not only the tyranny of the majority, but also of all those forms of government which claim to represent that majority faithfully.

**VI.21** We can understand why Rosmini, in the conclusion of his essay on *Communism and Socialism* had maintained the full correspondence between freedom and the catholic faith, as the inspiration of virtues which uphold and reinforce true liberty (cf. Rosmini, SCS, 115 ff). Only religion could, he argued, educate for that generous sense of heroism of which true liberty has an absolute need in order to survive in many moments of history: a freedom for which it is necessary to prepare the way with a path of real interior discipline which renders us capable of enjoying our rights because we really know how to direct our activities in the light of an effective spirit of moderation, prudence, patience and indulgence, and other qualities known only to a Christian soul. This does not mean depriving politics of its rightful autonomy nor confounding the role of the state with that of the Church. In confirmation of this, it should be said that "Rosmini's affirmations in this sense lay the foundations for the distinction between 'laicism' and 'laicità' the former which resolves religion in the conscience and affirms the self-sufficiency of religion, and the latter which instead recognises the autonomy of reason and the conscience in that which is defined by the limits imposed by the meta-empirical principles which transcend it. In this view, religion, and through it the Church, express the limit which must be recognised as applicable to politics, and consequently to the action of the state" (D'Addio,

LA, 269). Here Rosmini resumes in original fashion the two thousand year relationship between the temporal and the spiritual, recognising the *raison d'être* of the state while attributing to the Church the irreplaceable role of a guarantee for liberty in that it is capable of asserting the limits of the state itself.

# VII. THE DANGERS OF INVOLUTION IN A FREE MARKET SOCIETY

**VII.1** The theorists of a perfect society, who have caused some of the most dramatic aberrations in history, have been amply criticised by various liberals who have claimed that the market and its various logics are both more honest and more democratic. However, under this pretext not a few of these thinkers and economists have ended up, over the years, by exalting economic liberalism almost as if it were the sole and definitive remedy for all ills. In this way they have managed to forget that capitalism too is a product of history, and that it shows the vices of this, both in personal and social terms, if not indeed in terms of whole civilisations. Like all forms of economic development it must always be prone to self-correction, to take on board criticism, to satisfy the new needs and demands of the excluded. In itself, the logic of the market is not an abstract logic which can be adapted to any time and place; indeed it is often imprecise and deaf to certain innovations. It is true that liberal and market societies are capable of understanding novelties, and of "over-riding" them to bring them to a valid conclusion, but it is also true that on many occasions, overcome by their own contradictions, they have proved incapable of reading the signs of the times, and have hastened towards recession. Democratic thinkers of the most varied persuasions, and certainly not of revolutionary inclination, have drawn attention to this state of malaise, even though they may have remained unheard for long periods.

**VII.2** Those who believe as I do that economic development is easier where guarantees exist – i.e. juridical guarantees, consolidated and favourable to certain types of action – must certainly not forget that all this can become a convenient expedient for those who understand this institutional order in a purely defensive way (cf. Touraine, 7). This position, as I shall point out shortly, has already been clearly expressed by thinkers such as Veblen and Wright Mills, and it is one which those who seem to accept or impose (whichever happens to be the case) a strongly ideological interpretation, must keep clearly in mind; as, for example, when they maintain that globalisation has created a world order which is by its nature liberal thanks to the global market. The fact that this interpretation is ideological is demonstrated by all those enormous areas of the world subject, certainly, to the logic of the market, but completely deprived of the most elementary rights (cf. Touraine, 13). It is precisely in those areas that we are seeing the most deleterious effects of capitalism – among them corruption, which can certainly accompany any political system, bar none, but which spreads more rapidly where no certain rules exist, or where it is too easy to ignore them. The market society cannot pretend that nothing is wrong; indeed the logic of all times says that where there are greater riches and wider circulation of money, corruption is easier. Anyone who seeks to ignore this is a slave to a no less dangerous utopia, which someone described as utopian capitalism, and which always presents itself as a temptation and an illusion (cf. Rosanvallon, vi).

**VII.3** In order to throw a little light on these problems, it may be worth while to take a new look at some the classics, beginning, for instance, with *Das Finanzkapital* by Rudolf Hilferding, which a little less than a century ago dealt with financial capitalism, warning of the radical transformation of classical capitalism and already pointing the way to those dangerous vices which were likely to accompany economic acceleration. We need not necessarily accept his conclusions, but there can be no doubt that not a few false structures were to be built on that financial world, all of which collapsed in 1929. This crash took place, as J. K. Galbraith reminds us in his well-known work *The Great Crash*, because financial capital made itself capable for a while of maintaining a class which, from the heights of its well-being, was led to believe that such well-being could grow to an immeasurable degree.

**VII.4** The creators of the market society themselves, aware of the lessons of history, have been able to bring correctives to a system which, like democracy, may perhaps be held to be the best of all, but is certainly not without its defects. To take just one case, of which we hear little, and which would merit greater attention, the *Rhine model* may be cited. It seemed to have discerned the way, however banal, of avoiding the uncontrollable and chaotic effects of economic behaviour. As has rightly been stressed, by resorting to various financial and managerial structures, it was sought to avoid speculators making easy gains to the detriment of industrial entrepreneurs, and to prevent easy, short-term gains keeping the wealth of investment at bay for a long period: in short, a social market economy in which the political sphere acquires dignity as joint leader – as it has been called, a liberalist order which ensures liberty to the market, but which alone cannot regulate the entirety of social life. It needs elements of external equilibrium which are based on presuppositions of social policies established *a priori*, of which the state is a guarantor (cf. Albert, ch. V).

**VII.5** The most significant theorists of free exchange, or as some call it, self-regulation, offer the US as a definitive proof of the capacity of a market economy to function. These, however, base their analysis on an American situation in which the whole of society was growing strongly – i.e. up to the first world war (cf. Polanyi, ch. XVII). What followed after is considered by these theorists as virtually an accident *en route*. And yet similar incidents recur in history. How can we forget that Tawney himself had clearly stated that "societies, like individuals, have their moral crises and their spiritual revolutions". And yet these facts continue to be viewed with serene indifference (cf. Tawney, 271). And also included in this indifference are the criticisms which have come even from liberal spirits, who have perceptively highlighted the contradictions inherent in a mature market society. Among these Thorstein Veblen deserves a high place; he was able to show up clearly the contradictions of that leisure class, closely linked to financial capitalism, which ended, though obviously involuntarily, by being a drag on America's own productive society.

**VII.6** In order to understand Veblen, we must keep in mind the economic and social dimension of American agriculture in the late 1800s and early 1900s; the growing debates concerning socialism, and the more or less evident contrasts between the business-orientated and parasitic world of financial capitalism, and the industrial world with its ever-increasing stimulation from invention, genius and innovation. This contributed to ensuring that the economy could not be analysed completely by setting aside sociology and psychology, all of it included in an evolutionary framework which, however, preserved and at times exaggerated primeval instincts. In short the demands of war, rapine, speculation, and above all selfishness and emulation prove certainly to be more refined, but they are always there. With regard to emulation, Veblen maintains that, since there is a kind of antagonistic spirit present in this intention, it is from this that property, its genesis and development really spring. However, what is truly serious in his view, even though it is not the first time that it has appeared in history, is the fact that such a mentality is generating a parasite culture which in time gets in the way of development itself and brings about a crisis not only in the achievements of capitalism but in its basic motivations. This is the apogee of the *leisure class*. Out of this comes a little-explored theme, but one which I think is critical to my analysis: that capitalism, if it is not capable of renewing itself and remaining linked to the genuine presuppositions of liberal democracy, may regress towards barbarism, reaching the point of denying its own nature.

**VII.7** In the light of these reflections, we may accept the judgment of Lekachman in whose opinion Veblen had the great merit of perceiving that when human institutions (defined as mental habits) are too far behind the real socio-political situation, they are destined to be shipwrecked. It is certainly not a coincidence that his death, which took place in 1929, ended an epoch of whose outcome he had been in certain senses a prophet. The ruin of a society is due to a kind of struggle, even a class struggle, which, however, does not take place between those who control the means of production and the proletariat. The clash takes place between two differing mentalities, on the one hand the one formed by technicians, scientists, manual labourers – in short the world of doers, – while on the other hand we find the world of wheeler-dealers: a plethora of professions made up of idle gentlemen (cf. Lekachman, viii-x). A certain amiable inefficiency has always existed, because the so-called leisure class has never collapsed completely. With time, however, it discovers that its maintenance is constantly more costly, and leads (as I have described in the second chapter with reference to the Roman world), to forms of self-induced decomposition of the social system. The need for parasitic maintenance saps energy and resources from those who seek novelty, and thus the society loses its vital urge.

**VII.8** In this parasitic condition, the criterion of property itself becomes the most easily recognised test of a respectable level of success, the conventional criterion for esteem, instead of being the result of effort and the need for improvement.

Wealth becomes honourable in itself, and confers honour on those who possess it. To be rich and ostentatious ends up by becoming a necessary condition for respectability. Everything that exceeds the normal level of life becomes meritorious (cf. Veblen, 29-31). It seems almost as if the serenity of life is measured by the possession of a certain amount of goods. Such serenity becomes gratifying when one succeeds in possessing something more than others have got. It is certain that all this generates in too many people a chronic dissatisfaction, and in others an absurd but prestige-bringing ostentation. The fact remains that the need to accumulate becomes uncontrollable, because it is understood that from riches not only stems the sense of power, but also its dimension. Competition seems to detach itself from the just criterion of the method, but it becomes a sports stadium for the pursuit of spheres of command and respectability.

**VII.9** Idleness, in this context, becomes a fundamental element on the social plane. For the leisure class, the time is consumed in non-productive ways out of a sense of the indignity of productive work, almost as if to show one's own economic possibilities, which make it viable to live without working (cf. Veblen, 43). Idleness thus assumes an honorific character; it is not, as the ancients used to say, the father of all vices, but the demonstration of a special status. Being able to involve others, obviously by being able to maintain them, in this *conspicuous leisure* increases one's prestige and power. Idleness, however, does not seem to be sufficient in itself, there is a need for quite showy and visible consumption, even though at certain social levels one has an obligation to distinguish "noble" consumer goods from the vulgar type (cf. Veblen 73-4). Idleness and consumption must therefore be lived in a given way, bearing in mind that they can never manage without competitiveness, which obviously expresses itself not in violent ways, but in frivolous ones, such as festivals, gifts, etc. Hence the exhibitionism and the need to feel oneself esteemed in a certain way. The culminating point is reached when one becomes convinced that in order for there to be respectability, there has to be waste (cf. Veblen, 96-7). Thus one reaches the moment in which social competition becomes stronger than economic motives, properly so-called. At this point, we are faced with a paradoxical fact: in order to remain in a certain social status, one is prepared to sacrifice many domestic consumer-goods, or at least those relative to private life which, being secret, can remain anchored to miserable levels, while not rejecting those consumer goods which form part of the visible life (cf. Veblen, 112).

**VII.10** What we have been talking about here, unfortunately, does not remain simply a mere external fact. The norm of honorific waste may have a more or less direct influence on the sense of duty, on the sense of beauty and even that of utility (cf. Veblen, 116). But this is not sufficient, because for Veblen, waste impinges on moral principles and practice, and even on scientific truth. Everything, even the usefulness of objects, depends on their costly extravagance. Clothes and furnishings are an eloquent expression of this. But what is more incredible is that even human relations themselves are conditioned by all this. The ideal of love, beauty, of womankind, proves to be strongly conditioned by it. It was this way even in the prehistoric world when goods were the result of violent appropriation (cf. Veblen, 148-50).

**VII.11** In this way, what can be defined as a genuine "pecuniary culture" becomes installed in the mentality, with *cheap and nasty* as its motto, in the sense that everything that is low-priced is deplorable. This is why proverbs like *a cheap coat makes a cheap man* are coined, confirming that clothes too are signs of a style, but above all of a status in life (cf. Veblen 155-6). One's way of dressing comes to demonstrate a financial situation which becomes almost a superior and spiritual necessity; so much so that those who buy certain clothes usually do so to conform to a social standard of taste and respectability. Anything outside this standard ends up, too, by being considered of little functional use, so that the ostentation of wealth must ensure that clothes are little adapted to certain types of activity which the rich regard with repugnance. What we have said is especially true of women who, with body upholstery and high heels, come to wear a whole outfit of uselessness (cf. Veblen 169-171) It could be said that fashion, with its changes and its various ornamentations, responds to that primitive need for exhibitionism which is typical of the human spirit. Not a pure and simple exhibitionism, but one above all linked to the financial capacity of the exhibitor. Hence the need for constant innovation. This must not only be the most beautiful or perhaps more often the least displeasing, but it must be brought up to the current standard of extravagance (cf. Veblen, 174). The fact that the clothes do not please the wider public is of little importance; what is important is that they strike the few people who count, those for whom it is essential to dress in a certain way.

**VII.12** I think that the most paradoxical aspect which emerges from all this is that the leisure class ends up by denying the very nature of that economic liberalism which has produced it. By closing itself up it impedes that social osmosis which must characterise real democracy, and in contrast ends by generating such an obtuse conservatism that it leads it to lose contact with those forces of industrial change, and of work in general, which ensure progress to society. This is the source of the most extreme form of conservative capitalism, the existence of which some purists of the market theory consider impossible, but which in fact constitutes one of the latent dangers of liberal society.

**VII.13** Over and beyond this consideration, if we wish to relate Veblen's conclusions to what has been said, we must add that in this kind of conservatism we have the preservation of some archaic characteristics expressed above all in certain forms of survivalism, like those of fearless boldness, and in the belief in fortune. The games-oriented aspect of these societies is expressed in the enormous importance given to sport, which becomes more and more important the more it moves money and generates riches, and in the interest in gambling and betting, because of the easy ways of obtaining money which these forms imply. The dream of winning at various forms of gambling projects one immediately into that leisure class into which it is otherwise very difficult to enter.

**VII.14** In order to survive this dangerous involution, the various groups need new alliances. This issue was confronted by Veblen and other scholars of his time, and expressed unequivocally by Wright Mills. In his analysis the relation between the military, politics and industry is vital. The link between the first two groups has always been very clear, even if it is not always easy to discern which of the two exercises supremacy over the other. In periods of peace, the military have been defined as an instrument of politics. In moment of crisis, however, the military have sought to reduce the other institutions to the level of means for achieving their own ends. In short, arms have become the instrument of political struggle and brute force has substituted the rule of law. Everything has become more complicated in the modern world when, without the support of an industrial economy, not only political activity, but above all military activity, proves to be impossible: the army is an army of machines (cf. Wright Mills, 222-3). The very close link between the military and industrial powers, which has politicians as its intermediaries, is obvious. This link must not only be understood to apply to periods of war, but I believe that it is even more valid for times of peace. One only has to think of the resources dedicated to research and experiment which are only used for conversion to civil use as a kind of afterthought.

**VII.15** The military construct a power élite which is quite well-integrated with the political world, and with that of the economy. This fact surely implies moral questions of great import, but according to Wright Mills, these rarely concern Americans. They have always believed that politics is the result of the composition of many interests which, setting aside any moral consideration, only find some sort of bridle in the Laws. Offspring of the economic liberalism of the eighteenth century, they believe in the ideal of automatic equilibrium. Hence the idea that a certain system of checks and balances constitutes a perfect mechanism, capable of guaranteeing economic and political liberty, which will always hold tyranny at bay (cf. Wright Mills, 242). Unfortunately, the political events of the twentieth century, with their totalitarianisms and authoritarianisms of various kinds, have to some extent stifled the critical sense of the Americans, and have driven them to consider as perfect a political system which, like all fruits of human action, is always capable of improvement. Americans have closed in on themselves, and have avoided that constant confrontation which characterises every true democracy, and which in the past was the prerequisite and original feature of their own.

**VII.16** Wright Mills insists greatly on the system of balance of power, stressing how it can be understood in various ways: from the sense that no particular interest may impose its own will and conditions on others, to the sense that no interest, not even a political one, can be allowed to block the functioning of society. But he also warns that the system of balances, weights and counter-weights, can be understood as an alternative to the *divide and rule* dictum, becoming a trick to prevent any popular aspirations from having the possibility of expressing themselves more directly, and making institutions conform more and more to reality. His reflections on the composition of the Senate are revealing (cf. Wright Mills, 246-7 and note, 248-9). This Chamber has not been able to effect the transformation in its composition which happened to its namesake in the ancient Roman world, or in the British House of Lords.

**VII.17** In the opinion of Wright Mills, this static character of American institutions has favoured the spread of immorality. The politician, to *keep himself in the saddle* at all costs, has been forced to gain entry to bureaucratic and administrative cliques. His influence does not depend on voting for or against a law, but on entering into a clique which can have some influence on positions of command, but also and perhaps above all it depends on abstaining from investigating certain sectors sensitive to the interests of the clique. Through the politician in question, the middle class as a whole has found itself entrammelled in the mechanism of the state, politically and economically (cf. Wright Mills, 257-60). The reflections in which he places the union leaders in the same false position as the politicians are interesting. It follows that the form and significance of the power élite in these moments assumes a very particular significance. We have a military capitalism formed by two groups (industrialists and the military) who act within a system of formal democracy, hence a seriously weakened one – in which the politicians (who constitute the third group) depend, with regard to methods and viewpoints, on the economic and military powers. This means the convergence of the various interests, the decline of the true professional politician, and the absence of a bureaucracy independent of the pre-constituted interests (cf. Wright Mills, 276). If this fact is not perceived as a problem, it is because these élites, as in the American tradition, have no "boundaries" and fixed personnel, but indeed favour the continual entry of groups, making for an easy change of personnel capable of guaranteeing the increase in volume and importance of the dealings between the various sectors. In a perhaps somewhat over-pessimistic mood, all this determines what Wright Mills calls the "immorality of the high ranks" (cf. Wright Mills, 287-8 and 343 ff.)

**VII.18** Bureaucracy elevated to a system has given birth to a new social category – or rather caused it to develop to an excessive degree. This is the category of the *white-collar workers*. Wright had already dealt with this phenomenon in an earlier book than the one dedicated to the power élite; it is progressively supplanting the traditional professions, and redesigning the whole of American society. The professionals of the past were free individuals, who almost always acted in their own right, assuming risks for which they answered. In the new society, they have been reduced to salaried workers, trapped in the most important structures of the political system. As a result they end up by becoming the upholders of the system itself, providing that consensus without which the compromise of the power élites could not survive. In short the white-collar workers are the expression of a class of conformists already very far removed from that liberal class which had enabled the United States to be a true democracy. The white-collar workers seem to be truly aware of their status, but they have no possibility of changing a situation which would condemn them together with the economic system which they serve. Hence that state of malaise which renders them anxious and insecure, as so much of twentieth century literature has proved capable of describing so admirably.

## VIII. BUREAUCRACY:
## THE PURSUIT OF EFFICIENCY
### A gnoseological problem

**VIII.1** The development of rationality understood as the "logical coherence" of an intellectual-theoretical position, or a practical and ethical one, can result in the creation of a "power over people". All this has involved "a relative rational systematisation" of daily life, or one limited to the individual aspects or of life in its totality. The latter is the claim of all religions of "redemption"; above all those which have seen the nature of evil in a sublimated and interiorised manner (cf. Weber, Z, 480 and 484). It seems to me that a reflection of this kind could provide a useful departure point, even though I believe that the religions which have claimed to influence the whole field of existence are those which have conceived of evil in its exterior manifestation, since they have claimed, through revolution, to change the world and human relations, even though, at least up to this point, they have not had the possibility of exercising sufficient control over the interior allegiance of the individual. It is true, however, that the regular recurrence of certain determined conditions has always given greater strength to a certain kind of hereditary or bureaucratic "hierocracy". The latter has ended up by regularising a certain mode of action by conferring tranquillity and certainty of norms and objectives to the whole social context (cf. Weber, Z, 484). This security is especially valuable to economic activity, as long as it permits such activity to be carried on freely in the context of rules and guarantees. In other words, the bureaucracy must provide services, data, opportunities, etc., but cannot take the place of the economic operators themselves. Otherwise a planned economy would be the outcome, and in the long run, this will constitute the reverse of development. Before von Mises (cf. Mises, S, ch. V), Weber maintained that in this case, when the competition between individual interests in the market comes to nothing, the rational economy itself also comes to nothing. In fact, without conflict of interest and consequently without the estimates of monetary prices, no economic calculation is possible. Everything becomes abstract and impersonal, and even the formulation of hypotheses becomes impossible (cf. Weber, Z, 488).

**VIII.2** Weber makes a statement full of implications when he maintains that the growing rationality of the political order, (like the economic sphere also), causes growing tensions (cf. Weber, Z, 491). Individuals, in their economic activities, are led to act on the basis of motives that are almost always strictly personal. When these do not conflict with the rules of civil existence, they lead to widespread spontaneity of behaviour. By its very nature this behaviour is against the full rationalisation of life as pursued by, for example, a rigid state centralism. But spontaneous behaviour also flees from the total uncertainty which exists where there are no rules. The real problem, in much the same way as in politics, is that of determining the limits of bureaucratic action. This means assessing the real weight of the progress of political functions within the state apparatus, and above all, the weight of the resources which that apparatus consumes in exchange for the services which it provides. Only in this way can its efficiency and its real rationality be evaluated. Certainly, politics cannot be completely summed up in simple mathematical calculation, otherwise a whole series of activities which do not have any economic return would be excluded. And these are activities without which political activity would be nothing but "economicism". As Weber says, if the economic world were to be objectivised, it would cancel from its roots every form of sentiment, or rather every form of love, as a part of human action, obliterating everything that derives from it (cf. Weber, Z, 517). The fact remains, however, that every political action has a cost which, even if it proves necessary to undertake it, cannot be left to improvisation, or worse still, as an inheritance of future political action.

**VIII.3** We should not forget that politics too needs resources in order to survive. Everyone seems to agree with this conclusion even if there are quite a few who feel a notable revulsion against having to uphold it in practice. This probably derives from the fact that politics never seems to be satisfied with the resources which it possesses, and always tends to transgress the limits of those which are legally permitted. I think that Weber was thinking of this when he spoke about the bosses, who are described as the genuine capitalist entrepreneurs of politics. They have the power of supplying votes, organising parties and structures, in the sense that they have a capacity for collecting the money from the great magnates of finance directly. The boss has no specific or well-defined political principles, and because of this he may end up by being despised (cf. Weber, PB, 215-7). It would seem indeed that this is an inevitable destiny, in that it is logical that the great magnates of finance, who provide the political sphere with economic resources, do so to obtain special favours. This seems to be indirectly proved by the fact that in these circumstances parliaments appear to be reduced to a state of impotence, as those who seem to possess special qualities, when they realise the implications, avoid entering parliament altogether, or only become members for very brief periods (cf. Weber, PB, 218-19). In order to keep the political sphere within its proper limits, (and as a reflection of that, the economy as well), it is essential either that the former shall be satisfied with the resources which it has available legitimately, avoiding the creation of overweight, costly structures, or that it shall possess the autonomous capacity to increase its own resources; or finally, that it is capable of avoiding useless extravagance, beginning with the elementary rule, noted by Tocqueville, by which it is better to let the citizens do what they know best how to do, more speedily and with less waste and sometimes with no waste at all.

**VIII.4** Closely connected with the bureaucracy is the problem of administrative regulation, which in Weber's overall view should possess the capacity to regulate the actions of "the group". Its basic purpose should be that of regulating social activity by guaranteeing the possibilities arising out of such regulation. It is clear that administrative regulation confers special characteristics of both potential and actual power on the bureaucracy. The *former* characterises every possibility of making its own will prevail within a social relationship, even though opposition may exist. The *latter* defines its capacity to exact obedience (cf. Weber, WG, vol. I, 27-8). The problem of both characteristics, not only for economics but for the most varied forms of civil life, is that it is very hard to contain them within their boundaries. The intrusiveness of administrative regulation, and the consequent depersonalisation of responsibility, becomes transformed from a guarantee of the life of the individual to an insurmountable obstacle, part of a Kafkaesque Castle, within which we end up wasting both time and resources.

**VIII.5** It is the basic connotations of bureaucracy which confer certain powers on it. Weber sums these up in masterful fashion: obedience to objective official duties; existence of a hierarchy with precise areas of competence; employment on the basis of free selection, and on the basis of a contract that recognises specialised qualifications certified by a diploma and tested by examination; recompense based on a salary which gives the position held the character of a unique or principal profession; rigorous discipline and surveillance of work, which nevertheless permits career advancement based on the judgment of superiors. To all this is added the impossibility of appropriation of official position. The really important factor is that the birth and expansion of the bureaucratic administration constitutes the nucleus – and I would add, also the development – of the modern state machine (cf. Weber, WG, vol. I, 126-8). An obvious conclusion can be drawn from this: there can be no re-dimensioning of the power of the bureaucracy without a parallel re-dimensioning of the role of the state itself: making the bureaucracy more agile means reforming and re-dimensioning the power of the state machine.

**VIII.6** Giving a new dimension to bureaucratic power also means reducing the gnoseological claims of the state structure. This must concede that the private individual interested in gain, is superior within his field of interest, to the bureaucracy in terms of specialist knowledge and awareness of facts (cf. Weber, WG, vol. I, 129). The bureaucracy must keep in mind that re-structuring of its interventions in the context of the economy means not only guaranteeing that the latter can be more flexible and capable of responding with greater rapidity and vigour to the needs of civil society, but also rediscovering its own *raison d'être*, which can certainly not be summed up exclusively in its relationship with the economic sphere. The bureaucracy must, in fact (as Weber notes: WG, vol. II, 382-3), guarantee the most varied and elementary interests of the individual, which range from personal security to the needs of the family and the community. It must see to it that basic rights are not transgressed, and above all that the rules of economic competition are respected. If it goes beyond these tasks, the bureaucracy may risk going beyond the possibility of imposing a framework of rationality on economic activity; on the other hand, if it abdicates the task completely it will end by rendering the pursuit of private interest completely devoid of rules. Over-rational centralised control and leaving the irrational free to take over are the two extremes which the bureaucracy must combat. The *former* is a danger within its own ranks, the *latter* is external to it. The first danger is the more frequent because with regard to the latter, it should be remembered that the bureaucracy, as Weber maintains, is characterised by a deep contempt for the irrational (cf. Weber, WG, vol. II, 272-3). Moreover it arises from the attempt to rationalise certain activities, and thus make them more secure. But even extreme rationalisation, Vico would say, in its claim to become absolute, produces precisely its own contradiction: irrationality. Obviously, this is a different kind of irrationality from the anarchy which rejects any type of rule, but it is a more dangerous one, because in the claim to control everything, it generates fear, static conditions, and the death of imagination and creativity.

**VIII.7** If a process of rationalisation tends to give rules to the identity of a society for its own organisation, apart from displaying and limiting its own capacity, we can agree with Habermas when he maintains in the opening paragraph of his *Legitimationsprobleme im Späkapitalismus* that it is precisely from this that the causes of its crisis can be generated. This crisis, in fact, comes to a head when problems arise which cannot be resolved in the context of the organisation which society has bestowed on itself. His statement in the same context is also true, and may even be seen as a corollary – that "the states of crisis figure as a disintegration of the social institutions" – obviously, those institutions which already exist. It seems to me equally obvious that new social institutions are necessary for any kind of society which seeks to take the place of one which has entered into crisis.

**VIII.8** A measured and responsible bureaucracy is necessary, if for no other reason, to permit certainty in certain "passages" within civil society. Even those who have been the most relentless enemies of the bureaucratic state, especially in certain historical and cultural contexts, have generally admitted its utility. We may point to what Von Mises says (and for him a serious analysis of the bureaucracy can attribute neither condemnation nor blame: not even when those who hold office become transformed into irresponsible bosses). It is no use criticising the bureaucracy which, in itself, is neither good nor bad (cf. Mises, B, 9, 44 and 122). The activity of the bureaucracy depends on the way the political sphere is managed, and on how and to what degree it seeks to intervene in the sphere of private citizens. On this depends the intrusiveness or otherwise of the bureaucracy. But to the best of our knowledge, the harmful effects of bureaucracy may develop even within the private sphere of business management. Mises himself admits this, and considers it at times not to be the cause but the effect of crises in business. It is enough in fact for the inventive and tireless spirit of the entrepreneur, and his passion for innovation, to fail, and the whole enterprise degenerates into a sterile bureaucratic regime. Without willing it, the drying up of the special characteristics of free enterprise itself generates the bureaucrat (cf. Mises, B, 13).

**VIII.9** This is surely the reason why bureaucracy and bureaucratic method are more ancient than might be supposed, and always have been and still are present in the administrative structures of governments, especially those which extend their sovereignty over a wide area (cf. Mises, B, 15). Faced with this, as Croner points out, the development of rationalisation has ended up by giving a new face to the bureaucracy of the twentieth century. There has been a notable increase in the middle class of salaried employees, because of the multiplication and consequent sub-division of the functions that industrial and post-industrial states have had to cope with. This class has found itself in conflict with all the other groups operating in society, because of the ever-growing influence it has been assuming. Prior to Croner, Renner had pointed out that the growing number of salaried employees gives rise to a special group of individuals. These are neither capitalists nor workers in the classic sense; they are not owners of capital, nor do they create "added value" through their work, but nevertheless they end up controlling everything that others create (cf. Dahrendorf, 91-4). This structure, composed of salaried employees, has finally acquired growing power even in the effectively democratic states – perhaps for reasons that belong to their very nature. In fact the complete change of governments which is possible in such political circumstances in peaceful and rapid fashion, has increased the power of the only class which, by virtue of its capacity for rationalisation, provides a sense of stability even in the midst of the most rapid and justified changes.

**VIII.10** What Weber called "the administrative staff" is today present in Dahrendorf's view in all three classic powers of the state. But what is more surprising is the fact that, in addition to legislative, executive and juridical bureaucracies, we have also seen the growth of a bureaucratic system in strictly non-political structures, such as those of industry, the trade unions, or even simple associations (cf. Dahrendorf, 295). Each of these, as it gradually grows, tends to create upper ranks which fulfil an important role: sometimes, indeed, too intrusive a role, in the context of society, in which they consider themselves to have a determining influence. It should be said that the bureaucracy has been able up to now to count on the fact that part of its activity responded to the widespread need for a series of services which everyone could make use of, in order to justify its development: for instance the postal and telegraph services, and more generally everything relating to communications. It still remains to be seen, in a world which provides more and more opportunities for individuals to communicate without the assistance of structures, how those forms of bureaucracy which were previously dedicated to these tasks will evolve. Their suppression cannot be painless, in part because they will seek to transform themselves in order to survive. We only have to look at what is taking place in the traditional post offices, which are coming more and more to resemble banks. This is a sign that part of the bureaucracy tends to manage certain capital resources, at least those of savers, while thinking in future also of investment possibilities as a different way of justifying its survival.

**VIII.11** All this could mean a new development and further success for certain offices of the bureaucracy, which in some ways have an advantage over many other organisations. Apart from continuity in relation to certain purely political structures, the bureaucracy also shows one of its special characteristics with regard to industrial organisations, for example: its sense of authority and the pyramid of responsibilities, both based on the hierarchical structure. All this certainly involves the well-known slowness of bureaucratic procedures, but as has been usefully pointed out, it also means the total absence of conflict between those who hold bureaucratic positions (cf. Dahrendorf, 296). The slowness of decision-making is compensated by its certainty, which it is hard to challenge. All this should be borne in mind if a different bureaucracy is to develop, capable, once certain traditional functions are lost, of managing economic and financial resources.

**VIII.12** While it seems now beyond question that the bureaucracy expresses a rationality of its own, it should be pointed out, nevertheless, that it is extremely cold, because it objectifies human relations and their activities and almost crystallises them, though not always in the same way. The acceptance and the justification of the bureaucracy which the variety of individuals demonstrate in the life of society also depends on this. It is from the different way in which certain conditionings are experienced that the judgment on bureaucratic rationality varies. I believe that we need in fact to remember that in every society there are some people, such as small traders, artisans, restaurant owners and so on, who are not as free to express their convictions as others who possess greater rank or economic power (cf. Mises, B, 39). Is it not these people who provide the more or less conscious consensus for the bureaucracy in which they seek, according to the needs of the moment, protection and security? The need for stability, from which and for which a certain form of rationality is formulated, depends on a wide variety of needs. The important thing is that this rationality must find expression in legality, otherwise the bureaucracy operates in the most completely arbitrary fashion. Even Mises recognises that the bureaucracy must conform to the criterion, *nulla poena sine lege*. Beyond this criterion, the state and its administrative and bureaucratic structure exercise a limitless power. Prescribing limits for it is the function of the laws (cf. Mises, B, 42 and 76). The difference between the liberal democratic systems and those which are not such lies precisely in the definition and the respect for this limit.

**VIII.13** This limit cannot be ignored by anyone. As classic jurisprudence stated: *ignorantia legis non excusat*, but the law which must be put into effect within precise limits, apart from not tolerating ignorance by anybody, cannot even tolerate the disregard of the resources which needs in order to be actuated. These resources or means constitute the operative limit of the law itself, or at least, should constitute such in a genuine democracy. Financial statements are as binding as legal statements. Can it be allowable for an administration to spend more than what has been established, or, worse still, to spend it for reasons other than those intended? An important innovation in the context of bureaucracy could be that of promoting persons who, having performed their tasks, have done so not only within the context of the law and of their responsibilities, but also without having in any way increased state spending; or better still, having made it possible for a certain amount of saving to be achieved. In contrast, in the administrative hierarchy, access is by seniority and one arrives at the top, as more than one person has noted, when one is no longer motivated and near retirement, thus contributing to a further immobility in the bureaucracy.

**VIII.14** Certainly modern absolutist theory has contributed to creating the figure of the manager as a figure of power and immunity, but no less certainly, various totalitarian utopian notions have also contributed to this. Mises mentions a conviction shared by many: so many people among the so-called revolutionaries sang fervent hymns of opposition to the existing power and its machinery of state repression, but in their hearts they only wished to put themselves in the place of those they were challenging; in short, they were themselves ambitious for state positions (cf. Mises, B, 96). They did so because basically they were not creative and brilliant individuals, and so they sought for self-realisation by finding an arrangement within a society capable of rationalising their utopia, and making it real. Once they had succeeded in their aim, they prevented any change which might compromise their achievements. Because of this, they fought against innovative spirits and those possessed of genius. The latter, however, cannot be created by society. "A creative genius cannot be trained. There are no schools for creativeness". Geniuses are such because they are able to be masters, never disciples (cf. Mises, B, 13). However, I believe that this notion, despite its undoubted originality, is too drastic.

**VIII.15** We must all admit that both the process of rationalisation and geniuses have their importance. Without the former, novelty would never have any way of being appraised and put into effect; without the latter, novelty would not exist at all. Speaking in epistemological terms, we could say that the *bureaucracy*, or the process of rationalisation, takes shape according to a mechanism similar to that described by Kuhn with regard to *normal science*, in the sense that like the latter, it seeks to give stability to the social achievements of the past, but risks closing itself up in those achievements and seeking to prevent any innovative spirit – in other words any genius – from calling them into question. But the anomalies existing in everything that proves normal and solidly-based leap to the eye sooner or later. Society, like consciousness, cannot be other than cumulative, because the brightest social activists, like the best scientists, seek novelty. This cannot be handled in anarchic fashion on their part, because it must find the time to take root, to be assimilated – otherwise it cannot even be transmitted. One of the philosophers of the anarchy of consciousness, Paul Feyerabend, had to admit this implicitly in the ninth chapter of his book *Farewell to Reason* when he reminds us that even today someone like Galileo would have found difficulty in getting himself accepted in the academic circles of half the world, which only declare themselves open to novelty *a posteriori*. In the end, the conflict between bureaucracy and free enterprise is of the same nature. Both, however, prove to be useful to one another, if they manage to admit that the first, i.e. the bureaucracy, ends by suffocating life itself if it claims to direct the path of novelty, while the latter cannot make any progress and development if it does not find the stability which only its rival is capable of guaranteeing, thanks to legality and rationality. To break up this stability will never be a process which is an end in itself, because at the same time it is necessary to give life to new formulas of stability.

**VIII.16** Certainly the process just described is neither easy nor painless. Propaganda may spread lies, but the truth never has an easy path of self-assertion before it. For this reason, I do not find myself at all in agreement with Mises when he states: Propaganda is always the spreading of lies, errors and superstitions. *Truth has no need of propaganda of any sort*, it defends itself on its own (cf. Mises, B, 113). The first statement is not always true, but nor, alas, is the second: otherwise so many evident facts, such as that the earth is round, would not have found rapid acceptance, not to mention the truths of the spirit.

## IX. RISK LIMITATION AND THE CRISIS IN INTELLIGENCE

**IX.1** It is said, in the past, that education was supposed to be capable of preparing one to face the unexpected, and above all, the risks that life entailed. Not everyone showed signs of being prepared for these; to some extent because special natural endowments seem to be needed to confront them. However, in the past, risks could be placed on the same plane as unexpected events, while today it seems, quite rightly, that this is no longer so. "The modern business process also instills – and requires – the practice of a number of other virtues, among them diligence, industriousness, prudence in undertaking reasonable risks, reliability, and fidelity in interpersonal relationships" (Novak, BC, 127). This certainly does not preclude the courage to take decisions on difficult or special occasions. It means, though, that when we talk about economic development, we too often take for granted the moral capital "invested" by some operators and are ignorant of the effort put into building it, enriching and defending it. And if we fall into this trap, we forget that civic and economic virtues are the *sine quâ non condition* of a society which seeks to make progress but also to remain free. The modern world has made certain aspects of these virtues even clearer: the *virtue of creativity, the virtue of building a community*, and the *virtue of realism and concrete notions* (cf. Novak, BC, 125). It should be said, however, that even if economic progress has determined the development of individualism, this assertion will not be exhaustive, since the development of the person is something which goes well beyond that of the individual. This aspect of things deserves to be commented on more often. The enterprise itself, if and when it takes the person into account, already makes a major increase in quality. "The business corporation is also a mediating structure, that is, a social institution larger than the individuals who make it up but smaller than the state. An institution both voluntary and private, it stands between the individual and the state and is, perhaps (after the family), the crucial institution of civil society" (Novak, BC, 136).

**IX.2** But to return to the problem of risk. A classic text on the matter is *Risk, Uncertainty and Profit*, by F. H. Knight, who was the first to write about risks as distinct from uncertainty (though with the passage of time the distinction has been constantly losing substance). Risk seemed to be linked to all those activities which present greater variables than others. The latter seem less risky because they allow fairly sure prediction, and thus guarantee greater security. It is clear that in economic terms, risk means the possibility of losing, which reaches its culmination when investment becomes ruinous both for the investor and the producer. It is clear that, according to the means which one has available, risk also varies as a result of the profit that the operator expects from his action. The employment of means may be dependent on a psychological component which is not easy to measure, and which oscillates between aversion to risk and its attraction. However, I believe that it is ridiculous to maintain that the latter can be a characteristic of the economic operator, because his farsightedness always leads him to keep the risk factors to a minimum. If this were not so, what we have said up to now about the relationship between politics and economics would be immediately invalidated, and it would also prove to be impossible to explain why economic development almost always takes place under favourable political conditions – i.e. those which seem capable of reducing the margins of risk.

**IX.3** Uncertainty is a typical characteristic of the human condition, so much so that it is one of the components of everyday life. Because of this, financial institutions such as insurance came into being; these actually function on the basic nature of risk. As I said, it seems to me that there is a certain measure of aversion towards the latter on the part of those who work in the economic field. If, in fact, the springboard for economic action is the possibility of improvement and gain, it is logical that anyone would look with a certain suspicion on everything that might hamper such legitimate aspirations. So it is easy to understand why the problem of risk is one of the crucial themes of economic decision-making; so much so that there is not a manual or classic of economics which does not take it into account. Among many of these considerations, I begin with the clear discussion by Hal R. Varian in *Intermediate Microeconomics: a modern approach*. The aversion to risky activities bears witness to the role played by conditions of uncertainty in economic decision-making. This leads us to examine and describe the distribution of probabilities present in the decisions, which are described by means of certain parameters. Varian speaks of a "medium variance" model for the analysis of what he defines as a simple portfolio problem. Suppose that we are able to invest in two different activities, one *non-risk-prone*, i.e. guaranteed by a constant return $r_f$ such as Treasury Bonds; the other *risk-prone*, like, for example the purchase of a quota in a common investment fund which operates in the share market, a purchase which will be profitable only if the share market has a positive return. Logically, Varian maintains that since individuals are naturally averse to risks, they invest in risk-prone activities only when the expected return $r_m$ is superior to that of a non-risk-prone activity. The available wealth moves towards activities with a slightly more risky security margin only if there is the justified expectation of a higher return; in short we may assume $r_m > r_f$. The risk thus comes to assume its own price which measures the substitution between risk and return in the decisions made for the portfolio (cf. Varian, § 13.1).

**IX.4** It is clear that economic science has always been concerned with measuring risk, or rather with measuring its cost. The more the risk component grows, the more aversion to risk increases, and the more aversion to certain forms of investment in particular increases. At the same time the claims and costs of insurance which should aid or stimulate the investor and economic operators in general also increase, reaching the point of no return, from which it is no longer desirable to invest, because it is also no longer advisable to insure, given the low expectation of return. Varian goes on to talk about a beta index, which establishes a relationship between the risks associated with a certain action and the risks associated with the whole market. In these circumstances, if it does not prove possible to bring about changes, or rather corrections of the return in relation to the risk, both the possibility and the stimulus for any kind of economic activity vanish away (cf. Varian, § 13.2). If uncertainties in the political sphere are also added to all this, a phase of economic regression is generated. It is only possible to emerge from this if the socio-political conditions capable of bringing back confidence to the economic operators and stimulating a new readiness for risk are re-established. It seems clear that risk, while being a non-eliminable element in economic activity as in life in general, can certainly not be considered a leap in the dark. On the contrary, it remains feasible within precise limits and under determining political conditions.

**IX.5** In order to measure risk, economic operators not only need a system of competition to give value to the basic notions for economic calculation (as von Mises and some of his eighteenth- century predecessors remind us), but also need a certain social order. Without this, who is in a position to provide indications on the order in which the various alternatives and possibilities will present themselves to the economic operator in order to determine his preferences? (cf. Impicciatore, 54). The action of the player in the economic game, like that of any individual consumer, is thus free, but within a series of conditions from which it is not possible to escape. The decisions of the competing businesses, like the decisions which guide the consumer, revolve around certain schemes which, as we have seen in connection with risk, are not only of an economic nature, and hence affect much wider spheres. Here the relationship between politics and economics becomes closer. If the former does not provide the conditions for the free expression of the latter, it may fall into the hands of someone who, even by the use of brute force – one thinks of the Mafia, for example – can guarantee certain rules. By this I mean at least the possibility of financing social security, for which Sen speaks of *active public intervention* (cf. Sen, DF, 40). For this reason he reasserts the very close link which must exist between democracy and political incentives, which indeed was already widely anticipated by the Italian thinkers of the second half of the eighteenth century (cf. the last part of ch. IV).

**IX.6** The capacity of discerning, guessing or even foreseeing the risks is one of the best characteristics that anyone operating in the economic sphere can possess. It is a capacity which one can, up to a certain point, prepare and refine. It also depends on numerous aspects of daily life, and is based on practical and subjective experience which, in very many cases produces really excellent results. Such experience permits those who possess it to make choices at the right moment which will preclude long and improvised ratiocinations, but which will be successful in bringing together intuitions, past knowledge, and possibilities which, at times, it will be hard to repeat. These "heuristics", as such simple and rapid choices have been termed, meet the same limits and problems as anyone finds who makes decisions after having assessed the incompleteness of available data. This means, in the end, that the more associations of ideas, frequencies of situations, memories or data inherent to the phenomenon to be dealt with are available to the memory of the operator, the more the event can be judged successfully and with greater speed (cf. Oliverio, 103-4). From this, it can be assumed that a virtual culture of security can exist. The economic operator is led to make decisions with the whole of his "personality baggage". For him too, the choices are not improvised, in contrast to what it may seem. In the major operator, momentary euphoria must always be backed up by the capacity to control the data and to study events. This may be the way of bringing into being the decisions which are always the result of a long preparation, and of an entrepreneurial culture which springs out of an infinity of elements coming from the most disparate areas of knowledge, and from a humanity formed by the concurrence of such experiences. Where it has been impossible to conduct certain experiments, or where the data have been distorted by incorrect information, the unknown risk-factors increase substantially. Because of this, a *real economic democracy must allow all its members exactly the same access to certain information, and also to a certain kind of educational preparation.*

**IX.7** It is now a given fact that all investors prefer to invest in harmony with their own values of reference, even in the context of operations which permit a certain level of economic return, or at least the satisfaction of expectancies. Because of this less frequent activities are refused, not only because they are more risky, but also because they are emotionally less rewarding, in the sense that our feelings are less satisfied by them. This may be the reason why the young are more likely to prefer risky activities than the more mature, who have already made trial of certain experiences (cf. Oliverio, 117). In fact, one of the aspects which most characterises risk is the novelty which, because of its unpredictability, compels us to make improvised decisions at unexpected moments, and makes us seek to forecast future situations of need or conflict, so as to avoid succumbing in competition. Certainly a vast majority of operators prefer to concentrate their own activities on traditional activities, because they can be easily controlled. In doing so, however, they place themselves in a retrograde position, destined to be set aside as time goes on. It still goes without saying – and here von Hayek is right – that just because no one will ever be omniscient, risk will always be a component of economics, even if each operator tends, over a long time-span, to *lower the tolerability threshold of the risk itself.* Considering the relation between politics and economics, this consideration should also be something to be hoped for among politicians who, for their part, can certainly contribute to reducing risks.

**IX.8** Beck has rightly noted that risk seems to point to an invasion operated in the future. Because of this, risk has become a synonym for "nobody knows", even though it has the beneficial aspect of making our awareness grow (cf. Beck, 59). The real problem is that the risk can provoke consequences which are not always happy, and it is difficult to identify those responsible for this – one could cite the case of mad cow disease, for example. And yet it would seem logical that, if an economic operator may enjoy the benefits of a successful operation he has undertaken, he must nevertheless be held responsible for any harm caused to others when he does not succeed in predicting and controlling the risks inherent in his activity. As has been very rightly said, that fact that there is no right without duties cannot be applied only to the less well off (cf. Giddens, US, 33). This may be another aspect of what Soros describes as *moral hazard.* A concept of this kind derives from the fact that investors – though I would rather say economic operators in general – allow themselves to act imprudently in the awareness that someone else will pick up the bill if things go wrong. All this is not based on strictly rational expectations, and generates the possibility that someone who errs tends not to assume the full responsibility for his actions (cf. Soros, S, 58 and note 2). All this means that politics must not only offer guarantees for economic development, but also guarantee those who may prove to be victims of such development as a result of dishonesty.

**IX.9** *It is true that the private economic sector is not and cannot be a charitable institute, but it is also true that it cannot take cover behind the privilege of only responding to the laws of the market, and ignoring the laws of civil society.* This seems to me the just concern of those who, like Soros, speak of *market fundamentalism*. It is this view that, for example, makes it possible to shift capital with extreme rapidity from one part of the world to another, and often, when conditions are favourable, from the centre to the periphery without caring for what this may mean for whole geographical areas. It should be clear that all this happens because politics seems to be dreadfully behind economics. The latter, already on a global level, finds no adequate response in a political scene more and more embroiled in localism or in centres of power controlled by the economic world. It is no chance that control is permanently in the hands of the multinationals at the centre of the system, while the fringe suffers from the fact that its own concerns are not taken sufficiently into consideration (cf. Soros, S, 58-9). It should be clear, on the basis of what I have tried to show in this study, that I do not hope for a world in which the positions are reversed and the world of politics comes to suffocate that of economics, but neither do I believe that the present situation can continue indefinitely, because an economy left to itself will sooner or later run into disaster.

**IX.10** It is as a result of this that some people have suggested the need to review the tasks and functions of the *International Monetary Fund* and the *World Trade Organisation*, especially because, while there is much talk of free trade and a free market, access to both would seem to be far from free. The problem of loans, of programmes of restructuring, of provision for global well-being (to which no one seems to pay much attention) demand reliable and credible institutions which are capable not only of creating laws of international application, but also have the possibility, without which classical jurists would have termed them feeble efforts, of causing them to be applied, and of imposing sanctions (cf. Soros, S, 59). As the economists of Italy had already observed in the eighteenth century, international political organs should also "revitalise and encourage imagination", with a series of incentives which push people to invest where no one would normally do so, as happens, for example, within many states in relation to their own depressed areas. In this way, that absurd policy of loans which has accompanied the world economy for the last few decades would be avoided. This policy has in the end set aside the fact that, at the centre as at the fringes, nobody any longer assumes objective responsibility, but all retreat behind moral questions which, unfortunately, for many only represent a useless screen and in no way a real question of conscience.

**IX.11** Present international policies also pose problems of a logical kind, which concern the very bases of political legality. For the citizens of a state it may seem difficult to understand why a government, democratically elected, should obey the "abstract" regulation of an international economic organ (like the World Trade Organisation, for instance) which has not received the same explicit and direct consensus as a national political organ. Protectionist policies are certainly unjustifiable, even though they may be lauded by certain reactionary quarters, to respond to such effects, because they only serve to sharpen the divisions and provoke international crises in the long run, apart from impoverishing and isolating the states which apply them (cf. Gundlach, 114 and 116). This demonstrates yet again how unacceptable an anarchico-libertarian policy is, because in its uncertainty it causes risks not only to the economy. The risks are also political, because in order to favour development of any kind it is first necessary above all to foster dialogue, integration and the establishment of certain regulations. The old adage of certainty and reliability of the law, which is with us from the moment that we can begin to talk about civilisation, cannot ever be ignored, even though many rules must be re-written. Without rules, no honest competition will be set in motion, and there is no need to examine the etymology of the exquisite word "compete" in order to realise this.

**IX.12** Examples such as that of the Chinese economic situation confirm what has just been stated. The market economy is not enough in itself to guarantee an effective transformation from a state-driven economy, even though it may be the state which carries out the privatisation. Profound institutional reforms are required, as well as economic ones; these are needed to accelerate the processes of transformation. Without them, even prosperous and active centres such as Shanghai risk being suffocated and "despoiled" by thoughtless action on the part of an old-fashioned and irresponsible local bureaucracy. This obviously depends on an atavistic tradition, but also on the centralism of the monolithic Chinese Communist Party. This is also the key to the explanation of the great corruption which is a feature of states based on strong centralisation of economic decisions. This is why, despite the fact that there is always talk of administrative and financial reform, all this remains an insurmountable taboo in China (cf. Soler-Matutes, 143-5).

**IX.13** It is truly emblematic that states which seem most disposed to carry on international economic activities are those which have long achieved and regulated so-called economic regionalism. As has rightly been observed, and as a confirmation of the view upheld in this study, the collaboration between states operating within a well-defined geographical area is not summed up simply in finding solutions to certain economic needs. What is explicitly sought for is to "embrace the space of politics and security"; in short, there needs to be a reply to the complex problems typical of international relations (cf. Troiani, RE, 11). The expansion of economic regionalism will also tend to have an influence on relations with other states, creating the need for a new political and economic international order. All this will be made necessary by the passage from economic regionalism to economic globalism. Furthermore, if the major economic and financial phenomena "tend to take spaces away from the traditional sovereignty of the states" it is clear that sooner or later the necessity will be felt to find new regulatory systems, first of all by those who feel themselves to be weak in this new scenario (cf. Troiani, RE, 11). All this makes it clear that the present international phenomena, which we might define as economic in the broad sense, are in process of definition, even if some tend to be unaware of that necessity. It is clear that this is the task of politics, which if it were to abdicate from this responsibility, would in the long run compromise any form of economic activity.

**IX.14** So, turning to what Sen describes as so-called *active public intervention*, it must be said that this must be capable of keeping within established limits. It is necessary to make sure that this interventionism does not transform itself into *overactivity of the state*, which can only end in damage to the economy and to individual initiative. But it is also necessary to avoid pre-constituted interests causing a form of *underactivity* which ends up by causing the political sphere to forget the initiatives which it is its duty to undertake (cf. Sen, DF, 127). Somewhat as with blood-pressure, it is necessary to prevent it becoming too high or too low. It is normality which gives health and well-being to the organism, not excess. The outcomes of economic activity are never simply individual (we are not talking about mere gain), but neither are they completely collective or "general". The security which the economic operator enjoys to achieve the maximum reduction of his risks can and should produce advantages, if not for all, at least for a constantly growing number of people – and this is the task of the political sphere. To reclaim land which allows for safer agricultural activity does not bring advantages and revenue only to the agricultural entrepreneur, but also to the whole community which, in terms of health and environment eventually makes use of the general diminution of risks and the elimination of certain diseases.

**IX.15** These considerations convince me more than ever of the value of the basic thesis of this work. I believe that at the basis of the western mentality of the last three centuries there has been a developing misunderstanding which has ended by influencing a large part of the world. Despite what was maintained by quite a few theorists of the eighteenth century, the conviction has grown that to change the socio-political reality it is necessary first to change the economic reality, since the latter is the structure on which the super-structure is built up (this interpretation is the one which, though in different but mutually reflective ways, brings together Smith and Marx). History, however, is showing us that exactly the opposite is true. England, as I have mentioned several times, has been able to undergo the Industrial Revolution after having undergone and consolidated its revolution in rights; and this is how it has always been, in all places. Without the guarantees and the rights, no economic activity is activated. We have deceived ourselves that peace can be viewed as an objective, when in fact it is a precondition, as the ancient and mediaeval classical writers warned us. If politics does not recover dignity and autonomy from economics, we will be living in what Sen calls *dynamic instability*. What we need, on the other hand, is what I have frequently described as *dynamic order*, without which there is no progress, because there is no effective stability recognised by all. We should not forget, either, that when Britain became the first country to realise that it must intervene in the working world in order to regulate the inhuman conditions of workers, above all (but not exclusively), women and children, by introducing laws for the safeguarding of workers and guaranteeing trade union rights, it enabled another phase of great development to take place. Here again it was the initiative of the political sphere which avoided conflicts of the kind which could have sparked off a revolution. It was the so-called superstructure which prevented the crisis or, as some feared, the collapse of the structure. Certainly in many cases some believe that one of the tacit rules of economics is the one which implies that what the artful and cunning do is more convenient than respecting the rules. It is precisely from this that another essential task of politics derives: to carry out checks for conformity to the law on every economic activity. What some refer to as moral instruction, while certainly praiseworthy, cannot be sufficient in itself. To avoid some people getting away with fraud, I prefer to adhere to the judgment *ignorantia legis non excusat* rather than the Socratic judgment that only the ignorant err.

**IX.16** No doubt the notion of a world government capable of guaranteeing the rules, put forward on more than one occasion, may still seem quite utopian. But this backwardness should, I think, be attributed to western economic culture, which – to return to what I said about Smith and Marx, has too long held that the political question was a result of economic action, that in short the "artificial" society, i.e. the political superstructure, derives from the "natural" society, i.e. the economic structure. And yet a world organisation has become a necessity even it is, as Sen claims, premature. However, I am not in agreement with him when he says that much can be done by the International Court of Justice (cf. Sen, G). Not because I do not believe in the crucial role of law, as my study of the *Open Society* abundantly shows, but a law not backed up by the necessary force – legal force, obviously – ends up by being just one of those many good intentions which, as the popular saying puts it, pave the road to hell. In short, without what is erroneously called the superstructure, all the other structures fall in on themselves, suffering a process of involution.

**IX.17** Those who are disciples of Smith and Marx, however different their approaches, have justified their positions by saying that the rules are a consequence of a reality which is poor in consequential logic, in that in human affairs what predominates are the unlooked-for consequences, which are necessarily unpredictable and unintentional. However, as chance would have it, when economic risk is involved, as I have stressed in this chapter, certain unexpected events must be rationalised, and if this does not happen, economic activities cannot take place. Economic returns, without which no economic business is possible, need political stability, juridical certainty, strength of law; in a word, they need rationality and not uncontrollability. Sen rightly says that even if we wish to talk about unlooked-for consequences, this idea is not in any way opposed to the possibility of rational reform (cf. Sen, DF, 257). Many pessimists have spoken, with regard to economic activity, of individual urges due to irrepressible human selfishness. From the first pages of this book, I have preferred to talk about aspirations to well-being and improvement of life, but in these aspirations everything takes place in a framework of legality which, I repeat, is an attempt to rationalise; it is in the interest of all, in the first place and the long run, even if it may seem to be the contrary, of all the economic operators themselves.

**IX.18** To prevent the economy losing control of itself, there are those (cf. Boltanski-Chiapello) who maintain that in the future, structures and organisations which in the past were typical of the workers' movement will perhaps be led to expand and operate in the international world. This also seems due to the fact that since a crisis in the traditional model of social has occurred within the individual states, and above all the most developed ones, a weakening of the union movement has been generated, so that this movement can now find its *raison d'être* only by engaging itself in a much broader field of activity than in the past. Moreover, how is it possible to operate in traditional fashion in an economic situation in which capitalism is profoundly renewed – capitalism, which has passed from the managerial level to the patrimonial level? In the first of these, the objective of the Welfare State involved a logic of alliances between various institutions; in the second, however, there is a supremacy of shareholders with the consequence, as Minc points out, that even the objects of economic policy are changed. It is no longer equality but equity which becomes the fundamental objective of the new capitalist society. All this reconfers on politics a determining role, and revalues it in terms of the position of subjection to which the classic economic writers (and not only they) seemed to want to relegate it.

**IX.19** Again, it has been clear since ancient times and the Middle Ages that *political stability, certainty of law and the efficiency of institutions* favour the conditions for economic development. In fact peace, the expression of these elements, also generated *the spread of culture and the development of minds*. From Dante to Marsilio, passing through Ockham, this was quite a widespread conviction, proved by the fact that the flowering of academies and centres of study aided this development which prepared the technological leap of the Renaissance. In this era, commercial expansion and European policy towards the Indian Ocean and the east of Asia was possible because in those regions total political chaos reigned, which caused these ancient civilisations to regress (cf. Landes, ch. IV and VI); not to mention the fact that in the latter, there is no neat separation between the political and religious spheres, such as we find, on the contrary, in the whole history of the West, despite the fact that there have been various periods when the spiritual has attempted to override the temporal and vice versa. This separation usually disappears, or leads one power to succumb in relation to the other, when civil coexistence, tolerance, certainty of the rules and equity in applying them fail. All this not only generates uncertainty, but leads to living by expedients, and in a climate of widespread lack of confidence, increases risks and dulls minds.

**IX.20** The risks also decrease when the infrastructure is allowed to improve and render itself adequate to the degree of development that a nation has reached. Landes rightly holds that the Industrial Revolution developed in Britain because here there was timely attention to the efficiency of transport and the agricultural marketing system. Moreover, in contrast to what happened in other states, the British agricultural sector was not a bastion of conservatism. Similarly to ancient Rome (cf. ch. II), communications and (as Varro would have said) rationalisation of agriculture were conditions of development. To this were also added selection and competence of personnel, encouragement of initiative and competition, guarantee of rights, contracts, savings and investments, personal freedom and the possibility of defending oneself against abuse, and all the rest takes place of its own accord (cf. Landes, ch. XV).

# X. CONCLUSION OF THE WORK?

**X.1** In his famous treatise on the purpose of work, Jeremy Rifkin, in reviving some very acute reflections by Peter F. Drucker, maintains that the disappearance of the way of understanding work in the classical sense – i.e. in relation to production – is the critical unresolved question of modern capitalist societies, to such an extent that it is even possible to speak of a new type of unemployed person. From the productive level to that of services, there is no difference in the problem; indeed it seems even to be aggravated. We have only to think of what has happened and is happening in a city like New York, somewhat similar to other cities of the world which possess a developed third sector, where all repetitive services, and sometimes more complex ones too, are increasingly entrusted to machines. The actual work carried out in the commercial centres is running the risk of becoming more and more obsolete, given the diversifying of the systems of supply and sale. But Rifkin adds, quite clearly, that it is up to us to render our future absolutist, utopian (no less dangerous an aspect) or characterised by solidarity, as can be seen from the four final chapters of Part V. In order to save advanced society from a sure collapse, the commercial forces of the market will have to be tempered by the forces of solidarity characteristic of an effectively enlightened society. So we need to keep in mind that, if one of the trends of the present-day economy is that of seeing a reduction in the costs of production that can be attributed to intense labour in the classic sense, work in the context of solidarity demands calculations that are not always equal to those of a common economic activity; calculations which have some positive aspects, despite what some writers have maintained. In fact, not only does it enable many individuals to rediscover the sense of a common destiny which binds us together as a species, but it also seems to wipe out the myth of technocracy, which as Veblen pointed out in his well-known work, risked conferring an almost dictatorial power on the technicians. However this may be, the road of solidarity seems to be the only one possible if we want to avert the explosion of the planet. At the end of the thirteenth chapter of the work in question, Rifkin presents a clear alternative which should be available to all human beings who have any kind of political responsibility. Never has humanity been in a position to produce the present volume of goods and services which it can today, though by making use of a work force which is steadily diminishing. The more production increases, the more work diminishes. Demographic pressures, but other factors also, demand, if we think in traditional terms, the creation of 700 million jobs in the next decade. Geopolitics is not a fantasy but a brutal reality; we need the courage to think of the good of all, of what was once called the common good, if we do not want social dialogue to return to the law of the jungle.

**X.2** According to Rifkin, making the world more politically stable fends off certain tendencies typical of the era of so-called *Food Technology* (to paraphrase the title of a famous review belonging to this sector). While it is in fact true that many spices and products typical of the area of the world which suffer from unstable, climatically uncertain and scientifically retarded factors, can be obtained at low cost in laboratories, it is also true that once the above factors have been brought under control, new life can be given to traditional agriculture, obviously if supported by sufficient technology. If things do not move in this direction, growing instability will be created not only at international level, but also within the individual national communities, because we shall reach the point of having members of the same society who do not participate in the various benefits of the same economic system. When the sense of solidarity is lost, the sense of belonging also collapses, and individuals no longer identify themselves with the society in which they are living. The consequent social disintegration ends by damaging everyone. Perhaps because of this, Rifkin reminds us of the attempt undertaken by certain Japanese firms which tend towards binding their workers to them for the whole of the working lives.

**X.3** Social disintegration would bring growing uncertainty, from which many think that they can escape by retreating into the fortress of their own egoism. To lock oneself up in such a fortress in order to guarantee privileges and exclude others from every possible share in them could be the dangerous – though ultimately useless – temptation for some. In a more and more global reality, no one can claim to be fully secure in an insecure world: there are no more impregnable fortresses. The sharing of riches could help us to make notable steps forward, and it could stimulate the opportunity to create new work from non-work. This is not just a play on words. If it is true that the quantity of free time available is increasing for a growing number of people, helping to fill up this free time intelligently could create a large number of opportunities. We could have a great development of the so-called "leisure industry", if it is true – and it is – that the complete satisfaction of the human spirit is virtually impossible, not to mention, obviously, the dangerous contradictions which Rosmini already pointed out as possible outcomes of such satisfaction (see ch. VI). It has never been possible in history to speak of *industry as entertainment*, as we can today. Certainly we need to call in question the actual life styles and the many moral questions which are linked to it; for example the manner of investment of resources which are increasingly managed by a restricted number of individuals.

**X.4** The national states are demonstrating their incapacity to resolve certain problems because the economic stakes are proving greater than they are. This incapacity runs the risk of giving rise to perilous perfectionist utopias capable of causing leaps in the dark. As Rosmini warned, we need to have the humility not to seek for definitive solutions even if we need to commit ourselves to the way of progressive and secure betterment. To seek for possible solutions we need to consider the fact that at least in the economic and social spheres, no one possesses real solutions in absolute form (cf. Drucker, 109 ff.) Basic concepts of policy, ranging from participation to incentives, need to be re-discussed. The latter need to be rediscovered in order to urge people to those activities to which no one is any longer paying due attention.

## XI. THE STRENGTH OR WEAKNESS OF THE CHINESE ECONOMIC SYSTEM?

**XI.1** Despite what quite a few economists maintain, the conviction grew that the economic system had to be changed before changing the social and political one, since the economic system was the superstructure on which the latter was based. Smith and Marx have this interpretation in common in different but symmetrical ways. History, however, is proving precisely the opposite. England had her industrial revolution after consolidating the revolution in rights without whose guarantee she could not have implemented any economic initiative. Peace, based on rights, must be a precondition for development, as the classic ancient and medieval writers warned. The political world, in rediscovering its dignity, must, therefore, make an effort to bring about those preconditions without which true development is not possible. From what has been called congenital instability it is necessary to move on to a *dynamic order*, without which no progress can be assured.

**XI.2** Political institutions have the duty to reduce the climate of uncertainty that can call into question the success of economic action, while seeking not to encourage encroachments on other spheres. Uncertainty is inherent in human existence and is one of the components of our daily life. This is why financial institutions have been created – insurance for example – which operate directly in terms of the nature of risk. This is further proof of the fact that anarchical-libertarian positions are unacceptable in the economy. By their very nature they pose risks not just to the economy. It must be quite clear that in this situation there is absolutely no desire to allow politics to take unfair advantage of the economy or prevail over it. That would be harmful. The only wish is that each area should work towards its objective in harmony with the other.

### 1. A giant with feet of clay

**XI.3** Some distinguished experts ask themselves why Chinese state capitalism continues to grow so rapidly as to threaten geopolitical and hegemonic balances, disregarding that democracy which, in the opinion of many, has to be a characteristic of capitalism itself. I believe that this perplexity is unfounded. At other times, throughout ancient and recent history, the state has had a preponderant role in economic activities with results that have turned out to be catastrophic in the long run. This had already happened in ancient Rome when the "liberal" system of exchange and production, based on private law, gave way to an economic one that was increasingly controlled by the state. As has already been observed, this was one of the reasons for the crisis of the western Empire, and it has hardly been assessed. The colossus gradually revealed its feet of clay and ended up by being a little researched crisis model. Further study would be still be useful today to bring us closer to a better comprehension of phenomena such as the Chinese one.

**XI.4** The omnipotence of the state, the systematic control of every activity and an administration that was, to say the least, paternalistic, led to the gradual eclipse of the fortunes of private individuals. To this can be added increasing taxation as well as sea and land hazards as regards transport which helped to strengthen that climate of suspicion that penalized the economic freedom that had led to ancient prosperity. Over time, the guarantees offered by the central power turned out to be pious illusions. There was also the problem of the monetary crisis, since the various emperors began to alter the value of the currency (cf. points II.35 and II.36). From the silver standard, they moved to one of a partial silver content with a consequent alteration of its real value and the beginning of inflation. It must be recalled that this flow of silver towards China and the Indies, also involved the United Kingdom, as Marx himself recalls in *Capital*. This not only led to exchanges: it was also the cause of so-called loan capital.

**XI.5** Returning to the ancient world, it should be pointed out that trade with the entire Asian continent, from the Russia of today to China and from Sumatra to Indochina, privileged Roman support for India where free ports existed. Obviously, exchange took place through the use of precious metals. As Braudel reminds us, according to what Pliny the Elder said Rome lost millions of sesterces every year in trade with the East. Further proof of this is the fact that Roman coins are still found quite frequently in India today. This was only the beginning of a continual haemorrhage of precious metals that would strike Europe in various moments of her history, demonstrating her weakness (cf. Braudel, CM, 3, 17 and 615).

**XI.6** According to Strabon, trade with India through the Red Sea became almost a regular practice. This is even shown on the maps. The *Tabula Peutingeriana*, with its interesting annotations, should not be forgotten. These show that commercial exchanges were not at all occasional (cf. points II.30 ff.). Certainly the *pax romana* guaranteed all of this but nothing could resist the rigid rules of the monetary crisis. The expenditure of precious metals, which ended up in eastern coffers, led to a progressive loss of real wealth on the part of the buyers. To overcome the crisis, people thought of changing the alloy of coins but a currency that became in fact of lower value brought about an increase in prices and, what counts the most, a staggering increase in the public debt, as the state took over from private individuals in economic and commercial activities. As Pliny had occasion to complain: "every year, India takes no fewer than 50 million sesterces away from the Roman Empire" (Pliny, VI, 23, 26).

## 2. Analogies with the case of China

**XI.7** There are those who say that the development of China is due to the way socialism has developed as compared to what took place in Eastern Europe. The Chinese Communist Party brought about a true genetic "mutation" rather than managing the transition, as took place in other Communist countries. The far-sightedness of Deng Xiaoping was purportedly responsible for this (cf. Coase–Wang). The fact remains, however, that despite the supposed far-sightedness of some Communist leaders, China still has a significant number of typically Communist points of view or, whatever the case, those of a constructivist state. The *first* is that of pursuing a policy of power whose nature is typically totalitarian. The *second* is that a monopolistic conception of public property persists, despite all the purported openings up to the market. The *third* is that there is an almost total absence of any discussion of human rights and dissent, an almost total absence of debate on ideas – an issue which more than any other will end up by harming development in the long run.

**XI.8** It should be recalled that as far back as the 1970s "the new political leadership placed emphasis on economic development without allowing ideological considerations to interfere directly (seeking truth in the facts – said Teng at the eleventh Convention) and returning to the procedures of more organic planning" (Salvini, 78-79). This meant that the new Chinese ruling class intended to give more leeway to the economic system given the contradictions that had characterized the Maoist era (cf. Salvini, 84). The national party conferences "aimed at analysing the various problems of the sectors, all insisted on the principle that what is favourable to development of production was favourable to the revolution" (Salvini, 79). The new party leaders thereby intended to consolidate their positions, fighting against the more radical wing of the party (referred to as the Gang of Four) and promoting more moderate figures from the past, such as Teng Hsiao-ping. As Mao had done, he, too, when neutralizing his opponents, took care to create a group of possible successors (cf. Chang, 1-21).

**XI.9** The relationships between politics and economics were thereby turned upside down, privileging the principle according to which "the struggle for production prevails over the class struggle (*The Peoples' Daily*, 12 December 1977)" (Salvini, 79). There was a return to incentives that old-style propaganda would have called typically revisionist, since "the motivation of farmers and workers was shifting (…) material incentives were being favoured over ideological ones" (Salvini, 73). More than a paradox, this approach makes clearer "the dual nature of the eastern revolution – a love-hate relationship with the capitalistic West, the will to reject modernity coupled with a strong desire to wrest away from the invaders the secret of their power, etc. – as well as the objectively ambivalent nature of their results" (Pellicani, 88, note 73). This is why, on the one hand, great efforts were made on behalf of an industrial leap forward, and, on the other, incentives were provided for craftsmen and farmers, on whom the Chinese economy had always been based. However, these activities continued to take place under the direction of the bureaucratic apparatus (cf. Apter).

### 3. State Capitalism

**XI.10** In China, as far as labour is concerned, it should be recalled that "the party reduces its price by means of jails, immediate conquest, for anyone who might have the bad idea of going on strike". This has been one of the reasons – but not the only one – for growth, which, in various periods, has also surprised the West. It is not the only one because another aspect deserves analysis: investments made by the Chinese government are made more quickly than any other interventionist measure. The goals of private individuals need time to be carefully assessed and to gain the confidence of banks. In contrary fashion "despotism can quickly collect an enormous sum of capital and use it as it likes". Furthermore, the party, which sings the praises of equality, favours "a wider range of incomes than in any other place in Asia" (Alvi, 8 ff.).

**XI.11** Despite this policy, Chinese state capitalism does not escape some of the basic rules of capitalism, such as dealing with the data supplied by Western banks, and not only that. As confirmation of what von Mises maintains, the Chinese banks themselves depend on what happens on the American stock exchange; "the accumulation game" and periodic injections of capital are the result. In other words, a Chinese bureaucrat must engage in financial calculation with a high degree of rigour in programming production. This is indeed based on basic data which depend on capital, income, profits, costs, yields, expenses, savings, etc. If the Chinese economy were to close itself off, financial calculation would be absolutely impossible since in a planned economy (cf. von Mises, S, II/5 § 3 and II/6 § 2) – as history has amply demonstrated – everything becomes bogged down in bureaucratic inefficiency which costs much more than it should. The only things that increase are expenses. Socialist policy is the decisive factor in public expenditure; socialist needs govern tax policy; and in the socialist programme itself public finances come more and more to the forefront as socialists (bureaucrats) claim that the greater the taxation the better (cf. von Mises, S, V/34 § 7). Under real socialism one goes from the reign of liberty to that of taxation. This aspect is all the more evident in the Chinese tradition, where, for example, the Mandarins have claimed that "banks were not commercial institutions in China, but tools of political economy set up by the party" (Alvi, 14).

**XI.12** As Luca Fantacci pointed out in a carefully examined review in *L'Indice*: "Capitalism has shown itself to be better than Communism in making all people more equal". Rather than equality, one should speak of standardization and not forget that a similar "danger" of uniformity (standardization) inherent in capitalism had already been posited by a significant number of thinkers. What ought perhaps to be emphasized is that *both economic systems have* given rise to *aristocracies avid for gain who forget the most basic rules of social coexistence in order to make profits.* It must, indeed, be pointed out "all capital, western included, (…) has been perverted and denatured by the accumulation of wealth by capitalism (…) However, are the mad speculative ventures of the West more moral than the schemes and disputes among the Mandarins of the Mao dynasty?" (Alvi, 17). It is the system that has lost its foundations and this is typical of periods of transition.

**XI.13** In the light of all this, it is quite understandable that "the industrious Mandarins (…) in *China Can Say No* took heart and called the western notions of democracy and rights a demonic expedient to weaken China and subvert national unity". Moreover, the two economic systems are now so intertwined that they cannot harm each other to more than to a certain degree. If, in fact, "the West has turned the private debt of banks into a public debt to a degree that goes against any form of decency (…) the Chinese East finds itself with two trillion in reserves and possibilities for investments" (Alvi, 172-173 and 22). These figures are unimaginable in the West. These numbers are, for the most part, aimed at both internal and international investments. Although China is a latecomer, she seems to have discovered the political economy of Lord Keynes. It is quite curious – according to what *The Economist* points out – that in the last few years a debate has been underway among Chinese Communist Party leaders and their economists on the economic views of Keynes and Hayek on the very problem of investments (cf. Cox). Those of the English economist are considered by some as inadequate investments because, among other things, they are too "easily obtained". The ease of investing would bring any entrepreneur to imagine ambitious and often not highly remunerative investments. In other words, the orientation was towards "bad" investments that could conceal other aims.

**XI.14** Aside from the considerations of von Hayek that are in some ways debatable, the fact remains that in the East, as in the West, "capitalism has become more and more intertwined with the state, in the poor as well as the rich countries". This is shown by the fact that it is the "foreign policy" of a country like China, at least in the economic area, that demonstrates that it is in the interest of the state to display a different face at the cultural level to ensure a certain penetration in some markets and areas of important strategic value. The rediscovery of a thinker like Sun Tzu, considered a master of the *art of soft power*, fully demonstrates this. This thinker, of whom Mao "was a great fan", demonstrates that a policy of detente towards the enemy may in the final analysis be more effective than armed conflict (cf. 'Sun Tzu and the Art of Soft Power', in *The Economist*, 17 December 2011). For this reason, policy based on the *art of soft power* seems, for some time, to have become a priority of the "new" party which has become increasingly convinced that the greatest forms of excellence must never seek conflict "because the commencement of the battle signifies a political failure". For this reason, the Central Committee of the Chinese Communist Party has believed that only an *art of soft power* can ensure *conspicuous gains*. The watchword seems to have become "harmonise", a term, which, naturally, has no value for internal dissent.

**XI.15** This is obviously yet another attempt at state capitalism which returns to ancient wisdom to find political legitimacy. It is certainly interesting that Sun Tzu is the only great name in ancient Chinese culture who managed to survive Communist changes in a climate in which a figure such as Confucius created problems. Mao, indeed, considered his philosophy a sort of ideology for the ancient feudal system, one which had to be destroyed because it was seen as an obstacle to the development of Communism. Instead, by applying an *art of soft power*, it was surely easier to attack and defeat the economic strategy of the enemy ('Sun Tzu and the Art of Soft Power', in *The Economist*, 17 December 2011). Henry Kissinger himself (cf. Kissinger), in his book *On China*, speaks of having been struck by ancient Chinese wisdom which seems, indeed, to have dictated a winning strategy to the modern Chinese.

**XI.16** This Chinese wisdom has diversified China's state capitalism from what was once adopted from the USSR. Differently from the Soviets, the Chinese *do not engage in ideological aggression towards the outside world.* Nonetheless, they feel that they are a superpower and they have increased their current military expenditure considerably; indeed to a far greater degree than the United States and, obviously, Europe. Their purpose, at least the present one, is to keep the USA away from their geographical sphere of influence, and from crises in their relations with Taiwan, even if they do not desire these. Even though they do not reach the point of worrying an indolent West, actions of that sort are the subject of strong concern on the part of South Korea and Japan, as well as India and Australia (cf. 'China's Military Rise', in *The Economist*, 7 April 2012). This new confirmation of a fluid situation is not always easy to interpret.

**XI.17** While all of this has aspects, which for some may seem positive for international balances, one also must watch out for others such as "corruption, the exchange of favours between politics and business, the formation of a co-opted elite not based on merit and, above all, brutal practices to keep away from business those who do not have protection" (cf. Taino). The Chinese model, which can mean all this, has many imitators on a more or less concealed similar point. The result of this could give rise to an "anomalous" form of capitalism. Out of this could come an economic system that "rewarded oligarchies, increased income thereby leading to the destruction of capital, that is labour" (cf. Taino). Obviously, there is a need to add new and ancient dimensions, starting with moral ones, and this naturally encounters considerable resistance (cf. Giraud–Renouard) which seem those most lacking today and hence all the more necessary. If this road is not taken, there could be serious hazards. The state would, in fact, acquire a conservative function and not one of providing guarantees or stimulation. It would end up by ensuring and protecting the privileges of dominating oligarchies that are no longer capable of renewing themselves.

**XI.18** Some scholars have appropriately spoken of a China little inclined towards the inclusion of those many who do not take part in the life of a tightly closed political system (cf. Acemoglu – Robinson). This all leads to a not insignificant danger for future growth. There are a great many, indeed, who feel excluded and decide to go abroad for the sake of growth and development. Requests for an "immigrant visa", especially for the USA, are increasing appallingly and the result is a brain and capital drain. This should give food for thought to those who see Chinese development as something that is miraculous. Years ago, the same happened for the USSR. In 1961 Samuelson believed that the Soviet world would surpass the United States in gross domestic product by the end of the century. Yet that world collapsed miserably before the end of the century. It might be added that a state of that nature would end up being all the richer and all the more conservative. This is why China's two trillion in reserves and the possibility of investing in that country should at least make us think. Furthermore, the phenomenon is destined to assume far greater proportions, so that China's history will be more and more linked to our own, overthrowing that commonplace – typical of the entire West – of a country "outside history". The role of being a super power, which is performed with increasing aggressiveness, causes this state capitalism to meddle with another form that is now worn out and dispirited. Such interference is reaching the point of directing the policies of multinationals towards a position of conflict with the policy of those states which once operated in them and felt protected by their structures.

**XI.19** The result is what some might consider an actual mutation of the species. Classical capitalism, which according to Smith derived support from an almost providential, invisible hand, now finds support in what could be called *the visible hand*. The market itself, according to the definition of Jan Bremmer, is becoming a means to political ends. State capitalism, therefore, has become an inseparable and crucial element in contemporary geopolitical and economic phenomena; it is, in other words, an effect of globalization (cf. *The visible Hand*, in *The Economist*, 21 January 2012). On the contrary, is it possible to allow only private entities to manage policies, such as those concerning energy? In these cases, starting from oil policy in some countries, and not just the developing ones, the effective expression *petrostate capitalism* has been coined. The true danger, to be sure, is that only a new elite made up of a new generation of managers operating in the public sector will manage energy policy or, in any case, state capitalism. There is the danger of an anti-democratic negative tendency, as is in fact happening in significant number of countries, a sort of disguised authoritarianism – "a Leviathan as a minority" (cf. 'Theme and Variations', in *The Economist*, 21 January 2012). There is an oligarchy that is beyond internal and international control.

**XI.20** What has been described up to this point seems the fulfilment of a prophecy. Proudhon's criticism of Marxism appears to be borne out here. This sort of communism, changed into a form of state capitalism, became the ideological support of a China which seems to have found the theorem for power politics, the enhancement of the wealth of the state and centralized policies all at the same time. Is change in this state of affairs imaginable? Will China evolve in the direction of genuinely democratic approaches? Various answers might be given to that question but one premiss, in my opinion, cannot be avoided: if, as many people say, *the most powerful capital of a nation is its culture, it must not be forgotten that this is conditioned by this culture.* The problem is more serious because of a consideration that too many people tend to forget: Chinese aristocratic politics is not just the fruit of a party structure. The Chinese Communist Party has also had a military character – such was the Maoist vision – which has conditioned it for several decades, making it all the more sclerotic and monolithic, indeed, almost impermeable to outside impulses.

**XI.21** This consideration is located within a precise cultural tradition. As Braudel wondered, will China succeed in shaking off its Mandarin tradition? If not, everything will end up in the hands of the central power, variously interpreted, as happened in the second half of the sixteenth century when the Emperor Quianlong had his favourite minister Heshen killed and then confiscated his possessions (cf. Braudel, CM, 3, 53 and 62). Furthermore, China has often been politically aggressive – as have other empires – when politically strong. At the end of the seventeenth century, China tried to block Russian expansion and, in the following century, expelled Russian merchants several times from Beijing. The same commercial rivalry was to manifest itself with India as time passed (cf. Braudel, CM, 3, 578 and 634). It would perhaps be too obvious to recall that China, as Marx himself reminded us, exports more labour than any other country in the world because of the influence of its enormous population, and this gives it considerable weight at a worldwide level.

**XI.22** Furthermore, the diversity of the Indian merchants, as with their Russian counterparts, influenced the level of accumulation of wealth and the creation of those "castes" which, in India, would manage, despite exposure to forms of extortion and other dangers, to partially oppose the political power they supported and receive protection in return. Despite this sense of entrenchment, the Chinese, with the mentality typical of a great power, ever since the fifteenth century have never renounced far-off expeditions (cf. Braudel, CM, 3, 652 and 663). To do this, they anticipated that internal standardization which in the West only the recent consumers' society seems to have managed to achieve. John Stuart Mill had already discovered this danger to ancient oriental civilisation, a danger that could infect the entire world. This culture had progressively fought against individuality at all levels, thereby depriving humanity of that fruitful juxtaposition of mutual qualities and defects that leads to real progress. It is typical of Chinese tradition *to impress* a sort of wisdom or design for perfection (*upon every mind in the community*) and grant important positions "to those who have succeeded in assimilating that wisdom". This all appears to the Chinese to be *the secret of human progressiveness.* They have all become equal in the way they regulate their own thoughts. Even the educational system tends to confirm this cultural view (cf. Stuart Mill, OL, 80), and everyone knows how important academic freedom was to John Stuart Mill!

**XI.23** Up to that point, it had been the diversity of characters and cultures that had ensured the effective superiority of Europe. There was a great variety of paths, each of which led to something that was valuable. Yet Europe was "decidedly advancing towards the Chinese ideal of making all people alike". This subject had been anticipated by Tocqueville, in whose opinion, as Mill pointed out, the French of his day were far more similar to one another than those of the preceding generation, In the United Kingdom, as well, that variety was diminishing with every passing day. Such was the process characterized by the phrase "assimilation is still proceeding". It seemed that this development was unstoppable since all the same things were being read, listened to, and seen (cf. Stuart Mill, OL, 81). True public opinion was increasingly absent and this was spreading conformism. It would become steadily more difficult to oppose abuses and injustice. Everything that tried to free itself from standardization would become impious and almost monstrous (cf. Stuart Mill, OL, 82). Mill was a prophet for a world which does not seem to be aware any longer of the dangerous grip of such assimilation.

**XI.24** The concerns of the English philosopher went beyond mere cultural phenomena. The problem became political and economic – and with far-reaching consequences. He was more than convinced that every increase in functions attributed to the government was an increase in its power, both in the form of authority and, even more, in direct influence (cf. Stuart Mill, PPE, 328). Here, the danger, at least for the future, no longer concerned only China, whose model, indeed, seemed contagious, but the entire world, even liberal England. This was tantamount to saying that Mill's economic view certainly cannot be said to be an anarchic and liberal one of belief in an uncontrolled market. He well knew the importance of the political action of government and the benefits that could be obtained on behalf of the economy (cf. Stuart Mill, PPE, 366 ff.) but he maintained that the criterion of limits for all moving forces was the only guarantee.

### 4. A precedent of not so long ago

**XI.25** In National-Socialist Germany the economic system was similarly reduced to a form of state capitalism. Certainly the starting premises were different and Hitler secured the support of industrialists such as Fritz Thyssen but also that of small shopkeepers. The latter, who had at the outset been one of the most valuable sources of support of the party, were the first to be ruined and reduced to the ranks of salaried workers. Management of the German economic system passed totally into the hands of the state. The difficult economic situation of the 1920s was overcome and this bestowed unexpected prestige on Hitler himself. From six million unemployed, the number fell to less than one. Between 1932 and 1937 production increased 102%. The entire system of production was set in motion and Germany "seemed like a great beehive". Extensive public works and government credit (cf. Shirer, 357 and ff.) secured what could be called the German *New Deal*. This was all facilitated by another characteristic that is typical of highly centralized systems: general mobilization. In some ways it was precisely this that ensured the German economic recovery. It was an anticipation of what John Maynard Keynes was to make famous shortly afterwards with the concept of *deficit spending*: the creation of jobs through state orders. Public works, such as the building of motorways, and consumption for everyone, such as the "people's car" (*Volkswagen*), revived an economic system that had seemed to be in an irretrievable crisis. In this period – applying enlightened arguments – Keynes explained the profits of unproductive companies in terms of the building of pyramids or, simply, forms of earth moving (cf. Nolte, IV/8). Departing from different assumptions, Hitler aimed at the same ends.

**XI.26** Nazism, and particularly its leader, succeeded in communicating to Germany, then putting into practice, a simple idea: the German problem "around 1930 was not the lack of development, but improper use of its productive apparatus, hence employment of its workers". For some time, the Soviets had directed their attention towards the apparatus of production. Lenin had been "fascinated by the example of the *German war* economy" which had been disciplined as if it were a veritable army. This was to become characteristic of the Stalinist and then the Chinese economies. At the end of the

First World War, influenced by the German example, Soviet leaders applied the war economy to internal civil strife and then pursued it as a universalist ideology which saw itself as continually threatened (cf. Nolte, IV/8). In this perspective it is understandable why German workers, as is the case in all totalitarian systems, became cogs in the wheel of the system, veritable "serfs (...) increasingly tied to their jobs", directed not by just any boss, but by the state which "did not allow the individual to do things his own way". In return, workers had their jobs secured, but no other guarantee. German workers had "unions, collective contracts and the right to strike taken away". These organizations were replaced by *The Workers' Front* which was not independent in any way and strictly controlled by the Nazi system (cf. Shirer, 362 ff.).

**XI.27** As Fichte had foreseen, socialism, in its phase of development and rebirth, united with national socialism. Economic activity eventually fell under the control of the state which was said to be able to manage it better than anyone else because it was "rationally constituted" and, therefore, more capable of identifying the general problems facing individual economic operators. Only the state, in this approach, could place limits and impose methods for the trading of goods. Only this *super partes* prime mover could limit international conditioning effects through its constructivist ability to plan economic life and direct the various productive activities. This all came from a conviction typical of centralized systems: the possibility of organizing economic activity *by basing it rationally on philosophical and scientifically incontestable schemata.* This is what the Chinese system believes in and does today.

# XII. APPENDICES
## I

**XII.1** The reproduction on this page dates from 1974. It refers to a beermat found in one of the beer-halls of the West Berlin, obviously before the fall of the wall which divided the city during the years of the cold war. I believe this design is a good summing-up of what I said in the first chapter, and have re-asserted several times in this work, about the irrepressible aspiration towards well-being that leads humankind to overcome every obstacle. The most important thing is that everything should take place within the rules, and not to the detriment of others.

## II

**XII.2** Recently the Italian minister Tremonti has maintained that in order to give greater value to the European currency and avoid the growth of inflation, it would be more appropriate to make use of the one euro bill. I wonder how it is possible that experts of this kind only think of certain solutions *a posteriori*. I had similar doubts three years earlier, as this letter which I wrote to *The Economist* witnesses.

*Dear Sir,*
*I have been a reader of your esteemed journal, an acknowledged authority in its field, for many years. For this reason, I would like to put before you two considerations, which may seems a little naive or even banal, on the European currency which will begin to circulate in continental Europe as from next year. 1) Do you think that instead of a wallet, we will rather have to return for our day-to-day expenditures to a money-bag for coinage, since the smallest banknote will be one of 5 euros? In Italy, there will no longer be anything corresponding to the 1000, 2000 and 5000 notes, but in other countries of the EU too, much the same consideration will apply. Possibly the devisers of the smallest of the future denominations have made the assumption that there will be an initial and galloping inflation? 2) Despite the fact that the Euro has had a reference value which conferred on it parity with the dollar, and which in Italy was equivalent to 1936,27 lire (well-known to everyone – see the attached receipt), the recognised effective exchange rate of the most important financial centres of the world is at the moment a great deal higher (today it is above 200 lire to one euro). Is this not a further symptomatic sign of a forthcoming, and anticipated inflation?*
*With best wishes. Yours sincerely*
*Rocco Pezzimenti*

In reply I had this very brief but polite acknowledgment:

*9.5.01.*

*Dear Dr. Pezzimenti,*
*The editor thanks you for your recent letter, which has been passed to the appropriate person.*
*Thank you for having taken the trouble to write.*

*(in the editor's office)*

# WORKS CITED

ACEMOGLU D. - ROBINSON J., *Why Nations Fail: The Origins of Power, Prosperity and Poverty*, Profile Books, London, 2012.

ALBERT M., *Capitalisme contre capitalisme*, Éditions du Seuil, Paris, 1991.

ALFIERI V., *La partita doppia applicata alle scritture delle antiche aziende mercantili veneziane*, presentata da Antonio Fazio, Edizioni Studium, Roma, 1994. Ristampa anastatica dell'edizione del 1891 edita da G. B. Paravia.

ALVI G., *Il capitalismo. Verso l'ideale cinese*, Marsilio, Venezia, 2011.

ANDREAU J., *Declino e morte dei mestieri bancari nel Mediterraneo occidentale (II-IV sec. d. C.)*, in Aa. Vv. (a cura di A. Giardina), *Società romana e Impero tardoantico*, vol. I, *Istituzioni, ceti, economie*, Editori Laterza, Roma-Bari, 1986.

APTER D., *Political Religion in New States,* in C. GEERTZ (Ed. by), *Old Societies and New States. The Quest for Modernity in Asia and Africa*, The Free Press, New York, 1963.

BAGGIO A. M., *Capitalismo ed «etica cattolica». Osservazioni sull'interpretazione della dottrina sociale cristiana di Richard Neuhaus e Michael Novak*, in *Nuova Umanità*, anno XVII, n. 102, 1995.

BALBI DE CARO S., *La banca a Roma*, Vita e costumi dei romani antichi, Collana promossa dal *Museo della Civiltà Romana*, n. 8, Edizioni Quasar, Roma, 1989.

BAZZICHI O., *Alle origini dello spirito del capitalismo*, Edizioni Dehoniane, Roma, 1991.

BECK U., "Benvenuti nel mondo del rischio", in *Reset*, Settembre-Ottobre 2000, n°. 62.

BOLTANSKI L. - CHIAPELLO E., *Le nouvel esprit du capitalisme*, Gallimard, Paris, 1999.

BRAUDEL F., *Civilisation matérielle, économie et capitalisme XVe-XVIIIe*, 1. *Les structures du quotidien,* Librairie Armand Colin, Paris, 1979.

BRAUDEL F., *Civilisation matérielle, économie et capitalisme XVe-XVIIIe*, 2. *Les jeux de l'échange*, Librairie Armand Colin, Paris, 1979.

BRAUDEL F., *Civilisation matérielle, économie et capitalisme XVe-XVIIIe*, 3. *Le temps du monde*, Librairie Armand Colin, Paris, 1979.

BRAUDEL F., *La dynamique du capitalisme*, Les Éditions Arthaud, Paris, 1985.

BRAUDEL F., *Introduzione all'edizione italiana*, di I. Wallerstein, *The Modern World-System I. Capitalist Agriculture and the Origins of the European World-Economy in the Sixteenth Century*, New York, Academic Press, 1974, tr. it., Società editrice il Mulino, Bologna, 1978.

BRENTANO L., *Le origini del capitalismo*, Sansoni Editore, Firenze, 1978. The reference is to two essays which appeared in *Der wirtschaftende Mensch in der Geschichte*, Lipsia, 1923; the page numbers refer to the Italian edition.

BRUNI L., "Verso una razionalità economica 'capace di comunione'", in Aa. Vv., *Economia di comunione*, a cura di Luigino Bruni, Città Nuova Editrice, Roma, 2000.

CARACCIOLO A., *Introduzione* a F. Galiani, *Della moneta*, Giangiacomo Feltrinelli Editore, Milano, 1963.

CARAVALE M., *Gli ordinamenti giuridici dell'Europa medievale*, Società editrice il Mulino, Bologna, 1994.

CARROZZI L., *Introduzione* a Augustini (Sancti), *Epistolae, Supplemento (1\* - 29\*)*, in *Opera Omnia*, vol. XXIII/A, Città Nuova Editrice, Roma, 1992.

CAVALLI A. e PERUCCHI L., *Introduzione* a Simmel G., *Philosophie des Geldes*, Duncker & Humblot, Berlin, 1977, tr. it., *Filosofia del denaro*, a cura di A. Cavalli e L. Perucchi, U.T.E.T., Torino, 1984.

CHAFUEN A. A., *Christians for Freedom. Late-Scholastic Economics*, Ignatius Press, San Francisco, 1986.

CHANG P. H., *Chinese Politics: Deng's Turbulent Quest*, in "Problems of Communism", Vol. XXX, 1981, n°. 1.

CIARROCCHI B., MARTIN A., PAROLI L., PATTERSON H., *Produzione e circolazione di ceramiche tardoantiche e altomedievali*, in L. Paroli e P. Delogu (a cura di), *La storia economica di Roma nell'Alto Medioevo alla luce dei recenti scavi archeologici*, Atti del Seminario, Roma 2 – 3 aprile, 1992, Edizioni All'Insegna del Giglio, Firenze, 1993.

CICERO M. T., *De Officiis*, in *Opere Politiche e Filosofiche*, vol. I, a cura di L. Ferrero e N. Zorzetti, U.T.E.T., Torino, 1974.

CIMINO R. M. (Edited by), *Ancient Rome and India. Commercial and Cultural Contacts between the Roman World and India*, Munshiram Manoharlal Publishers Pvt. Ltd., New Delhi, 1994.

COASE R. – WANG N., *How China Became Capitalist*, Palgrave, London, 2012.

COCCIA S., *Il "Portus Romae" fra tarda antichità e Alto Medioevo*, in L. Paroli e P. Delogu (a cura di), *La storia economica di Roma nell'Alto Medioevo alla luce dei recenti scavi archeologici*, Atti del Seminario, Roma 2 – 3 aprile, 1992, Edizioni All'Insegna del Giglio, Firenze, 1993.

COX S., *Il pendolo dell'economia va da Keynes a Hayek*, in "La Stampa", 24 dicembre 2011.

D'ADDIO M., *Introduzione* a A. Rosmini-Serbati, *Filosofia della politica*, Marzorati Editore, Milano, 1972.

D'ADDIO M., *Libertà e appagamento. Politica e dinamica sociale in Rosmini*, Edizioni Studium, Roma, 2000.

DAHRENDORF R., *Class and Class Conflict in Industrial Society*, Routledge & Kegan Paul, London and Henley, 1976.

DELOGU P., *La storia economica di Roma nell'Alto Medioevo. Introduzione al seminario*, in L. Paroli e P. Delogu (a cura di), *La storia economica di Roma nell'Alto Medioevo alla luce dei recenti scavi archeologici*, Atti del Seminario, Roma 2 – 3 aprile, 1992, Edizioni All'Insegna del Giglio, Firenze, 1993.

DELOGU P., *L'importazione di tessuti preziosi e il sistema economico romano nel IX secolo*, in P. Delogu (a cura di), *Roma medievale. Aggiornamenti*, Edizioni All'Insegna del Giglio, Firenze, 1998.

DENIS H., *Histoire de la pensée économique*, vol. I, Presses Universitaires de France, Paris, 1965.

DOBB M., *Introduzione* a K. Marx, *Il Capitale. Critica dell'economia politica*, vol. I, Editori Riuniti, Roma, 1997; the page numbers refer to the Italian edition.

DRUCKER P. F., *The Future of Industrial Man*, The New American Library of World Literature, Inc., New York, 1965.

"THE ECONOMIST":
*What is Europe?*, in "The Economist", February 12th 2000.
*Sun Tzu and the art of soft power*, in "The Economist", December 17th 2011.
*Theme and Variations*, in "The Economist", January 21st 2012.
*The visible Hand*, in "The Economist", January 21st 2012.
*China's military rise*, in "The Economist", April 7th 2012.

ENGELS F., *Preface* to K. Marx, *Capital. A Critique of Political Economy*, volume II, *The Process of Circulation of Capital*, translated by S. Moore and E. Aveling and edited by F. Engels, Lawrence & Wishart, London, 1974.

FALCONE A., *Consuetudines Civitatis Amalfie. Le norme consuetudinarie di una città marinara*, Lumsa, Roma, 2000.

FAZIO A., *Presentazione* a Alfieri V., *La partita doppia applicata alle scritture delle antiche aziende mercantili veneziane*, Edizioni Studium, Roma, 1994. Ristampa anastatica dell'edizione del 1891 edita da G. B. Paravia.

FERGUSON A., *Principles of Moral and Political Science*, two volumes, Edinburgh, 1792.

FEYERABEND P., *Farewell to Reason*, Verso, London/New York, 1987.

FRANGIONI L., *Milano e le sue strade, costi di trasporto e vie di commercio dei prodotti alla fine del Trecento*, Cappelli Editore, Bologna, 1983.

FRANGIONI L., *Mercanti viaggiatori nel basso Medioevo: un nuovo contributo dell'archivio Datini di Prato*, SEGES, Dipartimento di scienze economiche, giuridiche e sociali, Università degli Studi del Molise, 1992.

GALBRAITH J. K., *The Great Crash*, Houghton Mifflin, Boston, 1954.

GALIANI F., *Della moneta*, Giangiacomo Feltrinelli Editore, Milano, 1963.

GIARDINA A., "Il mercante nel mondo romano", in Andrea Giardina e Aron Ja. Gurevič, *Il mercante nell'antichità e nel medioevo*, Editori Laterza, Roma-Bari, 1994.

GIDDENS A., *Capitalism and Modern Social Theory*, Cambridge University Press, 1971; the page numbers refer to the chapter and to the paragraphs.

GIDDENS A., "Una sfida chiamata governo globale", in *Reset*, Gennaio-Febbraio 2000, n°. 58.

GIRAUD G. - RENOUARD C., *20 proposte per riformare il capitalismo*, Éd. Flammarion, Paris, 2011.

GUIDOBALDI F., "L'edilizia abitativa unifamiliare nella Roma tardoantica", in Aa. Vv. (a cura di A. Giardina), *Società romana e Impero tardoantico*, vol. II, *Roma: politica, economia, paesaggio urbano*, Editori Laterza, Roma-Bari, 1986.

GUNDLACH E., "Globalisation: Economic Challenges and the Political Response", in *Intereconomics*, May/June, 2000.

HABERMAS J., *Legitimationsprobleme im Späkapitalismus*, Surkhamp Verlag, Frankfurt am Main, 1973.

HAYEK A. von, *Law, Legislation and Liberty, A new statement of the liberal principles of justice and political economy*, vol. II, *The Mirage of Social Justice*, The University of Chicago Press, Phoenix Edition, Chicago, 1978.

HILFERDING R., *Das Finanzkapital*, Wien, 1923.

HODGES R., *The riddle of St. Peter's Republic*, in L. Paroli e P. Delogu (a cura di), *La storia economica di Roma nell'Alto Medioevo alla luce dei recenti scavi archeologici*, Atti del Seminario, Roma 2 – 3 aprile, 1992, Edizioni All'Insegna del Giglio, Firenze, 1993.

HOLLIS M., *Trust within Reason*, C. U. P., Cambridge, 1998.

HOP P., "Il Profitto", in *Oikonomia. Journal of ethics & social sciences*, n. 2, 2000.

IMPICCIATORE G., *Introduzione alla moderna microeconomia*, CEDAM, Padova, 1998.

JA.GUREVIČ A., "Il mercante nel mondo medievale", in Andrea Giardina e Aron Ja.Gurevič, *Il mercante nell'antichità e nel medioevo*, Editori Laterza, Roma-Bari, 1994.

JAMES É., *Histoire sommaire de la pensée économique*, Éditions Montchrestien, Paris, 1959.

KIRZNER I. M., *Competition and Entrepreneurship*, University of Chicago, Chicago, 1973.

KISSINGER H., *On China*, Allen Lane, London, 2011.

KNIGHT F. H., *Risk, Uncertainty and Profit*, New York, 1921.

LANDES D. S., *The Wealth and Poverty of Nations*, W. W. Norton & Company Inc., 1999.

LAZZARI L., *Regine, badesse, sante: il contributo della donna anglosassone all'evangelizzazione (secc. VII e VIII)*, in "Studi Medievali", 3ª Serie – anno XXXIX, Fasc. II – Dicembre 1998.

LE GOFF J., *La civilisation de l'Occident médiéval*, Paris, 1964.

LE GOFF J., *Le Moyen Age et l'argent. Essai d'anthropologie historique*, Perrin, Paris, 2010.

LEKACHMAN R., *Introduction* to Thorstein Veblen, *The Theory of the Leisure Class*, Penguin Books, London, 1994.

LOMBARDI G., *Prefazione* a O Bazzichi, *Alle origini dello spirito del capitalismo*, Edizioni Dehoniane, Roma, 1991.

LONARDO A., *Il potere necessario. I vescovi di Roma e il potere temporale da Sabiniano a Zaccaria (604-752)*, Edizioni Antonianum, Roma, 2012.

MALASPINA E., *La terminologia latina delle professioni femminili nel mondo antico*, in "Mediterraneo Antico. Economie, società, culture", Anno VI, Fasc. 1, 2003.

MALTHUS T. R., *Principles of Political Economy considered with a view to their Practical Application*, John Murray, Albemarle-Street, London, 1820.

MARX K., *Capital. A Critical Analysis of Capitalistic Production*, volume I, translated by S. Moore and E. Aveling and edited by F. Engels, Lawrence & Wishart, London, 1974.

MARX K., *Capital. A Critique of Political Economy*, volume II, *The Process of Circulation of Capital*, translated by S. Moore and E. Aveling and edited by F. Engels, Lawrence & Wishart, London, 1974.

MARX K., *Capital. A Critique of Political Economy*, volume III, *The Process of Capitalist Production as a Whole*, edited by F. Engels, Lawrence & Wishart, London, 1974.

MARX K., GRUNDRISSE, in MARX-ENGELS, *Gesamtausgabe*, sez. II: *Das Kapital und Vorarbeiten*, vol. I: K. Marx, *Oekonomische Manuskripte 1857/58*, Erster Teil, Dietz Verlag, Berlin, 1976.

MCCORMICK M., *Origins of the European Economy. Communications and Commerce, A.D. 300-900*, Press Syndicated of the University of Cambridge, 2001.

MEEK R. L., RAPHAEL D. D., STEIN P. G., *Introduction* to A. Smith, *Lectures on Jurisprudence*, Liberty Press / Liberty Classics, Indianapolis, 1982.

MELIS F., *I trasporti e le comunicazioni nel Medioevo*, con introduzione di M. Mollat, a cura di L. Frangioni, Le Monnier, Firenze, 1984.

MELIS F., *I mercanti italiani nell'Europa medievale e rinascimentale*, con introduzione di H. Kellenbenz, a cura di L. Frangioni, Le Monnier, Firenze, 1990.

MERLEAU-PONTY M., *Les aventures de la dialectique*, Paris, 1955.

MEROLLE V., *Saggio su Ferguson, con un saggio su Milar*, Gangemi Editore, Roma, 1994.

MESLIN M., *L'homme romain. des origines au I$^{er}$ siècle de notre ère*, Editions Complexe, Bruxelles, 1978.

MICKLETWAIT J. - WOOLDRIDGE A., *A Future Perfect: The Challenge and Hidden Promise of Globalisation*, Times Books, 2000.

MINC A., *Www.capitalism.fr.*, Grasset, Paris, 2000.

MIRA G., *Storia del movimento operaio*, vol. I, *Storia del lavoro nel Medio Evo e nell'età moderna (sec. XIII-XVIII)*, Edizioni dell'Ateneo, Roma, 1949.

MIRA G., *Il lavoro nella storia economica medioevale e moderna*, (Lezioni tenute all'Università degli studi di Perugia), Roma, 1969.

MISES L. VON, *Socialism. An Economic and Sociological Analysis*, Liberty Fund, Inc., Indianapolis, 1981.

MISES L. VON, *Bureaucracy*, Yale University Press, New Haven, 1944.

MOLLAT M., *Introduzione* a F. Melis, *I trasporti e le comunicazioni nel Medioevo*, a cura di L. Frangioni, Le Monnier, Firenze, 1984.

MORGHEN R., *Il Medioevo cristiano*, Editori Laterza, Bari, 1951.

NOLTE E., *Der Europäische Bürgerkrieg 1917-1945. Nationalsozialismus und Bolschewismus*, Verlag Ullstein GMBH, Frankfurt/Main – Propyläen Verlag, Berlin, 1987.

NOVAK M., *The Spirit of Democratic Capitalism*, Simon & Schuster Publication, New York, 1982.

NOVAK M., "How Christianity Created Capitalism", in *The Wall Street Journal*, December 23, 1999.

NOVAK M., *Business as a Calling. Work and the Examined Life*, The Free Press, New York, 1996.

NUCCIO O., *Il pensiero economico italiano, 1. Le fonti (1050-1450). L'etica laica e la formazione dello spirito economico*, tomo secondo, Edizioni Gallizzi, Sassari, 1985.

NUCCIO O., *La civiltà italiana nella formazione della scienza economica*, Etaslibri, Milano, 1995.

OERTEL F., "The Economic Unification of the Mediterranean Region: Industry, Trade, and Commerce", in *The Augustan Empire 44 B. C. - A. D. 70*, in *The Cambridge Ancient History*, Volume X, Cambridge University Press, 1934.

OERTEL F., "The Economic Life of the Empire", in *The Imperial Crisis and Recovery A. D. 193-324*, in *The Cambridge Ancient History*, Volume XII, Cambridge University Press, 1939.

OLIVIERO A., "Investimenti finanziari, etica e rischio", in *Investimenti etici. Ricerche di psicologia economica*, a cura di A. Pedon e C. Galluccio, Rubbettino Editore, Soveria Mannelli, 2000.

PARSONS T., *The Structure of Social Action*, ed. Free Press, Glencoe, 1949.

PELLICANI L., *Il mercato e i socialismi*, Sugarco Edizioni, Milano, 1979.

PELLICANI L., *Saggio sulla genesi del capitalismo*, Sugarco Edizioni, Milano, 1988.

PENSABENE P., *La decorazione architettonica, l'impiego del marmo e l'importazione di manufatti orientali a Roma, in Italia e in Africa (II-IV sec. d. C.)*, in Aa. Vv. (a cura di A. Giardina), *Società romana e Impero tardoantico*, vol. III, *Le merci, gli insediamenti*, Editori Laterza, Roma-Bari, 1986.

PEZZIMENTI R., *Homo Metaphysicus. With letters from K. R. Popper, V. Tonini, L. Pauling, J. Eccles, H. Von Balthasar, P. Pavan*, LER, Napoli-Roma, 1992.

PEZZIMENTI R., *The Open Society and its Friends, with letters from Isaiah Berlin and the late Karl R. Popper*, Gracewing Fowler Wright Books, Leominster, 1997.

PEZZIMENTI R., *Dynamic Order. The Problem of Method in Evolving Nature*, Gracewing Fowler Wright Books, Leominster, 1999.

PIRENNE H., *Histoire économique de l'Occident Médiéval*, Desclée de Brouwer & C., Bruges, 1951.

PISANI SARTORIO G., *Mezzi di trasporto e traffico*, Vita e costumi dei romani antichi, Collana promossa dal *Museo della Civiltà Romana*, n. 6, Edizioni Quasar, Roma, 1994.

PLINIUS GAIUS S, THE ELDER, *Naturalis historia*, Oxonii, 1957.

PLINY, *Naturalis historia*, Oxonii, 1957.

POLANYI K., *The Great Transformation*, Holt, Rinehart & Winston Inc., New York, 1944.

POLANYI K., ARENSBERG C., PEARSON H.W. (Ed. by), *Trade and Marketin the Early Empires. Economies in History and Theory*, New York, 1957.

POSSENTI V., *Religione e vita civile. Il cristianesimo nel postmoderno*, Armando Editore, Roma, 2001.

QUILICI L., *Le strade. Viabilità tra Roma e il Lazio*, Vita e costumi dei romani antichi, Collana promossa dal *Museo della Civiltà Romana*, n. 12, Edizioni Quasar, Roma, 1990.

RICARDO D., *On the Principles of Political Economy, and Taxation*, in *Works and Correspondence*, vol. I, by Piero Sraffa with M. H. Dobb, Cambridge University Press, 1951.

RIFKIN J., *The End of the Work: The End of the Global Labor Force and the Dawn of the Post-Market Era*, G. P. Putnam's Sons, New York, 1995.

RODOLFO IL GLABRO, *Cronache dell'anno mille (Storie)*, a cura di G. Cavallo e G. Orlandi, Fondazione L. Valla / A. Mondadori Editore, Milano, 1990.

ROSANVALLON P., *Le capitalisme utopique. Histoire de l'idée de marché*, Éditions du Seuil, Paris, 1999.

ROSMINI-SERBATI A., *Filosofia della politica*, Marzorati Editore, Milano, 1972.

ROSMINI-SERBATI A., *Saggio sul comunismo e socialismo*, a cura di Clemente Riva, Edizioni Paoline, Pescara, 1964.

ROSMINI-SERBATI A., *La Costituente del Regno dell'Alta Italia*, in *Scritti politici*, a cura di U. Muratore, Edizioni Rosminiane, Stresa, 1997.

ROVELLI A., *La moneta nella documentazione altomedievale di Roma e del Lazio*, in L. Paroli e P. Delogu (a cura di), *La storia economica di Roma nell'Alto Medioevo alla luce dei recenti scavi archeologici*, Atti del Seminario, Roma 2 – 3 aprile, 1992, Edizioni All'Insegna del Giglio, Firenze, 1993.

ROVELLI A., *La circolazione monetaria a Roma nei secoli VII e VIII. Nuovi dati per la storia economica di Roma nell'Alto Medioevo*, in P. Delogu (a cura di), *Roma medievale. Aggiornamenti*, Edizioni All'Insegna del Giglio, Firenze, 1998.

SALVINI G., *L'economia in Cina 1949/1978. La via cinese da Mao Tse-tung a Hua Kuo-feng*, Milano, 1978.

SCHUMPETER J. A., *History of Economic Analysis*, Oxford University Press, New York, 1954.

SCHUMPETER J. A., *The Theory of Economic Development*, Oxford University Press, New York, 1967.

SCHUMPETER J. A., *Capitalism, Socialism and Democracy*, Introduction by R. Swedberg, Routledge, London and New York, 1996.

SEN A., *Development and Freedom*, Alfred A. Knopf, New York, 1999.

SEN A., *La globalizzazione non deve dividere*, intervista a cura di D. Taino, in *CorrierEconomia*, 25 settembre 2000.

SESTAN E., *Max Weber*, Introduzione a M. Weber, *L'etica protestante e lo spirito del capitalismo*, Sansoni Editore, Firenze, 1977.

SHIRER W., *The Rise and Fall of the Third Reich. A History of Nazi Germany*, Crest Books, New York, 1963.

SIMMEL G., *Philosophie des Geldes*, Duncker & Humblot, Berlin, 1977, Eng. trans., *The Philosophy of the Money*, edited by D. Frisby, translated by T. Bottomore and D. Frisby, second enlarged edition, Routledge, London and New York, 1997.

SMITH A., *The Wealth of Nations*, edited by E. Cannan, *Introduction* by R. Reich, The Modern Library, New York, 2000.

SMITH A., *Lectures on Jurisprudence*, edited by R. L. Meek, D. D. Raphael and P. G. Stein, Liberty Press / Liberty Classics, Indianapolis, 1982.

SOLER-MATUTES J., "Privatisation and Local Governments in Mainland China: A Critical Assessment", in *Intereconomics*, May/June, 2000.

SOMBART W., *Der moderne Kapitalismus*, Duncker & Humblot, Berlin, 1916, 2a ed., the page numbers refer to the chapter and to the paragraphs.

SOROS G., *The Crisis of Global Capitalism. Open Society Endangered*, Published in the United States by PublicAffairsTM, a member of the Perseus Book Group, 1998.

SOROS G., "Soros: questo capitalismo non mi piace", in *Reset*, Gennaio-Febbraio 2001, n°. 64.

SRAFFA P., *Introduction* to David Ricardo, *On the Principles of Political Economy, and Taxation*, in *Works and Correspondence*, vol. I, Cambridge University Press, 1951.

STUART MILL J., *On Liberty*, in *On Liberty and Other Essays*, Edited with an Introduction by John Gray, Oxford University Press, Oxford-New York, 1991.

STUART MILL J., *Principles of Political Economy*, Edited with an Introduction by Jonathan Riley, Oxford University Press, Oxford-New York, 1994.

SYLOS LABINI P., *Introduzione* a J. A. Schumpeter, *Teoria dello sviluppo economico*, Sansoni Editore, Firenze, 1977.

TAINO D., *Neo-statalista, rigido, legato al potere. Il Capitalismo ha mutato anima?*, in "Corriere della Sera", 21 Gennaio 2012.

TAWNEY R. H., *Religion and the Rise of Capitalism*, Penguin Books, London, 1990.

TOURAINE A., *Comment sortir du libéralisme*, Fayard, Paris, 1999.

TROIANI L., *Il Mediterraneo storico come confronto di civiltà e di economie*, in *Italia e Mediterraneo: le occasioni dello sviluppo*, a cura di S. Semplici e L. Troiani, Società editrice il Mulino, Bologna, 2000.

TROIANI L., "Regionalismo economico e multirateratismo internazionale", in *Oikonomia. Journal of ethics & social sciences*, n. 3, 2000.

VARIAN Hal R., *Intermediate Microeconomics. A Modern Approach*, W. W. Norton & Company, Inc., New York - London, 1996.

VARRO M. T., *De Re Rustica*, in *Opere*, a cura di A. Traglia, U.T.E.T., Torino, 1996.

VEBLEN T., *The Theory of the Leisure Class*, Penguin Books, London, 1994.

VEBLEN T., *The Engineers and the Price System*, B. W. Huebsch, New York, 1921.

VERRI P., *Della economia politica*, in Pietro Verri, *Del piacere e del dolore ed altri acritti*, Giangiacomo Feltrinelli Editore, Milano, 1964.

WALLERSTEIN I., *The Modern World-System III. The Second Era of Great Expansion of the Capitalist World-Economy*, 1730-1840s, San Diego, Academic Press, 1989.

WEBER M., *The Protestant Ethic and the Spirit of Capitalism*, translated by T. Parsons, with a Foreword by R. H. Tawney, third impression, New York-London, 1950.

WEBER M., *Zwischenbetrachtung*, in *Die Wirtschaftsethik der Weltreligionen Konfuzianismus und Taoismus*, Schriften 1915-1920, in Max Weber, *Gesamtausgabe*, Abteilung I: Schriften und Reden, Band 19, J. C. B. Mohr (Paul Siebeck), Tübingen, 1989.

WEBER M., *Politik als Beruf*, in Max Weber, *Gesamtausgabe*, Abteilung I: Schriften und Reden, Band 17, J. C. B. Mohr (Paul Siebeck), Tübingen, 1992.

WEBER M., *Wirtschaft und Gesellschaft*, 1. Halbband, Erster Teil (I), *Die Wirtschaft und die gesellschaftlichen Ordnungen und Mächte*, Verlag Von J. C. B. Mohr (Paul Siebeck), Tübingen, 1947.

WEBER M., *Wirtschaft und Gesellschaft*, 1. Halbband, Zweiter Teil (II), *Typen der Vergemeinschaftung und Vergesellschaftung*, Verlag Von J. C. B. Mohr (Paul Siebeck), Tübingen, 1947.

WILLIAMS E., *Capitalism and Slavery*, Chapel Hill, 1944.

WRIGHT MILLS C., *The Power Elite*, Oxford University Press, New York, 2000.

WRIGHT MILLS C., *White Collars. The American Middle Classes*, Oxford University Press, New York, 1951.

# INDEX OF NAMES

ACEMOGLU D., *252.*
ALBERT M., *201.*
ALBERTI L. B., *40.*
ALFIERI V.M., *24, 109-112, 117.*
ALEXANDER THE GREAT, *70.*
ALVI G., *248-249.*
ANDREAU J., *55, 65-67.*
ANTONINO OF FLORENCE ST, *101.*
APTER D., *247.*
AQUINAS, *23, 40, 96-97, 101-102, 119.*
ARENSBERG C., *269*
ARISTOTLE, *47, 101.*
ARNALDI G., *80.*
AUGUSTINE ST, *65.*
AUGUSTUS C. J. C. O., *55-56, 69-70.*
AVELLA PINZON J., *161.*

BAGGIO A. M., *29-31.*
BALBI DE CARO S., *53-55, 63-65, 67.*
BAZZICHI O., *98.*
BECK U., *229.*
BENEDICT II, *81.*
BENEDICT ST, *89, 93-94.*
BERNARD OF CLAIRVAUX, *95.*
BOCCACCIO G., *99.*
BOLTANSKI L., *236.*
BRAUDEL F., *113-117, 124-125, 245, 254.*
BREMMER J., *253.*
BRENTANO L., *45.*
BRUNI L., *42-43.*
BÜSCH J. G., *101.*

CAESAR C. J., *63, 70.*
CALIXTUS POPE, *92.*
CALLISTRATUS, *53.*
CARACCIOLO A., *143.*
CARAVALE M., *99.*
CARROZZI L., *66.*
CATO M. P., *47, 88.*

CAVALLI A., *28.*
CHAFUEN A. A., *118.*
CHANG P. H., *247.*
CHARLEMAGNE, *86.*
CHARLES OF BURGUNDY, *76.*
CHIAPELLO E., *236.*
CHRISTOPHER C., *113.*
CIARROCCHI B., *77.*
CICERO M. T., *38-39, 47-49, 52, 54, 62-64, 101.*
CIMINO R.M., *69-71.*
CLEMENT OF ALEXANDRIA, *90.*
COASE R., *246.*
COCCIA S., *77.*
COLLINS R., *108.*
CONFUCIUS, *251.*
CONSTANTINE IV, *70, 79.*
COPERNICUS N., *113.*
COTRUGLI B., *112.*
COX S., *250.*
CROMWELL O., *21.*
CRONER F., *217.*
CYRIL ST, *85.*

D'ADDIO M., *32-33, 184-196.*
DAHRENDORF R., *218-219.*
DANTE A., *237.*
DELOGU P., *77-79.*
DENG or TENG XIAOPING, *246.*
DENIS H., *87, 125-126.*
DIOCLETIAN, *74.*
DOBB M., *138, 154.*
DRUCKER P. F., *239, 243.*

EDWARD IV, *76.*
ENGELS F., *169.*
ENRICO DA SUSA, *101.*
EPICTETUS, *88.*
ERATOSTHENES, *69.*

FALCONE A., *98.*
FANTACCI L., *249.*
FAZIO A., *24.*
FERGUSON A., *128-129.*
FEYERABEND P., *222.*
FIBONACCI L., *100.*
FICHTE J. G., *167, 258.*
FRANGIONI L., *121-122.*
FREDERIC III, *76.*

GALBRAITH J. K., *201.*
GALIANI F., *143-146.*
GALILEO G., *28, 222.*
GIARDINA A., *100.*
GIBBON E., *78.*
GIDDENS A., *41, 154, 156, 158, 229.*
GIOIA M., *192.*
GIOVANNI DA VERRAZZANO, *120.*
GIRAUD G., *252.*
GREGORY THE GREAT, *77, 80.*
GREGORY II, *83.*
GUIDOBALDI F., *59.*
GUNDLACH E., *231.*

HABERMAS J., *216.*
HADRIAN I, *78.*
HARRINGTON J., *48.*
HAYEK A. VON, *48-49, 130, 172 229, 249-250*
HILFERDING R., *200.*
HITLER A., *256-257.*
HODGES R., *78.*
HOLLIS M., *43.*
HOP P., *102.*

IMPICCIATORE G., *227.*
INNOCENT III, *99.*
INNOCENT IV POPE, *108.*

JA.GUREVIČ, *99.*
JAMES É., *87.*
JOHN V, *81.*
JOHN VIII, *77.*
JUSTINIAN II, *79.*
JUVENAL D. J., *62.*

KEYNES LORD J. M., *249, 257.*
KIRZNER I. M., *179.*
KISSINGER H., *251.*
KNIGHT F. H., *224.*

KRIEDTE P., *38.*

LANDES D. S., *237-238.*
LAZZARI L., *78.*
LE GOFF J., *75-76, 95.*
LEO III, *84.*
LEO IV, *78.*
LEO THE ISAURIAN, *76.*
LEKACHMAN R., *203.*
LOMBARDI G., *98.*
LONARDO A., *80-84.*
LOUIS XI, *76.*
LUTHER M., *166.*

MALASPINA E., *78.*
MALTHUS T. R., *135.*
MAO TSE-TUNG, *159.*
MARABODUO KING OF CEYLON, *56.*
MARCUS AURELIUS, *88.*
MARIANA J. (DE), *118.*
MARSILIO OF PADUA, *34, 237.*
MARTIN I, *81, 84.*
MARTIN A., *77.*
MARX K., *9, 17, 37, 41, 45-47, 49, 101, 117, 136, 138, 142, 151-175, 234-236, 243, 245, 254.*
MAXIMUS THE CONFESSOR, *81.*
MCCORMICK M., *84-86.*
MEDICK H., *38.*
MEEK R. L., *133.*
MELIS F., *120-122.*
MERLEAU-PONTY M., *159-160.*
MEROLLE V., *128, 130.*
MESLIN M., *46.*
METHODIUS ST, *85-86.*
MICKLETWAIT J., *161.*
MINC A., *237.*
MIRA G., *87.*
MISES L. VON, *212, 217, 220-222, 226, 248.*
MOLLAT M., *121.*
MONTESQUIEU C. L., *34, 128, 132, 145.*
MORGHEN R., *74-75.*

NOLTE E., *257-258.*
NOVAK M., *20, 31, 35, 107-108, 223-224.*
NUCCIO O., *87, 100-102.*

OCKHAM W. OF, *98, 237.*

OERTEL F., *56-58, 68, 72-74.*

PACIOLI OR PACIOLO L., *23-24, 112-113.*
PAPINIANUS, *53, 101.*
PARSONS T., *42.*
PAULUS, *53.*
PECQUEUR C., *168.*
PELLICANI L., *35-38, 247.*
PENSABENE P., *59.*
PERUCCHI L., *28.*
PEZZIMENTI R., *13-15, 260-261.*
PIRENNE H., *74.*
PISANI SARTORIO G., *46, 59, 61-62.*
PLINIUS GAIUS S, THE ELDER, *56, 88, 245.*
PLINY, *61, 71, 246.*
POLANYI K., *76, 201.*
POSSENTI V., *17.*
PROPERTIUS S., *70.*
PROUDHON P. J., *253.*

QUILICI L., *60.*

RAPHAEL D. D., *133.*
RAYMOND DE PEÑAFORT, *100.*
REAGAN R., *15.*
RENNER K., *217.*
RENOUARD C., *252.*
RICARDO D., *135, 138-143, 155, 159, 161.*
RIFKIN J., *239-241.*
ROBINSON J., *154, 252.*
RODOLFO THE BALD, *95.*
ROSANVALLON P., *200.*
ROSMINI-SERBATI A., *29, 33, 35, 154, 178-179, 182-197, 241-242.*
ROUSSEAU J. J., *128, 164, 168, 189.*
ROVELLI A., *77, 79.*

SALVINI G., *246-247.*
SAMUELSON P. A., *252.*
SAVONA P., *9, 13.*
SAY J. B., *141, 177.*
SCHLUMBOHM J., *38.*
SCHUMPETER J. A., *27, 118, 177-179, 182.*
SEN A., *227, 233-236.*
SENECA L. A., *88.*
SESTAN E., *18-21.*
SHIRER W., *257-258.*

SIMMEL G., *27-29.*
SMITH A., *9, 17-18, 41, 49, 125-138, 140, 143, 149, 152, 158, 161, 164, 169, 234-236, 243, 253.*
SOCRATES, *48.*
SOLER-MATUTES J., *232.*
SOMBART W., *36-37, 39-40, 45, 71.*
SOROS G., *24-27, 32, 229-231.*
SPENGLER O., *113.*
SRAFFA P., *138.*
STEIN P. G., *133.*
STRABO J. C., *57, 69-70.*
STUART MILL J., *255-256.*
SUN TZU, *250-251.*
SYLOS LABINI P., *179.*

TAINO D., *252.*
TAWNEY R. H., *202.*
THATCHER M., *15.*
THYSSEN F., *256.*
TIBULLUS A., *70.*
TOCQUEVILLE A. DE, *20, 30, 33, 192, 194, 196, 214, 255.*
TOURAINE A., *200.*
TROIANI L., *114, 233.*

ULPIAN, *53, 55, 63.*

VARIAN HAL R., *225-226.*
VARRO M. T., *50-53, 238.*
VEBLEN T., *200, 202-207, 240.*
VERRI P., *146-149.*
VICO G. B., *145, 152, 186, 189, 216.*
VIRGIL P. M., *70.*
VITRUVIUS P., *61.*

WALLERSTEIN I., *116, 123-124.*
WANG N., *246.*
WEBER M., *18, 20-24, 35, 107, 116, 119-120, 211-216.*
WILLIAMS E., *21.*
WOOLDRIDGE A., *161.*
WRIGHT MILLS C., *200, 207-209.*

XENOPHON, *48.*

ZACHARIAS POPE, *83.*

www.ingramcontent.com/pod-product-compliance
Lightning Source LLC
Chambersburg PA
CBHW032020230426
43671CB00005B/144